Off T
Beaten Track

Off The Beaten Track

A Wexas Travel Handbook

Edited by Ingrid Cranfield
and Richard Harrington

WEXAS INTERNATIONAL LIMITED
LONDON AND NEW YORK
WILTON HOUSE GENTRY · LONDON

First published 1977
© Wexas International Limited 1977
ISBN 0 905064 30 5

Reprinted 1978

Published by Wexas International Limited,
45 Brompton Road, Knightsbridge, London SW3
and Wexas International Inc, Graybar Building, Suite 354,
420 Lexington Avenue, New York, NY 10017, USA
and by Wilton House Gentry Limited,
16 Regency Street, London SW1.

Designed by Bromley Arts Limited.
Filmset by Computacomp (UK) Limited, Fort William.

Printed in Great Britain by offset lithography by
Billing & Sons Ltd, Guildford, London and Worcester

Dedicated to the memory of
Eric Shipton
mountaineer, explorer
and traveller extraordinary

Contents

Introduction 7
Major Expedition Planning 9
Expedition Fund Raising 17
Major Expedition Organizations in the UK 19
The Expedition Vehicle 29
Expedition Vehicle Maintenance 37
Off-The-Beaten-Track Motoring 41
Vehicle Indemnity Insurance 45
Jetboats for Expeditions 47
Bargain Air Travel 51
Bureaucratic Hassles Overseas 55
Youth Hostelling 61
Maps and Map Reading 67
Expedition Travel and Your Health 71
Survival on Expeditions 85
Trials of a Freelance Travel Writer 89
A Traveller's Guide to Photography 91
Selling Expedition Photography 99
Overland and Adventure Trip Operators in the UK 107
Overland and Adventure Trip Operators and Agents Overseas 121
Expedition-oriented Organizations 137
Directory of Services 145
Personal Accounts of Expeditions and Travels 165
Useful Books 171
Periodicals 193
Maps 199
Embassies, High Commissions and Consulates in London 201
British Embassies, High Commissions and Consulates Abroad 204
Foreign Tourist Offices in the UK 208
Metric Tyre Pressure Conversion Chart 210
Representatives of Canadian, Australian, New Zealand and American Governments in
   Asia 211
Australian, Canadian and American Embassies, High Commissions and Consulates in
   Africa 215
Worldwide Voltage Guide 220
World Guide to Duty-Free Allowances 222
Worldwide Exchange Rates 226
Metric Conversion Table 228
Wind Chill Chart 229
Worldwide Average Temperature and Humidities 230
UK Passports 235
Useful Vocabulary: Europe 236
Guide to International Road Signs 238
Useful Vocabulary: Far East 241
WEXAS 243
Index 249
This Page is for You to Write 255

Introduction

The most difficult part of compiling this book was finding an appropriate title. We eventually came up with *Off The Beaten Track*, a title which we still regard as something of a compromise, since there is much in this reference book which will be of great value to the independent traveller who never strays too far from the beaten track. In putting this book together, we were obliged to leave out a lot; some of this material and more will find its way into the next edition at a later date.

Who is the typical person that this book is written for? The short answer is that there is no 'typical' reader. *Off The Beaten Track* is aimed at every open-minded traveller from the scientific explorer or the Everest climber to the trans-African hitchhiker or the South American railway enthusiast. Like the word 'expedition', the reader of this book defies classification. The nearest we can come to defining him is to say that he is not a tourist. He can be any age, any nationality. Nowadays, he is as likely to be poor as rich. 'He' is also just as likely, these days, to be a woman as a man.

So far as we know, no reference book quite like this has ever been published before. The first section provides essential information told from first-hand experience. The rest, apart from the temperature charts and so on, tells where to get the information you need. While it can never be exhaustive, you can help us to make *Off The Beaten Track* even more comprehensive by sending us information which can be incorporated in the next edition.

Bon voyage et bonne route!

Ingrid Cranfield and Richard Harrington

Major Expedition Planning

Major Kelvin Kent

Ethics

Nowadays I am quite often asked at lectures to answer such questions as 'which is more difficult, a jungle expedition or a Himalayan expedition?' Of course, the two can hardly be compared, but surprisingly there are many fundamental points which lead me to conclude that the basic principles of large scale expedition organisation are common to all expeditions.

I suppose the most vexed question of all is the one of ethics. Can the old-style amateur effort succeed? Can the really dedicated idealistic approach produce results? Can a small expedition manage to achieve a big aim? This is where it becomes difficult. Where do you draw the line? Obviously the small do-it-yourself expedition can and does succeed. The first-time organiser gets a couple of ulcers, loses a few pounds and learns a lot. Perhaps the financial outlay of the individuals concerned turns out to be more than forecast, but the rewards for those who do undertake these ventures definitely outweigh the inherent disadvantages and empty pockets. Even if an organised minibus party in Afghanistan is held up in a traffic jam of Australian professionals carrying cardboard Citroens over a small ditch, the experience is still unique for them. The fact that thousands of other people are doing the same thing doesn't matter.

The object and value derived are of a personal nature. It is the audio-visual effects with their associated memories which remain. The ability to absorb is maybe more important than just to have done. But in any case the value lies in going ahead and seeing for yourself. No one else's verbal or written accounts and pretty slides can make up for the personal experience which is interpreted differently by every one of us. If nothing else, in years to come you will be able to console yourself with the adage 'I'd rather be a has-been than a never-was!'

Getting it Off the Ground

In the bigger expeditions, the start point begins with the design of the all-important status symbol: headed notepaper, without which the project cannot be got off the ground. The trouble here is trying to distinguish between patrons and sponsors. If you can get the Duke of Edinburgh and Lord Hunt to agree to their names going at the top, you're well on the way to success. Additionally, it is advantageous to add an air of respectability by mentioning such 'sponsors' as Royal Geographical Society, Mount Everest Foundation, WEXAS, Scientific Exploration Society, Young Explorers Trust, Explorers Club, World Wildlife Fund and Survival International. The trouble is that whilst such bodies on your note-paper may impress some of the firms you write to, few such bodies will be in a position to offer financial aid themselves. The term 'Sponsor' in this context should therefore be watched. The other difficult problem to overcome is the chicken and egg syndrome concerning actual permission to use the names of some of these bodies on your notepaper. They will probably not agree until fairly detailed plans of the expedition are presented to them which adequately cover the viability of the venture physically and financially. This is a problem when, at this stage, all you want is a status letterhead to start fund-raising. Nevertheless, it's always worth a try, provided common sense, foresight and sheer optimism are there and don't amount to an outright bluff. The will to succeed before you start is thus of paramount importance. You may need a sound knowledge of interview techniques if you require nominal (non-financial) sponsorship from high-powered organisations or personalities.

Having embarked on the planning and setting-up stage, the next decision to be taken is usually the question of budget. Should you price all you want, go ahead and order, and then try to raise the necessary cash, or should you fix an expedition budget ceiling and arrange everything within that figure? The answer here depends on the views of the leader and on how much money his or her members can put in. For the bigger non-military epics, the time has really come to consider the concept of a limited company. Why not have shareholders who share the risk of failure, but equally, who hope to make a few pounds if everything goes well? Perhaps this is wrong. Perhaps no expedition should make a profit.

The only thing that is not in doubt is the time taken in getting help from sponsors. Cash is far more difficult a commodity to obtain than the actual merchandise of the firm concerned. Given, say, six months or more before an expedition, much of the equipment and food can be obtained free or at reduced prices. The main work involved is assessing the requirement and finding out who makes it — not who retails it.

Beware also of promising too much to would-be sponsors. It is so easy to promise articles, black and white negatives and colour slides, but on the ground, the ability to do so often falls far short of the mark and ends up in well motivated commercial firms feeling they've had a raw deal.

Applying for Cash

In the case of pure cash grants, the law as it affects charitable donations governs to a large extent what firms can give. Even if they themselves, for tax and PR purposes, budget a certain amount of money to aid expeditions, the sum is never enough to meet the ever-growing demand. There is no real remedy for success, but I do recommend a full description of the expedition aim and method of achieving it. This and other 'PR potential' details can be run off on the headed notepaper. A suitable covering letter (neatly typed) should be composed specifically for each firm.

Despite all, one principle remains strong. The more people you write to, the more you will get. In my experience for every ten letters that went out, three were not answered, four said no, two said they'd like to but ... and the tenth offered something.

Tana River Expedition white water team discuss the route.

Oh God — Not That *!? + ! Again

All who have been on expeditions know that food is responsible for about 90 per cent of conversation after just a few days. Food also constitutes nearly 50 per cent of expedition payload if prepacked ration packs are taken.

I have found that outweighing the concept of the perfect, medically designed pack of so many calories per man per day (which can never exist in reality) is the one simple rule: palatability. This is really more important than anything else, because each expedition environment produces a different requirement and at the end of the day, it is no use to anyone if half the ration is wasted. This is expensive in terms of weight and money as well as morale-deflating.

Obviously certain mouth-watering delicacies in the jungle won't be so successful on a rock ledge at 25000 feet and vice versa. But in both cases it is dangerous to assume that because you like mock turtle soup on Brompton Road, you will enjoy it in Ethiopia or Panama. My own recommendations are these:

1) Make the rations up into specific man/day packs. For example, on Everest we had 12 man/day packs for the approach, 8 man/day packs for Base up to Camp 2, and 2 man/day packs for the Face itself. The latter was a High Altitude Assault Ration.

2) Decide beforehand on the availability of local produce. From this, work out the proportion of weight that needs to be pre-packed at home base; e.g. an 8 man/day pack based on 2 lb. per man per day with a 1 lb. per man per day local supplement to be mixed in on arrival. Apart from being able to ring the changes with fresh rations, you can reduce the weight of the pack in this way.

3) Take a number of centralised luxuries which can be split up into goodie packs and distributed as and where necessary.

4) Bear in mind and try to get straight at the beginning:

a) The budget allowed for pre-packed food.

b) The budget allowed for local supplement.

c) The cost of and procurement of containers and packing for food.

d) Any weight limitations imposed. (A 10 man/day Army Compo pack weighs about 38 lb!)

e) Proportion of dehydrated materials (relates of course to weight and bulk).

f) Packing arrangements: if possible into porter loads (weight and size) so that when broken down, you still have correct packs for the task, e.g. on Everest, the assault ration was a 2 man, $2^1/_2$ lb. per man/day pack weighing 5 lb. Six of these packs were in an outer pack weighing 30 lb. which was the equivalent of one Sherpa's mountain load. For the approach march, two 30 lb. packs were bound together and pre-packed in a further outer container to make the total up to a full approach coolie load of approximately 65 lb. with container.

g) Ease of cooking; e.g. a tinned steak and kidney pud is not much use at high altitude because it takes too long (and therefore too much fuel) to cook.

h) Availability of what you think you want. Off the shelf items are obviously easy, but try arranging margarine in toothpaste tubes!

i) The time left to the unfortunate food member to do all this in his spare time.

It is just not possible to satisfy all of the people all of the time when it comes to food, but in my view it is the most important delegated job in an expedition. Good food produces good morale and a fit team. With these things, almost anything else can be achieved. Bad food and lack of thought beforehand can be the first thing to erode confidence and motivation. To this end I do not recommend too much dehydrated food. Apart from its slightly unnatural taste, it becomes monotonous faster than other foods, and in the case of mountain or arctic expeditions, takes a lot of effort and fuel in melting ice in which to cook it.

As we all know, the best combination is a blend of local and pre-packed food. Choose the cook carefully and treat him well. He is so important. Try also to introduce imagination into the cooking itself and make sure that at the end of each meal, things are cleared up and cleaned. This makes a great difference and helps overcome the lethargy towards producing a meal when attrition starts later on in the expedition.

Promotion, Media and PR

Whilst all this planning is going on it may become necessary (indeed imperative in the very big expeditions) to use a literary agent or a committee — sometimes both — to help promote the expedition as a third party and to work on your behalf before and during the expedition with such things as PR, newspaper and TV sponsors, publishers and big-time lecture or personal appearances. Good promotion beforehand is absolutely essential and requires a lot of time, visits and 'exposure'. The direct results are not easily seen, but the spin-off and long term rewards are considerable.

Every major expedition these days depends greatly on a lecture programme. This can be partly arranged before and during the expedition provided a wife, girlfriend, agent or secretary (paid or just friendly) can take it on. Within the same category of administrative responsibilities is philately and/or signed postcards posted from the country concerned. This type of postcard scheme can produce an income but involves a lot of work and may not be practical, despite the fact that it is a nice idea. On Annapurna, we all had to sit down to sign 8000 postcards (which is a hard day's work) and then despatch them to pre-typed addresses. For some reason which is still unexplained, fewer than half reached their destinations. Goodwill was not easy to maintain for a while!

The Dreaded Customs

Perhaps the most frustrating problem of all for many expeditions is importation and customs. If one is lucky enough to have a British Embassy who will assist, the problem is halved, but normally this is not the case. It therefore becomes necessary to write for information in advance about the procedures for obtaining an Import Licence and knowing how best to categorise and show the declared value for customs purposes. This is an art which is often learnt the hard way. There is no simple solution except the virtue of patience, combined with dogged perseverance and an ability not to annoy any link in the human chain of important officials.

Advance Information

Numerous other pieces of information also need to be gained beforehand. For instance, in a Himalayan expedition in Nepal, up-to-date rules of the Himalayan Society (the Sherpas' Union) are absolutely vital. For other countries, entry and exit points must be cleared first and a sound knowledge of the facilities existing there is important. It is no use taking a shortcut into a country and finding that their Customs Post hasn't got the authority to clear your stuff through.

Good Administration Pays Off

The very last point I wish to make in this article concerns logistics and the support side of an expedition. Most people understand the idea of a logistic pyramid but very few expeditions allow for sufficient manpower to be devoted to logistics and administration. The analogy of a football team with its five forwards and six support or defence players is about right. At the base of the pyramid, the work load can be enormous and needs good fit people to run it. Ideally, in a mobile expedition, the leader should always assume a centre half position with a firm grip on leading elements *and* the rest of the pyramid which is behind him.

It all really hinges on picking a balanced team who know their jobs and/or are willing to muck in as required doing anything needed, rather than relying on too many supermen with machetes between their teeth and flag-covered axes in each hand.

Finally, there is the importance of post expedition administration. It takes a great deal of effort at a time when everyone is shattered, but honouring the promises to sponsors with pictures, reports and letters of thanks is not only being honest, but also helping future expeditions. The accounts too need typing before audit, and it is always useful to produce a fairly comprehensive expedition report as quickly as possible after return. In the meantime, a small committee can get on with the work of picture allocation and transparency distribution and duplication for books, sponsors, lectures and exclusive articles. Only after this has been done should individuals get back their own negatives and remaining slides.

This and all the other associated work of expedition planning and organisation may not be glamorous and is often underestimated. It is therefore wise to be aware of the time and effort necessary to overcome the frustrations and problems of mounting an expedition epic.

Then again, perhaps a smaller expedition is better after all!

Sherpas carrying supplies on Annapurna.

A Cuna girl wearing a mola, the traditional embroidered blouse.

Expedition Fund Raising

Richard Harrington

A few words of advice to those seeking sponsorship in funds or in kind for serious expeditions.

Do not appeal indiscriminately, or to the wrong kind of organisation. Make sure that you have a well printed expedition prospectus, preferably with one or two 'names' on the cover who will act as sponsors/referees/patrons. This prospectus should be sound but not lavish, should list those from whom help has been received and those to whom an appeal is being made. It should contain a bibliography of the work already carried out in the field of inquiry, as well as an itinerary (preferably with a simple map) and a detailed costing. Expeditions that are over-ambitious in their research objectives and in their costings are courting failure from the beginning. Concentrate on a few, specific objectives. Offer to acknowledge all assistance in the final report and give a tentative date for its publication. Allow for report costs in budgeting. If you are undertaking a research expedition, do not plan to cover too great a distance or involve too many academic disciplines in your enterprise. Remember that an expedition carrying on the work of the previous year's party in a particular field is at an advantage since it is generally considered that 'follow-up' expeditions tend to be more productive than their predecessors. There is also, of course, the element of enhanced feasibility when some of the ground has been covered before, and credibility of this type is all important to any expedition. Remember to plan months, even years, in advance. No support will be forthcoming for a project put together at the last moment, or for a holiday trip disguised as a research expedition.

Certain soundly based and planned research expeditions have, on application to the Inland Revenue, been fortunate enough to be awarded charitable status. This has qualified them for assistance from the Charities Aid Fund of the National Council of Social Service (26 Bedford Square, London WC1. Tel: 636 4066), which simplifies the donation of money to charities by industry.

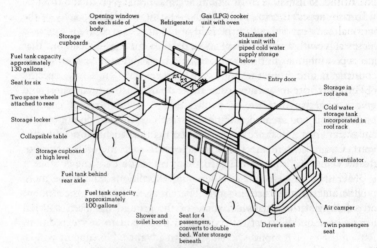

Major Expedition Organizations in the UK

British Mountaineering Council
Crawford House
Precinct Centre
Booth Street East
Manchester M13 9RZ

The British Mountaineering Council is the national representative body of British mountaineers. It offers members insurance schemes covering personal accident, third party liability, Alpine rescue and medical expenses at very competitive rates, information on equipment tests and access problems. It is also able to assist in negotiations with the Sports Council for grants for club huts.

The BMC organises a small number of specialist courses for Club members. Through its international exchange programme it is possible for hard and not so hard mountaineers to climb abroad as guests of equivalent continental organisations. The BMC is negotiating with the Sports Council and industrial sponsors for finance for expeditions to the greater ranges. Priority is given to the smaller amateur party.

BMC services also include a magazine *Mountain Life* every two months and an information service on books, brochures, leaflets and films dealing with specialised items of equipment and safety. The BMC offers advice on all aspects of mountaineering.

Royal Geographical Society
1 Kensington Gore
London SW7 2AR

The Royal Geographical Society is a focal point for geographers in Britain. Its large freehold building, facing Hyde Park, houses many services for the Society's Fellows and Members and for the promotion of geography in general.

The RGS was founded in 1830 and incorporated the African Association, which was founded in 1788. Since then the Society has sponsored or helped virtually all the famous British explorers — from Livingstone and Stanley to Fuchs and Herbert. The RGS continues to be very active in promoting exploration. It directly organises and finances its own scientific expeditions, and gives financial support, the loan of instruments, approval and advice to a great many more. The Society honours outstanding geographers and explorers with a series of annual medals and awards.

The RGS maintains the largest private map collection in Europe, with over half a million sheets. It has a staff of expert cartographers and the necessary drawing office and reproduction equipment to complement this service.

The Society's library, with over 100,000 books and periodicals, is an outstanding source of information on geography, travel and exploration. There is also an archive of historic records and expedition reports.

There are regular lectures, children's lectures, discussions and symposia in the Society's 760-seat lecture hall. Most of the leading names in exploration, mountaineering, and scientific geography have addressed the Society. But there are different types of meetings — some aimed at academic geographers, and others for the many Fellows who are members of the public with a general interest in the subject.

Anyone with a geographical interest can apply to join the RGS. Fellows and Members can meet one another over refreshments after evening meetings or at the Annual Reception and Anniversary Dinner. There are also comfortable Tea and Reading Rooms for Fellows in the RGS building.

The RGS publishes the *Geographical Journal* three times a year and is closely associated with the monthly *Geographical Magazine*. The Journal, now in its 140th volume, contains articles of a high academic standard and a full review section on the latest geographical books and maps.

On the academic side, the RGS organises meetings for sixth-formers and for geographers, planners, cartographers, surveyors and specialists in other related disciplines. The Society has committees for research, education, expeditions, publications and maps and instruments. Its building also houses the offices of organisations connected with geography, mountaineering or navigation, including the London offices of the Institute of British Geographers.

The Royal Geographical Society is a registered charity, supported by contributions, a government grant for the Map Room and Fellows' subscriptions. It seeks to help and encourage everyone interested in geography, from the general public to the professional geographer.

Scientific Exploration Society Ltd

Home Farm
Mildenhall
Marlborough
Wiltshire

Foundation and Aim

The Society was formed in 1969 by a group of explorers, many of whom had been together on expeditions. They appointed as their Chairman Major John Blashford-Snell, who had in 1968 led the first successful navigation and scientific survey of the Ethiopian Blue Nile and its gorge. It was after this expedition that some of its members decided to join together in a more permanent body to promote and carry out worldwide scientific exploration in the future. Experienced personnel and useful equipment were therefore not to be dispersed, but kept together for future undertakings. The Scientific Exploration

Society was launched with the intention of organising more expeditions and of helping other institutions — universities, schools, services and individuals — to organise their own.

It was to be a broadly based society — service and civilian, open to both sexes, all ages and nationalities, though for administrative reasons limited in size.

From the outset it was planned to maintain close links with commerce, industry, educational establishments, the services and other kindred scientific and exploration organisations.

The Society is now a registered charity, with a Council of ten experienced explorers, scientists, business men and servicemen.

What SES Does

SES Expeditions have taken place as follows:

Dec. 1969– Jan. 1970

The Dahlak Quest Expedition carried out a study of the Dahlak Archipelago in the Red Sea for the Ethiopian Tourist Organisation. A Report and 16mm film were produced.

Nov. 1971

The Alec Gale Memorial Expedition to the Dahlak Islands. A second visit to this Red Sea archipelago examined the feasibility of treating an unusual form of blindness found among the people there.

Dec. 1973–Jan. 1974

The Blue Mountains Expedition. Carried out a scientific survey of the northern slopes of the Blue Mountains in Jamaica and a historical/archaeological study of the sites of the Maroon Wars of 1729–39.

Oct. 1974–Feb. 1975

The Zaïre River Expedition 1974. Scientific research plus an attempt to navigate the complete Zaïre River.

The following expeditions were approved and supported by SES :

Mar. 1969

The British White Nile Hovercraft Expedition. Navigated parts of the White Nile by prototype Hovercraft to promote sales.

July 1969

Zoological Expedition to Guyana. A highly successful quest by a team of zoologists.

Aug. 1970

The British Jostedals Expedition. Dropped by parachute onto Norway's biggest mountain ice-cap and carried out glaciological and zoological surveys.

July 1971

The British Roraima Expedition. Parachuted into a little known area of Guyana and undertook zoological and other studies around Mount Roraima (the Lost World).

Nov. 1971–June 1972

The British Trans-Americas Expedition. 'The last great drive in the World' organised by the British Trans-Americas Expedition Committee. This important enterprise was largely mounted by SES. The team forced its way, with vehicles, through the last unconquered 300 miles of jungle and swamp in Panama and Colombia, which separated the northern and southern section of the Pan-American Highway. Two Range-Rovers motored from Alaska to Tierra del Fuego, completing over 17,000 miles in 7 months. Valuable scientific work was carried out and world attention was drawn to the need to complete the Highway.

Aug. 1972

The Sandhurst Ethiopian Expedition 1972. Made the first ascent of the volcanic plug Mt. Wehni, on top of which stands the ancient prison of the Princes. Scientific work was also carried out in the region of Lake Stephanie.

Membership

The Society has 250 members, many of them expert explorers in a particular field. All are eligible to take part in expeditions, but Honorary, Honorary Overseas, Associate and Corporate members support the Society financially or in some other way. The Council includes an Honorary Secretary, Honorary Treasurer, and a Quartermaster/Equipment Adviser. Fully sponsored expeditions generally appoint their own Leader, Secretary and Treasurer and many of their personnel from among the Society's membership. Other expeditions can be given the approval and support of SES by the Council and are then eligible to borrow equipment, receive advice and use the name of SES in their publicity.

A base is maintained in Wiltshire, as an administrative, training and briefing centre and equipment store.

Members have to be proposed and seconded by existing members, and then elected by the Council which meets about five times a year.

The Scientific Link

The Society depends on its connections with the scientific world. From the middle 1960s the Chairman and his associates have had an excellent liaison with the Natural History Department of the British Museum, the Royal Botanic Gardens at Kew, the Fauna Preservation Society, the Department of Archaeology at London University.

Young People
Considerable stress is placed on the involvement of SES with other exploration societies, and especially those that cater for young people. Close liaison is kept with WEXAS and the the Young Explorers' Trust.

The Future
As well as furthering scientific exploration, SES wants to play its part in improving Britain's post-imperial relationships with the Third World. It hopes to strengthen our ties with other peoples overseas by giving various forms of assistance, by seeking knowledge and by disseminating it at home and abroad. The Society from the outset has included members from many foreign and Commonwealth countries. It seeks to promote worthwhile, peaceful and possibly adventurous projects that will be of real service to mankind.

The Cost
Because of the high cost of travel, expeditions to distant places can be

very expensive. SES has no resources other than subscriptions from its own members, money from the sale of literary and film rights and from lectures, and the subventions of industrial and commercial firms and of individual well-wishers. It needs the support of everyone interested in scientific exploration, wild life conservation, closer links between the services, industry, educational and exploration organisations, and aid to developing countries.

WEXAS

45 Brompton Road
Knightsbridge
London SW3 1DE

WEXAS International Inc
Suite 354
Graybar Building
420 Lexington Avenue
New York
NY 10017
USA

WEXAS (for World Expeditionary Association) was founded in London in 1970 to provide an information and travel service for expeditions. Membership has since become open to anyone, and WEXAS currently has many thousands of members, spread over 83 countries. Offices are located in London and New York, and further offices are planned for the next few years. WEXAS has become predominantly a travel club for the majority of its members (for travel details and a WEXAS membership application form, see the 6-page WEXAS section in this handbook). On the travel side, WEXAS' appeal derives from its worldwide programme of low cost flights, and from its programme of 2, 3 and 4 week adventure holidays (at special low cost club rates) to such diverse areas of the world as the east coast of Greenland and the fiords of New Zealand's South Island. However the expedition information service has remained an essential component of the WEXAS range of services. Serious expedition organisers may, on joining WEXAS, receive useful contacts for their expedition planning, and names and addresses of the correspondents of expeditions at the planning stage. The Awards Committee of WEXAS makes financial grants to promising UK-based expeditions each year. It should be noted, however, that these expedition services are only available in the UK, and only to serious expedition organisers able to establish their *bona fides*. This means scientific expeditions, youth training expeditions or high-powered adventure expeditions. WEXAS' services outside the UK are limited to its Travel Programme, its Discoverers Programme of adventure holidays, and distribution to members of the extremely high quality *Expedition* magazine and other WEXAS publications. WEXAS members in the UK can attend regular film and lecture evenings presented by distinguished explorers and travellers. There are no restrictions on who can join WEXAS. Individual Membership costs £6.00 (£10 overseas) and Family Membership costs £12 (£20 overseas) — good value for money if only for the WEXAS publications, quite apart from the money-saving travel programme.

Young Explorers' Trust
(The Association of British Youth Exploration Societies)
c/o Royal Geographical Society
1 Kensington Gore
Kensington
London SW7 2AR

The Young Explorers' Trust came into being through the joint action of a number of societies and other organisations which promote or support expeditions of young people of school age. These bodies had wished for some time to join in establishing a national association for the promotion of youth exploration, and to provide a forum within which societies and individuals could exchange information and act together for their mutual benefit.

The Young Explorers' Trust is not a commercial organisation with services to sell, and it does not organise its own expeditions, place individuals on expeditions, or make travel bookings. It is a registered charity whose members work together to share their ideas and experience.

Membership is open to any group or society which wishes to take part in the Trust's activities; to contribute to as well as benefit from its meetings, courses, information and other activities; and to improve their own standards and those of the youth exploration movement as a whole. In seeking to promote appropriate standards of safety, organisation and fieldwork on expeditions of young people, the Trust is particularly anxious to help and advise societies who do not have a great deal of experience, and who wish to be put in touch with others with relevant

Malay fishermen preparing fishing traps.

knowledge. Applications from small societies — school, youth groups and others — are especially welcome.

Associate Membership is available to individuals and bodies who are interested in this work, but who are not active in running their own expeditions of young people.

Present members include all the major national and regional bodies active in this field, as well as school and university groups. Close links are maintained with the Nature Conservancy, the Field Studies Council, the Royal Geographical Society and the Association of Education Committees, all of whom are represented on the Council of the Trust.

The administration of the Trust is vested in a Council of twenty representatives of member groups and societies.

Meetings, courses and conferences are held in different parts of the country, covering a wide range of topics connected with expeditions. There is an annual general meeting and symposium on a topic important to exploration. Study group conferences debate aspects of expedition work in detail. Courses are arranged on various topics.

Study Groups report on matters concerning the areas in which expeditions operate; and other groups are concerned with practical matters such as food supplies, equipment and training.

An Iceland Unit provides help with the special problems of the large numbers of expeditions visiting that country.

Leaflets are published giving summaries of information on a wide variety of topics.

A Bulletin is published twice a year, and there is also a quarterly newsletter which is intended to have a very wide distribution.

A Reference Library of reports and other relevant materials is being built up.

An Expedition Index enables members with particular problems to be put rapidly in touch with others who have relevant advice to offer.

Guidance to leaders is available from the Executive Officer, and the Council has set up a scheme for giving advice and approval to school/youth expeditions; financial help is available to approved applicants providing requests are made before the middle of November of the year preceding their expeditions.

Membership of the Trust as defined in the Rules is open to: 'national and regional organisations and school, college, university or other clubs and societies which have among their purposes the organisation for young people of expeditions which involve significant elements of discovery and exploration.'

The Expedition Vehicle

Roger F. Hamer

There are three factors to be taken into account when deciding on the transportation method to be used to and on an expedition: (a) time, (b) cost, (c) load.

The type of project will dictate whether you have a number of small vehicles, or one prime-mover which will get you there and back and act as a base from which you can trek on foot, and which can move ahead to set up next base with all the bulk stores.

Such a decision is affected by budget more than anything else, and also by the numbers you can afford to have tied to the steering wheel. Trucks do not move on their own. I am a great believer in changing transport as infrequently as you can possibly manage.

The Vehicle

There are three old and well-tried favourites in the field:
1. The Long Wheel Base Landrover.
2. The Ford Transit Minibus.
3. The Bedford (RL) 3 Tonner.

These three have the advantage of being known worldwide, and consequently there are few countries where spares are unavailable. Also their performance is well tested in all climates.

Your decision as to which to use depends on numbers, the need for 4-wheel drive or not, and cost. There is, of course, the factor of driver capability. The Landrover and the Minibus can be handled by the domestic car driver; the Bedford takes you into the realms of the HGV (Heavy Goods Vehicle) Licence.

The Landrover 22/23 mpg

Can carry eight people in comfort and is reasonably economical on fuel, providing it is driven properly and is well maintained. With a roof-rack fitted, the Landrover can be made into a very pleasant, self-contained expedition unit that will get you anywhere.

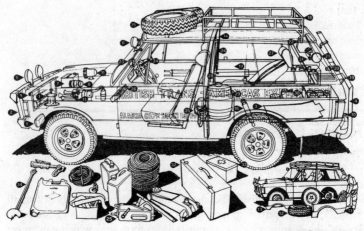

1 Front mounted capstan winch 3,000 lb capacity	15 Roof mounted spare wheels	25 Tirfor jack
2 Reinforced bumper/cow catcher guard	16 Special low-temperature shock absorbers	26 Stereo-tape player and radio
3 Petrol tank undershield	17 Insulated body panels	27 Reclining seat with full safety harness and headrest
4 Raised exhaust extension	18 Roof rack	
5 Four Quartz-Iodine spot and fog lights	19 Steps on tailgate	28 Built-in safe
6 Two swivel spot lights	20 Power point in rear of vehicle for cooker etc.	29 Water keg
7 Split charge two battery system	21 Heated rear screen	30 Partitioned stowage lockers
8 Heavy duty alternator	22 Wiper/washer equipment for rear screen	31 Inspection light, 26ft lead
9 Radiator muff	23 Extra instruments — tachometer, oil pressure and temperature gauges, ammeter for split charge system	32 Fully comprehensive tool kit
10 Four extra towing eyes		33 Medical supplies
11 Sirens and air horns		34 Extra equipment, hand winches, ground anchors, cable, tow ropes etc
12 Swamp tyres		
13 Removable wing panels	24 Map reading and interior lights	35 Coffee maker
14 Roll-bar		

Range Rover converted for expedition use.

The Transit Minibus 20 mpg

Can carry sixteen people in comfort and again will not give you too many headaches on fuel costs. With a roof-rack, it will suit any reasonably large party on road or track in most countries, and in most climates.

The Bedford 3 Tonner 12 mpg

The ideal expedition work-horse for up to twenty people, but can be heavy on fuel. With ingenuity, the 3 Tonner can be structured to carry all the bodies and their stores inside the truck, It is a vehicle that really will go anywhere, and get you out of anything.

Fuel:

With the present cost of petrol, go for diesel. Apart from cost, diesel is more often available even in the most remote places. Performance may be less dramatic and the noise level higher, but at least you know you can obtain fuel.

Trailers

Because of numbers or load you may have to take a trailer behind the vehicle. But my advice is — DON'T, if you can possibly do without. They can be an infernal nuisance, particularly in bad terrain. The trailer is an encumbrance and has a mind of its own. It will get stuck in soft sand, it will slip into ditches, and it will overturn whenever it gets the chance. If you have a trailer on the back, you can be sure that you will one day take a narrow track by mistake, and have to turn round, when without it you could have reversed.

Roof-racks

Useful, but a word of warning. Make sure that you have it made and fitted for expedition work and weigh the stores you are putting on the roof, or you will find that you have exceeded the front axle safe load, and end up nose-down, stranded, in the least inhabited area, with a smashed axle or cracked chassis. And if you have a roof-rack, always remember it is there. It may sound silly, but only last year I saw a school expedition drive off the ferry in France — out of the car exit. The roof-rack was taken clean off and all the stores ended up in a heap. Not a good way to start. The same thing can happen with low bridges or telegraph wires in remote areas.

Buy or hire your vehicle?

Buy where possible. You can always use it again, or resell — and you can make certain that it is in good condition. No doubt you can sue a hire firm if you have a bad vehicle, but that is no consolation if your expedition has been ruined.

New or Second-hand?

If you are doing a lot of this sort of thing, start new. Otherwise, there are a lot of good second-hand vehicles on the market. If the structure is sound, you can renew the engine and practically rebuild. Mileage, within reason, is no gauge of reliability. There was one Long Wheel Base Landrover, bought secondhand at 15,000 miles, that successfully completed six journeys from London to Nairobi and back over three years with different owners, and was showing a slight loss of power on the last trip. 'Nelly', as she was affectionately called, was quite a well-known Saharan character, and as far as I know is still going strong.

Well-driven and well-maintained, these three types of vehicle are nearly indestructible and keep their prices.

How many vehicles do you need?

Obviously, this depends on numbers, and on the need for mobility in the expedition area. If you are to be fairly static once you have reached your expedition base, you can manage with one vehicle. A second vehicle can be useful for emergency back-up or for small party transport. One can be used for base, as a centre for stores, cooking, etc, while the other can do the running about. If you are working in sticky terrain, two vehicles can get each other out of trouble, but each vehicles doubles your fuel bill, and with four-wheel drive and a few strong shoulders you ought to be able to sort out any problems of bogging-down. There is absolutely no point in taking four Landrovers, where one and a Bedford will do.

Spares

The size of your spares kit depends on where you are going and the mechanical ability of the driver. It would be nice to have two of everything, but hardly practical. Basic sets of gaskets, filters, plugs, hoses, bulbs, etc for roadside repairs, and a comprehensive tool kit — tyre levers, spanners, jacks, etc should suffice. At least two spare wheels and a tow chain are essential, and if you are going into desert areas — a set of sand ladders.

The essence of keeping out of trouble is good and sensible driving. Most broken axles, blown tyres, etc can be laid at the door of an inattentive or over-enthusiastic driver.

The key to an untroubled expedition is in routine checks and maintenance. If you make a habit of casting an eye over the vehicle at all stops, looking for leaks, etc and make a regular check of oil and water levels, tyre pressures, etc at least once a day, the major problems can be avoided and early remedial action taken. A vehicle is much like the human body — treat it right and it won't let you down; neglect it and you are in trouble. Before leaving, get a list of service points in the area of your expedition from the manufacturers of your vehicle.

Tyres

Start with new and have two new spares. Better to be safe than sorry. Like the rest of the vehicle, treat them properly. Make sure that they have the right pressures. Don't scuff them on kerbs or rocks (if you can help it). Unless you are operating in extremes of terrain, there is absolutely no need to equip the vehicle with special sand or studded tyres. Those recommended for the vehicle will do, of heavy duty pattern. Use radials and tubed not tubeless tyres.

Security

Whatever vehicle you are using, make sure that you have a strong steel box welded or bolted in the cab, and fitted with a good, solid lock. In it, you can carry vehicle documents, passports, traveller's cheques, etc. Just to lock these things in the cab, in full view of the passing crowd, is insufficient. Brief-cases, suitcases and suchlike attract the thief. Never leave your vehicle unguarded. In Morocco or Algeria, a truck can be stripped of all movables faster than *piranha* fish can strip a carcass. Don't issue a challenge to the light-fingered; you will always lose. Apart from the inconvenience, you are putting irresistible temptation in their way, and the resulting contact with local petty-officialdom may turn you into a raving idiot.

Documents and Permits

Find out your requirements early. In most countries on the periphery of Europe, the information services of the RAC or AA can give you all you need and make your arrangements. But if you are going further afield, you will hit some problem requirements — bail-bonds, *carnets*, border tariffs, etc. These can take months to obtain from some of the African states, and can only be got from the capitals concerned. Some visas are only valid for seven days. You may have to detour to one centre in the country for an extension, which is quite likely to involve a lot of patient waiting on the whim of a power-crazy bureaucrat. This is all part of planning. Make sure that you have all the necessary documents before you start, or that you know what you have to do or where you have to go to get them.

Vehicle Preparation

It may be great fun to carry out all the preparation of the expedition vehicle yourself, but unless you really know what you are doing, it is seldom wise. There are a number of firms which specialise in the design and preparation of expedition trucks. By using their expert services, much time and trouble can be saved on the road, and in the long run it could be cheaper to have the job professionally done. Not only that — these firms are a focus for the buying and selling of vehicles designed for the job, and are a good source of second-hand vehicles suited for heavy duty in off-the-track conditions.

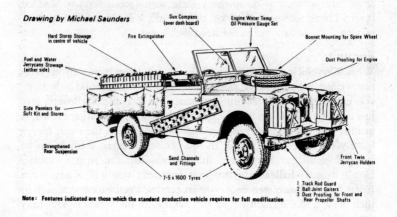

Drawing by Michael Saunders

Sun Compass (over dash board)

Engine Water Temp
Oil Pressure Gauge Set

Hard Stores Stowage in centre of vehicle

Fire Extinguisher

Bonnet Mounting for Spare Wheel

Fuel and Water Jerrycans Stowage (either side)

Dust Proofing for Engine

Side Panniers for Soft Kit and Stores

Strengthened Rear Suspension

Sand Channels and Fittings

7·5 x 1600 Tyres

Front Twin Jerrycan Holders

1 Track Rod Guard
2 Ball Joint Gaiters
3 Dust Proofing for Front and Rear Propellor Shafts

Note: Features indicated are those which the standard production vehicle requires for full modification

Local or Rented Transport

If you are going overland, it is better to move from your home base lock, stock and barrel. For a group of any size, getting on and off buses, trains, etc can be a nuisance. Although cheap local transport is generally available, you have to weigh up the merits or demerits of its use. The feasibility of fitting into time-tables (if they exist), the chances of getting all your party on one bus, your lack of mobility at your destination — all these have to be considered. You have far greater flexibility if you are self-contained and move *en bloc*.

It is possible to rent a vehicle for self-drive in most countries these days, but again you can be landed with a bad deal. Or you can hire a vehicle with driver, but there you have the possible snag of incompatibility between driver and group, compounded by language problems.

A few overland firms in the UK specialise in the supply of transport, drivers and equipment for specific group projects, and will provide these facilities in many of the areas to which expeditions commonly go. This is more expensive than doing it yourself, but can take many problems off the shoulders of the expedition leader, who is often the driver as well.

TRANS AFRICAN

London to Johannesburg   16 weeks

London to Nairobi   12 weeks

☆☆☆☆☆☆☆☆☆☆☆☆☆☆☆☆☆☆☆☆☆☆☆☆☆☆

REGULAR FILM SHOWS
Send for full colour brochure   Now

PLAYMATES

EUROPEAN CAMPING EXPERIENCES

North Africa 6 weeks   Morocco 3 weeks
Munich October fest 8 days
Greece Turkey 4 weeks

☆☆☆☆☆☆☆☆☆☆☆☆☆☆☆☆☆☆☆☆☆☆☆☆☆☆

PLAYMATES

165, Kensington High St, London W.8.

Enquiries Africa Tel: 01-937 5964

Europe Tel: 01-937 3028

Points on Driving in Extreme Conditions:
Hot Climates

Heat affects the vehicle and the human body in comparable ways. It strains the circulation, clogs up the respiration, and is hard on the feet. In the same way as you slow down your pace in hot weather, do not expect or demand Formula 1 performance from your vehicle. You will need more water as you will find that you get a wastage from evaporation. If you drive too fast on tracks in the desert, your tyres may overheat and all blow out together. Most dramatic.

Make sure you have a good water reserve, check your mileage to the next fuel stop, and keep an eye on your filters. Above all, take it steadily and sensibly. Then you will be as happy as a sand-boy, and so will your truck.

Cold Climates

Don't let things freeze up. Check your anti-freeze, give the engine a chance to warm up before blasting-off on the first run of the day, and watch out for accumulations of ice around your axles. Make sure you are using the right oils and have them with you for topping up.

In both hot and cold climates, consider how you are feeling. The chances are your truck is feeling the same, and will behave just as you would. Trucks break down under extreme conditions through lack of thought on the part of their drivers, and because the possible hazards have not been evaluated beforehand.

Pre-Planning

There is an old army saying: 'Time spent in reconnaissance is seldom wasted.' Much reconnaissance can be done from maps, books and full use of the expert information services that are available. But nothing beats the on-the-spot knowledge of people who have been there before.

The success of an overland expedition largely depends on the depth and detail of the planning. Once you are on the way, it is often too late, and if you have the wrong transport, you are stuck with it.

Expedition Vehicle Maintenance

J. R. Williams

Are you planning to travel on a private expedition? Do you have any talent for mechanical matters? Do you enjoy 'mucking about' with cars? If the answer to each question is 'yes', then you will already have volunteered to be the Expedition Mechanic. It's highly probable you will come to regret this rash action so I suggest you reconsider now, before it's too late.

First, think about the conditions you work under at home — fairly clean garage, good lighting, tea-breaks whenever you like, nearby motor shops with plenty of spare parts, friends who can lend you a hand and tools, and so much more. Now imagine what it will be like in the middle of nowhere. There is dirt everywhere and lousy lighting. Spare parts and tools disappear mysteriously. There are extremes of heat and cold. Regrettably, your companions won't show much enthusiasm for sharing the dirt and discomforts whenever a second pair of hands is required. There aren't any shops handy for parts. As for tea-breaks, nine times out of ten you can forget about them.

Minor troubles like punctures, blocked fuel pipes and slipped ignition timing occur regularly; they are merely irritating inconveniences, though after a while people will wonder whether the vehicle is in as good shape as you have claimed. Worse is to come. The important events in the life of the Mechanic never happen while you are travelling through a town with a quiet side-street handy for repairs. Instead, they always take place on a rutted dirt road that has seen no grading or maintenance since the time of Genghis Khan. This makes it very awkward when you have to squeeze under the car.

The bare and desolate countryside has an immediate and profound effect on the Mechanic. It makes him feel depressed and discouraged even before he hauls out his toolbox. In addition the nearest main road is 100 miles away with a further 45 miles to what passes for a town in that region.

After rolling and squirming under the car for five minutes looking for the right   nuts and bolts, you may think the manufacturer's handbook has it all wrong. Don't give up before it becomes apparent that everything is camouflaged by serveral years' accumulation of grease and dirt. All this muck must be scraped off before the spanners will fit. The problem of identifying parts is not helped by the fact that the complete underside is just a murky grey mass of chassis and transmission gear. In contrast, there is a bright bank of light between the ground and the lower edge of the car. Each time you look away from the job in hand a malevolent beam of light stabs the eyes, resulting in a throbbing headache.

But before this headache starts, other discomforts become apparent. Your neck aches to such an extent you wonder how it can continue to support your head. Arms ache intolerably, knees are bent at an awkward angle *and* start to tremble; to cap it all you keep thinking that you have slipped a disc. There is more: small stones make their presence felt. While their distribution under your body is quite random there is always one that digs into a shoulder. No matter how many times you change position, it's always there. You can reach back, grope for it and throw it far away. Two minutes later it is digging into a shoulder again, even more painfully. Continue throwing stones from under the car all you like, there will always be one under a shoulder. It is part of the job, something you learn to live with.

Another discomfort inherent to the job seems at first to be only slightly irritating; so innocent, people automatically adjust to it under normal circumstances. This discomfort is very simple and is spelt thus: SWEAT. The head is the first part to be affected. Sweat runs in small trickles down the face, getting in the eyes and nose before finding its way down the breastbone to form a puddle in the navel. Dust, and there will be plenty of it, is inevitably attracted to any moisture. The mixture so created on the navel and chest has the same effect as a sheet of gauge oo sandpaper trapped between the skin and shirt. Each slight movement produces an abrasive effect which is unbelievable. A hot sweaty face attracts every fly within a radius of 2 miles. You know very well that they cannot be brushed away but you try anyway. What happens? Four bolts drop into the dust, a heavy transmission part falls and gives you a bloody nose, and your wrist comes into contact with the hot exhaust pipe. Very painful indeed.

Surely by now you are having second thoughts on taking this job? Why not take on the job of Quartermaster, ensuring the group always has a good supply of food? He usually does his paperwork at a pavement café; at worst, in the car. Your resolve hasn't weakened yet? No? I'll go on.

Remember that most mechanical gubbins are lubricated by that marvellous stuff called OIL. When you are under the car you can be sure that some oil will splatter in the eyes and more will jet into your open, panting mouth. Yet more oil (it seems to be everywhere) covers hands and spanners. While one end of a spanner slips on the rounded corners of a stubborn nut, the other slips out of your oily grasp and flies away to land just out of reach. Knuckles become badly scraped and nicked of course. That should go without saying but I thought I should remind you of it.

Trials and tribulations of the Desert traveller.

Stand back for a while and imagine waiting for the Mechanic to complete his repairs. It may be a longish wait so you may as well have a brew-up. He will certainly appreciate it when he's finished. Eventually he appears and gets to his feet with a few grunts and groans; take a good look at him. He is covered from head to foot with uneven patches of sweat-soaked oil and dust. His clothes are crumpled. Legs and arms are a-tremble. His hair is tangled and standing up in all directions; and note the eyes: they are either dull and lifeless or staring wildly. Before he can collect his thoughts and speak coherently, sit him down. Push a mug of the afore-mentioned brew into his hands. It won't be ingratitude that makes him spill a great deal of it over his knees and your boots. It is caused by the lack of any real strength in his trembling hands.

Work in the engine compartment *may* seem easier — flies and perspiration are not real problems — but the only parts readily accessible are the radiator and fan belt. Space round the motor is so restricted that arms and hands have to be bent at unnatural angles to make the spanners fit. Even so, a nut is so far away that your arms are at full stretch most of the time. You can stand on the front bumper or kneel on a wing but after a while your back, arms and knees tell you it would be better to face twenty-four hours of interrogation by the Spanish Inquisition, rack and all.

By now you should be seriously considering another responsibility within the group. If you are determined to be the Mechanic, it is obvious you are either a mechanical wizard or a super optimist. I hope these qualities continue to keep you going when you are 'on the road'.

Off-The-Beaten-Track Motoring

Colin McElduff

Basic Route

Major road networks will no doubt be used as much as possible. Maps will be needed to study alternative approaches and ultimately to provide the distance in miles or kilometres the expedition is likely to travel. Many other relevant factors may emerge, such as back-up between habited areas, distance between refuelling and water points, how to carry extra supplies. The route chosen may present hazardous obstacles, such as river crossings, precarious bridges and appalling road and track conditions which will increase fuel consumption.

Time

Time is of the essence and one of the most important ingredients of any expedition. Every aspect of the trip should be studied in detail to ensure that you have allowed sufficient time to arrive at your destination. The distances out and back, together with any shipping involved and possible waiting time, must also be taken into consideration.

When to go

It is important that those chosen to take part in the expedition are available when the climatic conditions are right. You would not normally travel through mountainous countryside in the depth of winter, nor would you want to be in low-lying areas which are liable to flood in a rainy or monsoon period. Climatic conditions in all the areas you are to travel in must be examined at the planning stage.

Travelling companions

Many an expedition or protracted overland journey has fallen apart through lack of foresight by the organisers in looking into the personalities of the participants. Living in close proximity with others for maybe the first time often brings out unknown personal qualities, some of which in no way improve conditions when the going is tough.

Great care therefore must be taken in choosing the right team. The participants' health, physical condition, age, temperament, knowledge and general ability should be studied fully.

Political situation

The political scene in many countries changes from one week to the next. This may affect border crossings. You should keep up to date on the political situation in the countries you will pass through. Ask yourself the question: 'What do I do if this or that country's borders are closed to me?'— alternative planning is needed here. Certain areas, districts, and provinces within some countries may be restricted and permits will have to be applied for. In some cases you may even, on entering or transiting through a country, be subjected to further restrictions. Research the situation well in advance in case special permits have to be applied for.

Vehicles and Supplies

It is vital for any long distance motoring project that the right vehicle is chosen. It must be one that has good spare parts potential wherever it goes and is capable of carrying the occupants comfortably over great

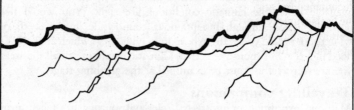

distances with their personal kit, equipment and spares. Range too is important for on some sections of the journey, habitations where fuel, water and food may be obtained may be non-existent. Check in advance on the length, height, weight limits of the vehicle in relation to regulations for ferries, bridges, etc. Remember too the overall weight of the equipment as a whole and that of the occupants. The vehicle should never be subject to a gross weight above that recommended by the manufacturer. Technically, you should be able to diagnose mechanical faults that may occur and be able at least to keep the vehicle going under all normal circumstances, other than a major breakdown which may necessitate obtaining parts not normally carried.

Finance

Because of the ever-changing conditions that will be encountered, (e.g. local price variations, political developments, loss of time due to adverse weather and road conditions, all factors which can affect the ultimate cost of the journey as a whole) a contingency must be built into your estimates.

Various emergency funds should be set aside. Remember that it is better to overestimate than to underestimate. Currency regulations of the different countries to be visited will have to be studied thoroughly and notes made of any reference to minimum amounts required for entry, together with any bonds or guarantees that may have to be supplied. You must ensure that you have sufficient funds available to get to your destination and/or return, together with an emergency fund to be used in case of accidents, especially those that may necessitate the repatriation of one or more of the participants. Additional expenses will have to be taken into consideration for personal and vehicle documentation such as visas, *carnets de passage en douane*, vehicle and medical insurance, ferries across rivers, toll bridges and roads, camping, gratuities, and, last but not least, pocket money. Do not skimp on the allocation of funds.

Iguiddi Moulay rides "El Horof" or the "sheep-camel."

Vehicle Indemnity Insurance

Richard Harrington

Indemnity *carnets* (touring guarantees) are a form of insurance that is often not fully understood by those taking vehicles outside Europe, especially through the Middle East. The following explains briefly how this form of bond or guarantee operates.

You may be contemplating taking a vehicle through various countries without paying duty.

Some countries allow a vehicle to pass through 'ex duty' on a *carnet de passage en douane* provided the vehicle does not remain in that country longer than the period permitted by the local customs authorities. This period varies from country to country.

If *for any reason* a vehicle remains in any country for longer than the specified period, local customs authorities may claim the duty at once. If an indemnity carnet has been arranged through the AA or RAC, the customs authorities may claim direct from the motoring organisation.

Before issuing a *carnet* (and before the vehicle can leave the UK), the motoring organisation will demand an indemnity from the owner to cover itself against any possible claims. This can be dealt with in one of two ways:

a) A lump sum can be deposited in the UK with the motoring organisation, before the vehicle leaves the country.

b) An insurance company handling *carnets* can provide the necessary guarantee or 'stand in' for the required amount, subject to a proposal form being completed satisfactorily.

It should be clearly understood that this does not relieve the owner of paying the duty should the necessity arise. The insurance company is entitled under the indemnity to recover the amount paid out from the vehicle owner. The guarantee merely enables the owner to take the vehicle out of the UK without having to 'freeze' a lump sum in the UK.

The amount of indemnity required is entirely a matter for the motoring organisation concerned. However, premiums tend to be about 4 to 6 per cent of the value of the vehicle, higher rates being more likely if the vehicle is to pass through high risk countries, especially those at war. Assuming that you could even get into a country without a *carnet* or without putting up a bond on entry, you could well end up in prison if the local authorities had reason to claim the full *local* value of the vehicle from you and you were unable to pay. Remember that the local value of the vehicle may well be two or three times its value in the UK.

To sum up: the carnet is the foreign customs authority's guarantee that it will receive payment if necessary (e.g. if you write off the vehicle and leave it by the roadside, or if you sell it illegally and get caught). The insurance bond you put up (by paying a premium) is the motoring organisation's guarantee that it will not be left out of pocket. Theoretically, the insurance companies could issue a *carnet* themselves, but the system is standardised by all insurance companies working through the AA or the RAC.

Arussi women of Ethiopia's Lake District.

Jetboats for Expeditions

Ralph Brown

From earliest times man has used streams and rivers, nature's highways, to explore new territories and to carry on trade and commerce. The first craft were crude rafts of logs, reeds, or air-filled animal skins. Later came oars and sails. Then Archimedes invented the screw from which the propeller was developed. All of these systems, however, ran into difficulties when it came to going upstream in a swift whitewater current or where the craft were liable to damage from rocks or shallow water.

Man has long dreamed and experimented to overcome these problems by use of a water jet to propel his boats. Patents were applied for early in the nineteenth century for systems that would actually propel a boat forward, but each had a drawback that made it impractical. The first successful system was developed by a New Zealander, Bill Hamilton, in 1954. His major breakthrough was in the nozzle design which directed the jet out through the transom above the water line. He was able to achieve a speed of 17 mph and to navigate successfully up the fast-flowing rocky rivers in the high country near his home. For six more years he worked at perfecting his unit and finally, in 1960, his son Jon felt ready to tackle one of the world's major river challenges, running up the Colorado River through the Grand Canyon of Arizona. This is now down in the history books as the first jetboat expedition up a major river with big whitewater rapids. Since then many of the world's roughest rivers have been conquered by jetboat.

A marine jet is simply a water pump driven by a conventional marine engine that sucks water up through a grill in the bottom of the boat near the stern and squirts it out through a nozzle in the transom. Since there is nothing protruding below the bottom of the hull, it only needs enough water to float the hull, and at high speeds when planing along the surface of the water, this can be as little as four inches.

Jetboats can even be bounced over short sand or gravel bars that are out of water. A modern jet will operate at approximately the same fuel economy and top speed as an inboard or outdrive with the same hull and horsepower, but it has more acceleration and will get a heavier load up on the plane. It is also much safer since there is no exposed propeller to chop off an arm or leg and, since there is no underwater gear to damage on a rock or in shallows, you are much more sure of getting home! Jetboats are more manoeuverable at low speeds if the proper driving technique is used, a technique that varies considerably from that used in driving a conventional inboard. At high speed, a jetboat can be turned end for end in virtually its own length or can be put in reverse and stopped in two or three lengths.

I drove one of the two eighteen-foot Hamilton boats on the Zaïre River Expedition, the first boats ever to go, up or down, through the world's largest rapids from Kinshasa to Inga (collectively known as the Livingstone Falls), the ultimate achievement in expedition jetboating. The Zaïre River is for most of its 2,800 miles, slow, wide and deep; however, below Kinshasa, the placid river enters a gorge and turns into a wild churning monster with a depth of up to 1,500 feet (the bottom is below sea level). The volume is as much as 7,500,000 gallons per second (70 times the size of the Colorado), making it the second largest river, by volume, in the world. (The largest, the Amazon, has no rapids along its main route.) The eighteen-foot jets with their greater manoeuverability and power were able to go up and down through rapids that turned back giant forty-foot inflatables. Of these rapids Stanley spoke a hundred years before: 'no boat could hope to survive'. And few other types of boat could hope to survive.

On the Zaïre, the jets were used to recce each big rapid, taking the helmsmen of the inflatables through for a look. This enabled them to determine the best position to enter each rapid for, with the river anything from half a mile to ten miles wide, there were a great many possible routes. Without this reconnaissance, the crews of the inflatable boats would have found it extremely difficult, on their own, to find the best way of going through. With the jets, it was possible to go to the head of a rapid and, whilst facing upstream and running at the same speed as the current, to hold long enough to examine the rapid below. The jets would move across the river from point to point until the entire rapid had been surveyed in this manner. A similar procedure would then be followed at the bottom of the rapid, by holding the boats in the eddies and working across the river point to point.

Rivers can be rather unpredictable. I am writing these words from the banks of the Tana River in northern Kenya. Old records indicate that during the rainy season, it was once possible for paddle steamers to navigate the lower reaches of this river. However, after five years of drought, the river is a series of mudholes with a trickle in between. In places you can wade across ankle deep. Even the inflatables run aground. Consequently we are doing our share of pushing and pulling.

Another problem in Africa is having to share the boatable channel with hippos and crocodiles. Since hippos apparently feel secure in deep water, they will head for the deepest channel if disturbed. As this is often the only boatable channel, you may end up in a race to avoid being 'cut off at the pass'. We usually carry thunder-flashes, but don't do what one crewman did. When we came to a herd of about twelve hippos, he got so excited that he threw the thunderflash over the top of the herd so that it exploded behind them, causing a stampede directly towards the boat. Fortunately we were faster than they were and got through just in time. Certainly nothing can improve one's concentration and the precision of one's driving more than seeing hippos or crocs slide into pools ahead!

Although jets may seem too expensive for a lot of expeditions, remember that a good boat can cross sandbars with only a few inches of water, dodge and weave its way through boulder-studded rapids and claw through whitewater as high as the boat is long. Jetboats can carry half a ton or more of people and equipment at cruising speeds of 25 mph or more. If there is a waterway roughly parallel to the expedition's route, a jetboat can be used to ferry people and supplies, to take scientists off to set or to collect traps or nets, and to extend the area of scientific study, thereby accomplishing far more than the same group could on foot or by rubber boat. Taking into account the cost of keeping an expedition in the field, it might well be possible to save more than the cost of the jetboat by being able to achieve all the objectives of the expedition in a fraction of the original time planned. Anyone organising an expedition along a waterway would be well advised to give serious consideration to the use of jetboats.

Bargain Air Travel

Richard Harrington

For the last ten years, the UK has been the world centre for cheap air tickets, the result of an excess of empty seats on the airlines of the world. Cartels have always held together with difficulty, and the International Air Transport Association is no exception. To it belong most of the world's large airlines. In theory, they are committed to selling tickets at agreed rates thereby avoiding the need to compete on price. In practice, many airlines, especially but not always those with fewer obvious advantages (particularly Third World Flag Carriers and those of countries desperate for hard currency), have been obliged to operate outside the price cartel for their own survival. This led in the late 1960's to the growth of the so-called 'bent' scheduled ticket market and a proliferation of so-called 'bucket shops'. Many of these made it their business to sell discounted scheduled air tickets, as well as seats on charter flights operating under the auspices of a spurious group affinity in order to bypass what had by then become a series of completely out-dated regulations. (Six months' club membership, club meetings, no advertising of travel services, etc.)

The picture has changed radically since the late 1960s and early 1970s. Bucket shops still abound but are less inclined to be thriving. The regular travel trade has caught up a lot of ground and capitalised on the cheap end of the travel market on which the so-called 'bent' retailers did such a marvellous entrepreneurial marketing job in the late 60s/early 70s . The airlines began to offer more attractive promotional fares. ABC charters arrived in 1972, based on the advance purchase principle pioneered by British Airways' Earlybird flights (whose invention is, so far as I know, anonymous).

So what is the picture today? Are fares still available at rates below those available from the High Street travel agent? The answer is 'yes.' Not as many as five years ago. Discounts are not as big as they were.

And thanks to the oil crisis and inflation, the full fares that discount rates are based on are at least double the rates of three years ago.

Certain publications carry advertisements for 'bucket shops.' With very few exceptions, these outlets will produce tickets, at varying rates of discount (as the seller makes his profit), in return for your money. There are disadvantages however. Stopovers will not usually be possible, outward and return dates may have to be fixed in advance and may not be changeable, refunds on unused ticket portions may be subject to heavy 'cancellation charges.' However depending on the bucket shop you buy from, greater disadvantages may still be to come. You may have to pay entirely in cash, and even though you book months in advance, you may not see your ticket until a few days or hours before the flight. You may never even see it or a receipt at all, but instead be given a rendez-vous where you will meet with fellow passengers and a courier carrying 'tickets' on your behalf. He will check you in discreetly at the airline's desk at the airport. So far so good, give or take a little sweat, but what about the return flight tickets? You may have to call at a travel agency whose address you've been given in Delhi or Singapore and hope that the tickets will be produced when you breathe your name, or if you're lucky, produce a special voucher you've been given in London. Is it really worth the hassle? Of course it isn't always that bad, and the vouchers and the secret street/ hotel rendezvous seem to be on the way out.

What I'm leading up to is that there are bucket shops and bucket shops. Most operate on low margins and even lower overhead budgets. In short, there's not much money to pay for the sort of service you might (if you're lucky!) have come to expect from your local travel agent. Result: uncooperative bucket shop retailers, inadequate flight information, joining instructions, etc., very late ticketing, all of which leaves you sweating, with no assurance that your money is in safe hands, and perhaps considerable difficulty in getting a reasonable refund in the event of cancellation, and so on. Of course there are helpful, efficient bucket shops. In general, they tend to charge a little more than the rest, so if you're shopping round, remember that. If peace of mind about your flight out (and you flight back 12 months later, or whenever) is important to you, it may be worth paying that extra £10 or £20.

Which brings me to WEXAS, now the largest travel club in Europe selling cheap travel to most long-haul destinations. WEXAS began life in 1970 selling cheap tickets to students and especially student expeditions. Today WEXAS still sells cheap tickets — but also provides a worldwide adventure holiday programme (WEXAS Discoverers) and publishes *Expedition* magazine.

The reason for WEXAS' exceptional growth in a field where so many have failed is really very simple. When WEXAS began as a small university-oriented travel club in 1970, the national papers were constantly filled with horror stories of 'bent' charter passengers stranded at airports, or 'fly-by-night' operators disappearing with the life savings of little old ladies planning to visit their grandchildren in Australia. From the beginning, WEXAS set out to put service before all else. At times, the limitations imposed by the airlines selling discount tickets made it impossible to be 100 per cent efficient (late ticketing was the major problem in the early years — today the airlines generally know better). But the service provided came far closer than anything provided elsewhere in this field to being efficient and honest. While WEXAS concentrated on quality rather than growth, it did not take long for word-of-mouth to outstrip paid advertising as a source of members, and growth followed naturally. Today WEXAS has members in 83 countries and 40 per cent of new members live overseas. A New York office was opened in February 1977 to sell the WEXAS Discoverers programme of Adventure Holidays. Overseas offices in a number of key cities around the world are envisaged for the 1980s.

So what bargain air tickets are available now in the late 1970s? Well,

Campsite on the way to find a new butterfly genus in the Sierra Nevada.

there are still some straight discounts on 12-month full fare tickets, with discounts occasionally going as high as 40 per cent or 50 per cent. And for some cities, these fares are operative *to* as well as *from* London. Then there are the excursion fares, with varying minimum and maximum stay requirements, and stopover possibilities, according to the route. Still cheaper are the three types of advance purchase ticket available: APEX and Earlybird on scheduled flights and ABC on charters. The advance booking period on most of these is currently 45 days, and may come down to 30 days in the future.

Then there are the GIT (Group Inclusive Tour) fares sometimes sold in conjunction with genuine land arrangements, and just as frequently sold without these IATA-required price-boosters aimed at keeping fares high enough to stop the various elements of the market (businessman, independent traveller and so on) from being tempted, possibly, into the cheaper fare category of the passenger sitting next to him. Nowadays, bargain tickets tend predominantly to be of the GIT variety, and IATA seems less concerned about this form of ticket bending than about the straight discount variety. The only problem here is that GIT tickets are usually limited to stays of 2, 3 or 4 weeks. If this suits your plans, they're one of the best travel bargains around.

The fall in the value of the pound sterling against the world's major currencies in the last few years has resulted in a situation whereby it is cheaper for Europeans and Americans travelling to Africa or Asia to buy their tickets in the UK. IATA fares have rocketed everywhere in recent years, but had IATA increased them even further in the UK to compensate for the fall in the pound, airlines operating out of the UK would have been priced right out of the market. Hence IATA meets periodically and 'weights' each country against every other. Against the USA, for example, the UK is weighted to give a differential of around 35 per cent at the present time. The USA is itself negatively weighted. Switzerland, with one of the three strongest currencies in the world, is positively weighted and has a differential of over 40 per cent against the pound. In simple terms, this means that the American or the Swiss flying to say Nairobi can save around 35 per cent and 40 per cent by flying via London, less a certain amount because of the indirect routing. Add to this a possible discount that may still be available in London (and almost certainly not in New York or Zurich), and you have potential overall saving of as much as 50 per cent. Add in a high level of efficiency and reliability and it's not difficult to see why an organisation like WEXAS has been able to develop and diversify.

Bureaucratic Hassles Overseas

Richard Harrington

Whatever the brochures may say, travelling outside the so-called 'developed' world isn't a bed of roses all the way. Often the reverse, in fact. A book could be written about the hassles that the single or group traveller may have to face in Central or South America, Africa, Asia and the Middle East. Here I'll limit myself to a few of the more common problems.

Your troubles may start before you leave home. Just getting a visa from the embassy may be an ulcer-provoking experience. Bureaucracy seems to grow in inverse proportion to the rank of the functionary one is dealing with. One embassy required three photos, three forms and three signatures from my 5-week old son before they'd issue a visa. I won't go into details, but the long lunch hours and early closings at the embassy didn't help much. Their country was much the same way, right down to the Voluntary Tourist Development Fund donation at the airport on leaving — you donated voluntarily or you didn't leave at all.

But let me tell you of the joys of a certain African Airport at 3 am. Of being hauled before the Airport Chief of Police and his armed henchmen, dark glasses and all, of being interrogated for half an hour while my passport was scrutinized, only to be told that they had decided to make me 'leader' of our group of transit passengers. Our passports taken, we were dumped on the rubber tyres in the back of a van and herded off across the city ($1^1/_2$ hours): I was to be responsible for ensuring that everyone paid for the compulsory sightseeing trip which our group had joined at our hotel in the belief that the ancient taxis had come to take them back to the airport for the onward flight. At least we finally made it back to the airport in the end. Those of us smart enough to spread a few dollars around accidentally, got their passports back just in time to make it to the check-in desk, where a few further dollars secured for me the only seat left on the plane — leaving behind eight bewildered Brits wishing they'd never left home, clutching their confirmed seat tickets, protesting to a now slightly richer check-in clerk, complete with the moustache that is *de rigueur* among all Third World airport bureaucrats, as he gazed through them as inscrutable as the sphynx. Too bad the next flight wasn't for a week....

By now, you'll have gathered that my lingering memories of hassles abroad have a lot to do with airports. That I cannot deny. However at least I have not fared as badly as the passengers transiting through Baghdad who were put up in the local prison for the night. Apparently the overnight hotel in Moscow wasn't much better five years ago. Maybe now the situation has improved.

Make sure your papers are in order before you go and that you can meet all the health and currency requirements. Some countries like Ghana and Zaïre now demand a minimum expenditure per person per day (currently $40 for Zaïre which seems a lot until you realize that it's $100 for Bhutan) in order to discourage poor tourists. (Yes, they've finally realized that not all tourists are millionaires.) In case you think you can cheat, be warned that for the growing number of countries adopting this type of policy, you have to buy currency vouchers before

you leave. If you plead convincingly at the Embassy/High Commission that you're going on a serious research expedition and can provide letters from potentates in the country to prove it, you may become an exception. But don't count on it. The guys who wrote the rules for a lot of Third World countries didn't think too hard about exceptions to anything, and you may quickly come to realize that whatever the bureaucratic jungle at home, at least your own system is flexible.

Customs is really a matter of commonsense, as is immigration. Immigration officers are usually superior in rank to customs officers, and therefore entitled to be additionally arrogant. Which they almost invariably are. What about the smiles and the welcomes and the flower *leis*? Forget it. Did you really believe that brochure rubbish anyway? But maybe I should be honest and admit that things aren't always all that bad. My wife and I, having been given the dirt treatment by the customs men on duty in Tangiers, stopped at a building a hundred yards further on to ask the way. It turned out to be the Customs HQ. Since it was the Muslim feast of Ramadan and it was after sundown, the off-duty officers were busily eating their first meal in over 14 hours. To the delight of my wife and myself, they not only showed us the way, but insisted that we stay for half an hour and share their meal. Friendlier customs men I have never met anywhere, which goes to show that it is dangerous to generalise.

My attitude to hassles improved after I spent a year studying social anthropology — the best cure for ethnocentricity and national prejudice. I began to understand why Singapore Airport provided barbers to cut the hair of those whose locks exceeded a statutory length indicated on posters hung around the building; and why mini-skirts have been banned in certain African countries; and why so-called hippies have finally been kicked out of Kathmandu and dope has been made illegal there.

I also understand why having a small blond-haired boy of under 2 years of age was a great ice-melter in most countries — an object of intense curiousity amongst blacks, and of great affection amongst the Latins of the Catholic countries, who have almost a reverence for small children. Only amongst the Arabs is a child of little interest. So if you can manage it, take one along on your travels. If he's under 2, his airfare is only 10 per cent anyway.

Ideally you should always wear glasses (not dark ones, which are the prerogative of the police), a dark suit, a white shirt, a dark tie and carry an umbrella. In practice, this is often not much fun when the temperature is 115°F in the shade, the humidity is 100 per cent, and your luggage weighs 35 kilos. Nevertheless, try to keep your clothes clean, use a suitcase rather than a rucksack if you're not backpacking/hitching, shave, and get your hair as close to a crewcut as is possible without looking like an astronaut. A moustache is better than a beard, but avoid both if possible. Don't try to smuggle anything through customs, especially drugs. Hash and grass may be common in the countries you visit, but be careful if you must buy any. Remember that a local dealer may be an agent of the police.

In dealing with airport officials, and with police and other government officers (and airline clerks for that matter), adopt an attitude that is neither servile nor arrogant. A friendly smile, even in the face of rudeness, will go a long way, and you should make every effort to be cooperative. As often as not, you'll have to turn the other cheek, but tell yourself that foreigners are like your own countrymen — they're all individuals and you can't judge the behaviour of them all by that of a few. There's no doubt that the white man's colonial legacy has had a lot to do with the hostility that you may encounter. Put it down to the arrogant selfish attitudes of some of your compatriots who have been there before you. It's not for nothing that the most difficult people you'll encounter in Third World countries are the ones who have the most contact with foreign visitors. It's true that every country has an abundance of friendly people willing to welcome you into their homes, and that generally speaking, the further you get off the beaten tourist track, the more hospitable the people get. That in itself is a good reason for heading away from the tourist trails. In a country where the immigration officer tosses your passport back at you, and where city youths shout abuse as you drive past in your hired car, you may still find people who will make you wonder how your own countrymen could be so cold. Adopt an understanding attitude and you'll have some tremendous experiences where you really feel you're beginning to connect. Learn the language fluently and it's hard to go wrong.

A few tips to close with: if you must spread around a little 'dash' (West African) to oil the palms that facilitate your progress, do so carefully after checking out how to do it properly from a friend who knows the ropes. You may have to do it, say to avoid a few days in a Mexican jail for a mythical driving offence. On the other hand, you could end up in a jail somewhere for trying to bribe an officer of the law — then you might have to bribe a lot more to get out rather than rot for a few months waiting for a trial. The $10 bill tucked in the passport is

the safest approach if you do decide on bribery, as you can always claim you keep your money there for safety. But since almost all officials ask for identity, make sure you don't go through more dollars than necessary.

Don't carry firearms for protection. You'll probably get caught with them on arrival (assuming they haven't been picked out by airport security X-ray checks on departure) and in most countries, importing firearms without a licence is illegal. It's very unlikely you'll ever be in a position where you'll need them. You may get robbed but if you give what you have quickly, you're unlikely to get hurt. Shoot someone and I don't fancy your chances of survival. On the other hand, learn karate and use it if you have to. It almost certainly won't provoke the use of guns.

Always carry your passport with you for identification purposes. If you're driving a vehicle, keep yourself clean-shaven and tidy as you'll be stopped frequently by the police in many countries — if only as a routine check. Be courteous and have all your car papers and your driving licence in order. Be careful to camp at night where you're not likely to get picked up by the police. It's a good idea to have a local friend travelling with you. He'll not only speak the language, but will probably be able to sort out any problems with officials.

There's no excuse for failing to research the countries you intend to visit. Talk to people who have lived in or visited them and find out what problems you may encounter. If you go prepared and adopt a sympathetic, understanding frame of mind, you should be able to manage without trouble.

Youth Hostelling

John Carlton and Diane Johnson

The off-beat traveller will inevitably meet others going to stay at a Youth Hostel and may well want to know what they are all about. The first point is that, although the facilities offered are designed primarily for young people, there is no age limit for staying at Youth Hostels (except in Bavaria, Germany) and they are used by 'the young in heart' of all ages.

The second point is that Youth Hostel facilities are provided by a club run not for profit, but to help young people to travel, to know and love the countryside and appreciate other cultures, thereby promoting international friendship. Each country runs its own hostels independently (usually by committees from its own membership) and the national Youth Hostel Associations of each country are linked through the International Youth Hostel Federation. The Federation (a United Nations sort of organisation) lays down basic standards for its members, but each National Association's interpretation of these does inevitably vary in the light of its own local culture. Theoretically, membership of an Association is necessary for all individual members of hostels but this rule is lax in some countries outside Europe. However membership is very worthwhile for the traveller who thinks he might be using hostels, and those resident in England and Wales should apply to YHA, Trevelyan House, 8 St. Stephens Hill, St. Albans, Herts. (or in person to YHA Services Ltd, 29 John Adam Street, London, WC2). In England and Wales the annual subscription is currently £2 for those over 21 or £1.40 for those between 16 and 21. Scotland and Northern Ireland have their own Associations and their headquarters' addresses are 7 Glebe Crescent, Stirling, and 93 Dublin Road, Belfast, respectively. It is possible to obtain YHA membership at an Association office (and sometimes at a hostel) outside one's country of residence, but one then pays a much higher fee.

Once a member, you can stay at hostels in 49 countries throughout the world. Basically a Youth Hostel will provide a bed in a dormitory of size varying from 4 to 100 beds. There are toilet and washing facilities and a communal room where members can meet, all at a cost of the local equivalent of from 50p to £2 for the night. In most countries, members will find facilities to cook their own food. Cooking utensils and crockery are provided but not always cutlery. Some countries' Youth Hostels offer cheap meals cooked by the warden or staff in charge.

A feature of Youth Hostel life is the sheet sleeping bag — a sheet sewn into a bag with a space for a pillow. Any traveller intending to make much use of Youth Hostels should have one, though there are some Hostels at which sheets may or indeed must be hired, so as to protect mattresses. Most Hostels provide blankets and consider that these are adequately protected by the traveller's own sheet sleeping bag. In this respect, as in others, Youth Hostel customs vary from country to country.

A full list of the 4,000-odd Youth Hostels of the world (published annually) can be obtained at YHA Services Ltd, 29 John Adam Street, London WC2. Ask for the International Handbook — Volume 1, *Europe and the Mediterranean*, and Volume 2, *The Rest of the World*. Each volume costs 65p (80p by post). As well as listing the addresses and facilities of each Hostel, the handbook summarises the local regulations for each country, including prices, lower age limits, facilities for families, etc. However all the information given is subject to correction as circumstances change during the year and of course prices will inevitably rise in time.

We attempt below to make a quick survey of the Youth Hostel facilities of the world.

Europe (including many countries in Eastern Europe but not Russia) is well covered by Hostels and the wide variation in their characteristics reflects the local culture of each country. The British Isles Hostels are perhaps now unique in expecting a small domestic duty from members before departure, but this does help to emphasize to members that they are part of a self-helping club. This idea may be less apparent in some countries, where the Hostel is often run, with the agreement of the National Youth Hostel Association concerned, by the local municipality as a service, and relations between members and staff are strictly commercial. The club atmosphere is stronger also in France, Holland and Greece. For Hostel atmosphere try Cassis; situated in an isolated position on the hills overlooking the *calanques* of Marseilles, 20 miles from the city. In West Germany, where the Youth Hostel movement started, Youth Hostels are very plentiful — mostly large well-appointed buildings, but lacking members' cooking facilities and largely devoted to school parties. Scandinavian Hostels are also usually well-appointed, many having family rooms, and there is therefore more emphasis on family hostelling. Spain still has one-sex Hostels, but these seem to be rapidly disappearing. Iceland has six simple Hostels.

In North Africa there are Hostels in Morocco, Tunisia and Egypt. These too reflect the local culture. Try calling at Asni, a hostel in a Moroccan village 40 miles south of Marrakech on the edge of the High Atlas mountains. Here the warden has three wives and will talk to you with great charm in French.

The Kenyan YHA has eight Hostels, two of which are on the coast. Kanamai, about 15 miles north of Mombasa, has an idyllic setting amongst coconut palms, a few yards from a deserted white sandy beach. Nairobi Hostel is a meeting point for international travellers, and at Nanyuki the hostel is close to one of the routes up Mount Kenya. Kitale Hostel near the Ugandan border is part of a farm with accommodation for eight people and the one room serves as a dormitory, dining and common room.

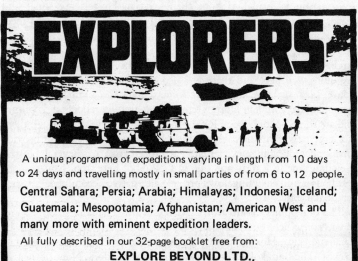

Apart from a few Hostels in the Sudan, the rest of Africa is devoid of Hostels until one reaches the south. Lesotho has one Hostel, Mazeru, which is well worth a visit. Local young Basutos use the Hostel as a youth centre, so travellers have a chance to meet with them. There is a South African YHA but because of the country's *apartheid* policy, it cannot be a member of the International Federation; this ruling also applies to the Rhodesian Association which has two Hostels. The membership cards of white members of the Association in the International Federation will, however, be accepted in these countries. The South African YHA Handbook can be obtained from YHA, PO Box 4402, Capetown. The Hostel at Camps Bay is in a beautiful situation, looking out across the Atlantic Ocean with Table Mountain almost immediately behind it. Unfortunately Port Elizabeth Hostel, a lovely old Victorian house, is very scruffy by South African standards but in a good position near Kings Beach.

Israel has a well-organised Association of some thirty hostels, the smallest having 100 beds. All provide meals and a members' kitchen and many have family rooms. Although there have been hostels in Lebanon for many years, owing to the civil war there, no recent information is available about them. Syrian Hostels are small and reasonably equipped. Many hostellers travelling to or from India meet at the one in Damascus.

Travelling eastwards, there are three Hostels in Iran, one in Kabul, Afghanistan, and a good network in Pakistan. The Pakistani Hostels are quite well kept and there are also a number of Government rest houses open to Hostellers, as are some schools in certain areas during school holidays. Indian Hostels tend to be mainly in schools and colleges and are therefore only open for short periods of the year, although there is a large new permanent Hostel in Delhi. Some Hostels do not provide any kind of bedding, even mattresses. Sri Lanka has several Hostels including one in Kandy and one in Colombo; here, too, Government rest houses and *dak* bungalows provide alternative accommodation at a reasonable price.

The Philippines, South Korea, Malaysia and Thailand all have some Hostels of which the Malaysian ones are particularly well organised. In Thailand, some Hostels listed in the International Handbook appear not to exist. The Bangkok Hostel, however, certainly does. None of the five Hong Kong Hostels is in the city itself.

Japan has the most extensive network of Hostels outside Europe. There are two kinds of Hostel — western style with the usual bunk

beds, and the Japanese style with a mattress rolled out on the floor. Television is a common feature. Several Hostels are on the smaller islands of the country such as Awaji, an island in the Inland Sea. Japanese food is served in most Hostels — a bowl of rice, probably served with raw egg, fish and seaweed and eaten with chopsticks.

Australia has over a hundred Hostels with most of them in New South Wales, Queensland and Western Australia. Distances between them are great. The smaller, more remote Hostels do not have a resident warden and the key has to be collected from a neighbour.

New Zealand has Hostels throughout the country on both the North and South Islands. They are fairly small and simple with no meals provided but have adequate cooking facilities. Many are in beautiful country, such as the Hostel near Mount Cook.

The Canadian and United States Youth Hostel Associations are the only ones now imposing the restrictions on motorists that were at one time applied by all Associations. The North American Associations ask that those using cars should stay at least two nights at a Hostel and not use their car in the intervening day. There are not many Hostels in North America, considering the size of the continent. There are a few Hostels in some of the biggest cities. (In the USA a city Hostel will often turn out to be a YMCA offering rooms to YHA members at reduced rates). Most are in isolated areas of scenic interest not always accessible by public transport. There are, however, chains of hostels in New England, Colorado and the Canadian Rockies. A feature of United States hostelling is the 'Home Hostel' where accommodation is offered to members in private houses. The Canadian government runs a network of hostels on a temporary basis in addition to those of the National Association. The government Hostels are not associated with the International Federation and do not require Youth Hostel membership.

In Central and South America, Youth Hostelling has not yet caught on seriously, although there are a few hostels in Mexico, Argentina, Chile and Uruguay.

Although in the poorer countries of the world you can often obtain other accommodation as cheaply as in the local Youth Hostel, members have the advantage of being able to look up an address in advance at points all over the world. They can then stay at the local branch of their own 'club' finding (albeit minimal) common standards of accommodation and be sure of meeting and exchanging experiences with fellow travellers.

Maps and Map Reading

Ingrid Cranfield

Women often claim, and men just as often prove, to be incompetent when it comes to map reading. Yet maps are simple tools and their efficient handling depends only on the understanding of a few basics.

First, there is scale, the measure that relates distances on the map to corresponding distances on the ground. A small scale map gives a broad overview of a sizeable area, while a large scale map shows a limited area in greater detail. One source of confusion about scale is the phrase 'on a large scale', which, in common parlance, means extensive: yet to show a 'large scale' feature on a map may require a *small* scale. One way of remembering the difference between small and large scale maps, therefore, is to note that features on a small scale map *appear* small, those on a large scale map, large. For most practical purposes, maps at a scale of about 1 : 1,000,000 or smaller are generally considered small scale; those of, say, between 1 : 20,000 and 1 : 1,000,000 large scale. Scales larger than 1 : 20,000 are used on town plans, maps of individual properties or installations and the like.

Map readers may find it useful to make a mental note of one scale and the measure it represents; all other scales can then be compared with it. Thus a scale of 1:250,000 (more accurately 1 : 253,440) means that a quarter of an inch on the map represents a mile on the ground. Metrication in mapping has meant a transition from scales representing round distances in miles (1 : 63,360 = 1 inch to 1 mile; 1 : 253,440 = $^1/_4$ inch to 1 mile) to scales using multiples of ten (1 : 50,000, 1 : 250,000 and so on). The official body that produces maps of the United Kingdom is the Ordnance Survey, which in the last five years or so has been phasing out its maps based on the mile and replacing them with metric maps. The standard unit for a moderately large scale O.S. map is now no longer 1 : 63,360 but 1 : 50,000.

The choice of scale in a map naturally depends on the purpose for which the map is intended. A motorist planning a route cross-country will probably find a map at 1: 500,000 quite satisfactory. A rambler, eager to note smallish features in the field, be they *tumuli* or pubs, will be well advised to acquire a map, or, more frequently, several adjoining map sheets, drawn on 1:50,000 or 1: 25,000. Many official mapping authorities base their map series on a national grid, a network of lines which divides the country into small units and represent the edges of individual map sheets. An index for the series (available for consultation at the map retail outlet or in some cases printed on the back of each sheet in the series) shows which map sheets are needed to cover the area of the purchaser's interest.

Another basic distinction to note is that between topographic and thematic maps. Topographic maps (which include most O.S. maps) show the general nature of the country: the lie of the land, the location and extent of built-up areas, some indication of land use and land cover (forests, marshes, farmland), the courses of roads, railways and other lines of communication, the presence of waterways and any other salient features, whether natural (e.g. mountains, sea-cliffs) or man-made (e.g. airports, quarries). A trained geographer, it is said, can study a topographic map of any area and 'read off' from it a large amount of information about the way of life of the area's inhabitants: where and how they live, in what pursuits and how successfully they earn a living, and something of their social, cultural and religious customs.

A thematic map focuses instead on a particular aspect of the country: relief, communications, climate, land use, population distribution, industry, agriculture. Thus a road map gives — or should give — detailed information on the road network and on associated features and amenities (e.g. petrol stations, motorway exit points, mileages between towns); but it may give little or no indication of relief, built-up areas or features of interest to travellers. Similarly, a 'tourist' map will show attractions for the sightseer — castles, museums, lakes, archaeological sites, parks — but will most likely skimp on information on the exact road pattern, sizes of towns and other features of, presumably, peripheral interest to the tourist. Thematic maps can be extremely useful provided they are chosen with care, bearing these limitations in mind.

All maps employ symbols and it is a good policy to familiarize oneself with the symbols used before taking a map into the field. Some mapmakers use representational symbols, i.e. simplified drawings of features; others use abstract or geometric symbols, e.g. triangles of different colours to represent different products at industrial sites. The representation of relief is the subject of much variation: methods include hill-shading, which simulates the appearance of the terrain as it might look from the air, spot heights, and contours (lines joining points which are the same height above sea-level). Recently the Ordnance Survey, having lately altered the symbols used on some of its maps, was compelled to issue a warning bringing to users' attention the vital distinction between the symbol for parish boundaries and the rather similar symbol for tracks (both broken lines): confusion between the two might have had disastrous results.

Apart from scale and content, what criteria should be used in selecting an appropriate map? Legibility is one: a balance should exist between the provision of information, especially of place names, and the prevention of a cluttered look; and a clear type face and size are of course most important. The map's main features should make a strong and unequivocal impact, e.g. colours should be graded logically to convey the correct impression of a variation in altitude, concentration or any other scale or continuum. Language and place name variants may have a bearing on the map's usefulness in some circumstances. One series of excellent Italian road maps of northern Yugoslavia, for instance, gives Italian instead of Slovene place names, which may cause the user some difficulty in pinpointing locations. Poor physical design in a map — the ease with which it folds, whether or not it is waterproof, the presence or absence of a folder or cover — may cause disproportionate inconvenience in the field.

Official map publishing continues to bear the stamp of colonialism, so that, for example, the best maps of former British colonies and territories are published by Britain's Directorate of Overseas Surveys, and former French possessions, e.g. Chad, Algeria and many other countries in north and west Africa, are covered by series published by the Institut Géographique National in Paris. Excellent maps of their own countries are produced by many of the old Commonwealth and other rapidly developing industrial nations (e.g. Australia, Canada, Israel); and the USA is in the course of being mapped at a scale of 1 : 25,000, a series which numbers many thousands of sheets.

The publications of commercial map producers however often rival those of the national authority in quality. In Britain there are a number of fine map publishers such as George Philip and Son, Geographia and John Bartholomew. The latter for many years published a series of maps of Britain at a scale of $^1/_2$ inch to 1 mile, which obviated the need for the Ordnance Survey to do the same. Map publication is not of course the exclusive province of specialists and the road, tourist and other maps put out for the purposes of promotion or information by, for instance, petrol companies and tourist offices are often of a high standard and should not be overlooked.

For the prospective map purchaser in Britain wishing to know which maps are available to cover his field of interest, a trip to one of the public map libraries, e.g. at the Royal Geographical Society or the British Library, is recommended. Here he may consult maps, discover where to buy them, make his own notes or copies from the maps, or arrange for them to be photocopied for his private use. (Note: the laws of copyright generally prevent maps from being photocopied for reproduction. Also note: if a photocopy is a different size from the original, it is also a different scale.) Maps may be purchased from specialist outlets (e.g., in London, Edward Stanford Ltd., 12–14 Long Acre, WC2) or from other stockists (e.g. Harrods).

The traveller proposing to stray from the beaten track may well expect to find 'his' area mapped poorly or not at all, and be surprised, even dismayed, to find that this is not so. The increasing use of aerial and satellite photography in mapping makes it virtually certain that the mapmakers have visited or surveyed the area before him. If however he looks upon maps as the informative, reassuring, perhaps even lifesaving devices they are, he will surely find that the security afforded by possessing a good map more than outweighs the mild disappointment of having been, so to speak, pipped to the post.

Expedition Travel and Your Health

Dr Peter Steele

The unprepared and the unwary are those for whom expeditions abroad can end in misery and expense. You are off on the trip of a lifetime. If you are a wise traveller, you prepare documents, check equipment and carry spares in case of emergency. It is logical to take as much care of your health for if this lets you down you may be throwing away a great experience and risking huge cost.

This article aims to guide you when visiting out-of-the-way parts of the world where certain health hazards exist. Whatever your reasons for travelling and wherever you plan to go, the medical problems you meet vary little; but disregard them at your peril.

The art of travelling is learned by building on the experience of previous journeys, but the objective always seems unattainable when poring over a map laid out on a comfortable sitting-room carpet. I have never lost the feeling of awe that goes with undertaking a new journey — and I hope you won't either.

Preparations

Besides your travel documents, do not forget to take with you:

Form E.III or your medical insurance policy (see later).

Medicines with which you are already being treated. The dosage and pharmacological name should be written on the bottle since proprietary names vary in different countries.

Personal medical information which can be imprinted on a bracelet or medallion; blood group, allergy, diabetic or steroid treatment dosage. This is safer than a card carried in the pocket and may be life-saving in an emergency.

Spare spectacles and your lens prescription.

Medical checks: a chest X-ray before will allow comparison later in case you contract tuberculosis, which is still wide-spread in some under-developed countries. Tooth fillings tend to loosen in cold so a dental check-up may save agony later. If you suspect piles, seek an examination. Feet should be in good shape as much will be expected of them.

Insurance

Falling ill abroad can be very expensive. The European Economic Community (Belgium, Denmark, France, West Germany, Ireland, Italy, Luxembourg and the Netherlands) have reciprocal arrangements with our own National Health Service. The detailed workings of the scheme are laid out in Form SA.28, issued by the Department of Health and Social Security. This explains how the certificate of entitlement to medical treatment (Form E.III) may be obtained. It is not available to self-employed or unemployed persons. (Students beware!).

Similar arrangements for free medical care exist in Bulgaria, Poland, Norway, Sweden and Yugoslavia. The embassies of these countries should be consulted for details.

Elsewhere, the cost of consultation, medicines, treatment and hospital care must be paid for by the patient. As this could be financially crippling, full health insurance is a wise precaution. A typical 'package deal' insurance includes baggage, personal accident and medical expenses up to £1,000. Routine dental treatment is not usually included in the policy. Insurance covers the cost of medical treatment abroad or of flying the sick person home. This may be safest and cheapest in the long run. Don't forget to insure every member of the party.

If you incur medical expenses, present your policy to the doctor and ask him to send the bill direct to your insurance company; if you pay cash, keep a receipt which will be honoured on your return.

If you are going to take part in 'high-risk' sports you will need a more specific insurance cover. Consult a company who specialises in this field and will give you an individual quote; one such is West Mercia Insurance Brokers, Orton Lane, Wolverhampton.

Immunization

Immunization can protect you from certain infectious diseases that are common in countries abroad but rare at home. Your local District Community Physician's Department will advise you on the inoculations necessary for a particular country you may wish to visit and how to obtain them, either at a clinic or through your family doctor. Do not leave it to the last moment as a full course can take up to three months.

Immunization is not obligatory in Europe or North America, but it is wise to be protected against:

a) Typhoid, paratyphoid A & B and tetanus (TABT). Two injections are given one month apart. An unpleasant reaction, with a sore arm and headache is not uncommon and you must avoid alcohol for 24 hours. After a wound from a dirty object or an animal bite, you should obtain a booster dose of tetanus toxoid.

b) Smallpox, yellow fever and cholera. Although not obligatory for Europe, it is wise to keep up to date. Smallpox is compulsory for Asia, Australia and parts of Africa; yellow fever for Central and South America and central Africa. A valid International Certificate must be carried. Smallpox immunity lasts three years and yellow fever ten years. Cholera immunization will soon no longer be compulsory. It may partly protect the individual for a short period but its value in international control of the disease is in doubt.

c) Diphtheria, poliomyelitis and tuberculosis (BCG). Immunization is given to most children and lasts, so usually need not be repeated.

Three months should be allowed for a full course of immunization, but in emergency, a 'crash course' of smallpox, TABT, yellow fever (and cholera) can be given in 15 days.

d) Malaria is not a danger in Europe, North America and the near east, but if you visit a malarial zone elsewhere in the world, a course of prophylactic anti-malarial drugs should be prescribed by your doctor starting one week before departure and continuing for at least a month after return.

Human gamma globulin has gained a reputation as a universal protector, especially against infective hepatitis (jaundice). Passive immunity lasts up to 3 months.

Advice

Now you are ready for the journey: rucksack packed, pockets crammed with documents and wallet bulging with travellers' cheques. Have a happy, healthy holiday. The following advice aims to help you avoid illnesses commonly met abroad, most of which can be treated by yourself in the first instance. If, however, the condition rapidly worsens or does not improve within 24–48 hours, you should consult a doctor. Several different drugs can be used to treat any one illness. Those recommended here are included in the suggested medical kit at the end of the article. Approved names of drugs are generally used; proprietary preparations are set in *italics*. Unless otherwise stated, a medicine should be taken four times a day. Children's doses are usually half the adult dose.

Traveller's Diarrhoea

Gippy Tummy, Delhi Belly, Kathmandu Quickstep — traveller's diarrhoea has as many names as patent remedies. It strikes most travellers at some stage in their journey, making more trouble than all the other illnesses mentioned here put together. The causes are usually untraceable but may include gluttony, change in climate and an upset in bacteria that are normal and necessary in the bowel. Infection with disease-causing organisms carried in water and food is less common.

Much of the pleasure of travelling abroad comes from eating local food and drinking wine; it is hardly worth going all the way for beer, fish and chips. Be moderate to prevent the tummy upset that will spoil your trip, and even make you into a useless member of the party.

Precautions

Water warrants the utmost care; carelessness may be very costly. In some clean hotels and restaurants, the water is safe to drink. Stream and river water is likely to be polluted unless it comes directly from a hillside spring, and glacial mud or mica in alpine rivers is especially irritant to the gut. If in doubt, sterilize all drinking water.

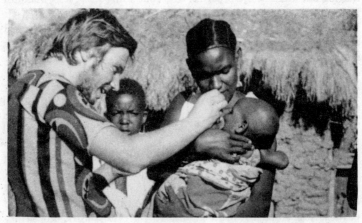

Tana River expedition (Kenya) carries out medical check on local inhabitants.

Boiling briskly for a few seconds kills most organisms (including amoeba cysts and infectious hepatitis virus). So drink tea or coffee.

Water-purifying tablets. Chemical treatment is less effective than boiling, takes longer and leaves a taste of chlorine, but is useful if boiling is not practicable.

Filters get rid of the murky colour of suspended organic matter but purify waters less surely than boiling.

Drinks: Bottled fizz is usually safe, so Coca Cola, almost universally available, may become your safest standby. Wine and spirits drunk in moderation are harmless, but mixing them with water has no 'sterilizing action'.

Food: Thoroughly cooked food is safe since any bacteria will have been killed by the heat. Avoid pre-cooked and handled foods, especially when flies abound. Peel fruit and vegetables. Thorough washing is only second best so beware of salads, lettuce and watercress. Keep to well-advertised brands of ice-cream, and risk shellfish only if you have a tough stomach.

Hygiene: Lavatories abroad are often dirty. You may have to squat and keep your balance by holding on to the walls. Wash your hands carefully with soap as soon as possible afterwards. Take your own toilet paper as newsprint is rough and fragile. At campsites, dig a latrine hole well away from the tents and your water supply.

Brush your teeth in clean water only — chewing gum is a useful temporary cleaner.

N.B. CHOLERA: 1973 saw a worldwide epidemic, notably in parts of Italy. The Cholera organisms come only from the human intestine and are spread by faecally contaminated water, not by direct contact or inhalation. Raw shellfish collect the bugs so are particularly dangerous. A sudden onset of profuse watery diarrhoea in an epidemic area calls for immediate attention.

Treatment of Travellers' Diarrhoea

The illness usually clears up on its own in 2–3 days. You may also vomit and because a lot of body water is lost, you may feel groggy. Go to bed and drink unlimited fluids (at least a pint an hour). Avoid eating — except dried toast and peeled grated apple gone brown (pectin). A binding medicine will speed recovery. A dose of the 'Everest Blunderbuss Cocktail' constipates most people for a week: kaoline powder 2 tablespoons, tincture of morphine (chlorodyne) 4–6 drops, Codeine phosphate 30 mg., and **Lomotil** 4–6 tabs. or any of these singly if all are not available. Antibiotics, though fashionable, should not be used blindly since they kill normal bacteria, which are protective, as well as poison-producing ones.

Dysentery
If diarrhoea does not stop within 24 hours on this treatment, or if blood appears in the stools, consult a doctor since you may be suffering from dysentery. If you cannot find help, the best drug to start with is Cotrimoxazole (*Septrin*, *Bactrim*). Bacillary dysentery starts suddenly with acute diarrhoea, fever and malaise. Amoebic dysentery causes slimy mucus and blood and warrants laboratory investigation and treatment. Its severity builds up slowly over several days.

Worms
Worms are common in tropical countries. They cause an itchy bottom and can often be seen in the stools. Take 1 Peperazine (*Pripsen*) sachet.

Indigestion
Magnesium trisilicate gets rid of wind and may even help a hangover.

Constipation
Drink plenty and eat fruit. If this fails, take two laxative tablets (*Senokot*).
N.B. Beware the person who feels sick, has no appetite, a dirty, coated tongue and pain in the belly. If the abdomen is tender, particularly in the right lower quarter, suspect appendicitis and visit a doctor.

Waterworks
Urinary infection is more common in women, and begins as frequent passing of urine with burning pain. Drink a pint of water hourly with a tablespoon of bicarbonate of soda and take an antibiotic if it does not improve in a day.

General infections
Antibiotics must not be eaten indiscriminately, but if you develop an infection with a high fever and rapid pulse when you are away in the wilds on your own, blind therapy with a broad spectrum bug-killing drug may be justified. Cotrimoxazole (*Septrin*, *Bactrim*) or Amoxycillin (*Amoxyl*) should be taken for a full five-day course.

Local infections
Eyes: If the eyes are pink and feel gritty, wear dark glasses and put in

chloromycetin ointment. A few drops of Amethocaine will anaesthetise the cornea so you can dig out a foreign body. Homatropine dilates the pupil and relieves spasm but will temporarily blur the vision.

Ears: Keep dry with a light plug of cotton wool but don't poke matches in. If there is discharge and pain, take an antibiotic.

Sinusitis gives a headache (felt worse on stooping), 'toothache' in the upper jaw, and often a thick snotty discharge from the nose. Inhale steam with Tinct. Benz. or sniff a tea brew with a towel over your head to help drainage. Decongestant drops may clear the nose if it is mildly bunged up, but true sinusitis needs an antibiotic.

Throat: Cold dry air irritates the throat and makes it sore. Gargle with a couple of Aspirins or table salt dissolved in warm water; or suck antiseptic lozenges.

Teeth: When brushing teeth is difficult, chew gum. If a filling comes out a plug of cotton wool soaked in oil of cloves eases the pain; gutta percha, softened in boiling water, is easily plastered into the hole as a temporary filling. Hot salt mouthwashes encourage pus to discharge from a dental abscess but an antibiotic will be needed.

Feet take a hammering so boots must fit and be comfortable. Climbing boots are rarely necessary on the approach march to a mountain; gym shoes or flip-flops are useful. At the first sign of rubbing, put on a plaster.

Blisters: Burst with a sterile blade or needle (boiled for three minutes or held in a flame until red hot). Remove dead skin, spray with Tinc. Benz. Cover the raw area with zinc oxide plaster and leave in place for several days to allow new skin to form.

Athlete's foot: Wash with soap and dry carefully between the toes; then dust with antifungal powder and wear open sandals.

Muscle ache: Rub Methyl Salicylate (Wintergreen) ointment deeply.

Cramps: Take extra salt in your diet or use salt tablets. Modify exercise until you are fit.

Sun

The sun can be a stealthy enemy. Sunlight reflects strongly off snow and light-coloured rocks; its rays penetrate hazy cloud and are more powerful the higher you climb. Until you have a good tan, protect yourself with clothing and a hat. An ultraviolet barrier cream (*Uvistat*) screens the skin but with excessive sun it merely acts as fat in the frying process. Rationing sunlight is cheaper and more effective.

Sunburn: Calamine soothes shrimp-pink prickly hot skin; if you turn bright lobster and blister you are severely burnt and should obtain a steroid cream.

Sunstroke: If you develop a high temperature and feel ill after being in strong sun, cool yourself with cold water sponging or ice packs, drink ample fluid and take Aspirin to lower your temperature and relieve headache. Collapse from sunstroke warrants urgent medical help.

Snowblindness is caused by an ultraviolet burn of the cornea, resulting in intense pain and swelling of the eyes. It can be prevented by wearing dark glasses or goggles; horizontal slits cut in a piece of cardboard will do in emergency. Amethocaine drops will ease the pain enough to reach camp. Then put Homatropine drops and chloromycetin ointment in the eyes and wear dark glasses or cover with eye-pads and a bandage if the pain is severe.

Travel Sickness

If you know you are prone to suffer, take one anti-histamine tablet. (Promethazine, *Phenergan* 25 mg.) before the journey and one more if sickness continues. A long and tedious journey will pass in a soporific daze, so do not drive. Chlorpheniramine, *Piriton* 4 mg. may be used instead if you have to keep alert.

Nature's Annoyances

From flies and mosquitoes, bees, wasps, ants and hornets; from fleas, lice and bedbugs; from sea urchins and jellyfish; and from a host of other creepy-crawlies we pray deliverance. Repellent sprays (containing Dimethylphthalate) only last a few hours; DDT may repel a few creatures. If you are unfortunate enough to be attacked, itching is the basic problem. If there is a sting, remove it. Treat the pain and irritation with Calamine cream or lotion, and Promethazine or Chlorpheniramine tablets. Scratching with grubby finger nails may cause the bite to go septic.

Arthropods: Lice, fleas and bedbugs are kept at bay by Lorexane.

Mosquitoes are usually only a bother at lower altitudes. A net makes sleeping more comfortable but does not guarantee protection from malaria.

Snakes: Clean the area and suck the wound. Do *not* slash the skin with razor blades or urinate on it. Remember only poisonous snakes cause snakebite poisoning, which is quite rare. Local hospitals probably carry the anti-serum against common local snakes. If possible, kill the snake and take it with you for identification.

Dogs: Bites always warrant an anti-tetanus booster. Rabies is rare but possible.

Leeches are most troublesome during and shortly after the monsoon in the tropics. You do not feel them bite and may only notice a bootful of blood at the end of the day. Open sandals let you see them early and insect repellent discourages them — a lighted cigarette or salt makes the leech drop off.

Wasp stings — vinegar. *Bee stings* — bicarbonate of soda.

Bilharzia is widespread in parts of Africa so avoid swimming in slow-flowing rivers and lakes where the flukes breed.

Poisoning: Try to make the person sick by giving him a salt solution to drink or sticking fingers down his throat.

Injury

Nature is a wonderful healer if given adequate encouragement.

Cuts and grazes go septic quickly so must be taken seriously. Wash thoroughly with soap and water or an antiseptic solution (gentian violet or potassium permanganate). Cover with a sterile plaster strip or non-stick (*Melolin*) gauze. Antiseptic cream may be used if the wound is difficult to clean adequately, but it tends to make the dressing stick and keeps the wound moist, which delays healing. Anchor dressings are useful for awkward places; e.g. fingers, heels. If the cut is clean and gaping, bring the edges together with *Steristrips* in place of stitches.

Deep wounds: Firm pressure on a wound dressing will stop most bleeding. If blood seeps through, put more dressings on top, secured with absorbent crepe bandage, and keep up the pressure. Elevate the part if possible.

Burns: Superficial burns are simply skin wounds. Leave open to the air to form a dry crust under which healing goes on. If this is not possible, cover with *Melolin* dressings. Burn creams offer no magic. Deep burns must be kept scrupulously clean and treated urgently by a doctor. Give drinks freely to replace lost fluid.

Sprains: Apply a firm crepe or elastoplast bandage. If painful movement and swelling persist, suspect a fracture. Cold compresses help reduce swelling.

Fractures: Immobilize the part by splinting to a rigid structure; the arm can be strapped to the chest, both legs can be tied together. Temporary splints can be made from a rolled newspaper, an ice-axe or a branch. Pain may be agonizing and is due to movement of broken bone ends on each other, and needs full doses of strong pain-killers.

Pain: Pain-killers fall into three strengths for different grades of pain:
Mild: Aspirin (lowers the temperature but can irritate the stomach).
Paracetamol is a useful alternative.
Moderate: Pentazocine *Fortral* (can cause hallucinations).
Strong: Pethidine, Morphine (may depress the breathing dangerously.
Only available on special prescription).

Unconsciousness
The causes range from drowning to head injury, diabetes to epilepsy.
Untrained laymen should only attempt to place the victim in the
'draining position' — lying on his side with the head lower than the
chest to allow secretions, blood or vomit to drain away from the lungs.
Hold the chin forward to prevent the tongue falling back and
obstructing the airway. Don't try any fancy manoeuvres unless you are
practised, as you may do more harm than good.
Fainting: Lay the unconscious person down and raise the legs to return
extra blood to the brain.

Exposure
Mountain hypothermia occurs when the temperature of the central core
of the body falls below about 35°C owing to the combined effect of
wind, wet and cold. Exhaustion and low morale worsen it. If someone
behaves in an uncharacteristic manner — apathetic, stumbling,
swearing, uncontrolled shivering — be on your guard. He may
suddenly collapse and die.

Stop and shelter the victim; i.e. tent, polythene bag, lean-to.
Rewarm him by skin-to-skin contact. Dress him in dry spare clothes
and put him in a sleeping bag. Give him hot drinks. A nip of alcohol
can do no harm and may give him the boost he needs to get down by
himself after he is rested and rewarmed. If his condition does not
improve you will have to call help to evacuate him by stretcher.

When at base, he should be slowly rewarmed in a water bath at
42–44° C.

High Altitude Ills
Up to 12,000 ft. you have little to fear — no more than on an ordinary
mountain walking holiday. If you are not shaping up too well,
reconsider the wisdom of climbing higher for you are entering the
realm of the high, thin, cold, dry air. Slow ascent is the secret of easy
acclimatization to altitude. Breathing and heartbeat speed up; a
thumping headache and nausea make you feel miserable. At night, sleep

is elusive (*Mogadon* 1 tab.). You may notice a peculiar irregularity in the pattern of breathing (Cheyne Stokes respiration) when, for a short period, breathing appears to have stopped and then gradually increases in stepwise fashion until it eventually falls off again. The normal output of urine may be diminished and very dilute.

The unpleasant symptoms of acclimatization usually pass off in a few days, but they may develop into Acute Mountain Sickness. This rarely starts below 15,000 ft. so is unlikely in the Alps, but may occur in Africa, the Andes or Himalayas.

If you begin to feel more ill than you would expect for your own degree of fitness and acclimatization, go down quickly and stay down rather than battle on for glory — and end up under a pile of stones on the glacier. Acute Mountain Sickness can quickly develop into High Altitude Pulmonary (lung) Oedema, or Cerebral (brain) Oedema, i.e. swelling due to abnormal retention of water. Women are more susceptible in the days before their periods. This is a potentially lethal disease, the cause of which is not understood, but it can affect all ages, the fit and unfit, those who have risen quickly and those who have not.

If someone suddenly feels, and looks, puffy in the face, goes blue round the lips, has bubbly breathing and even pink frothy sputum, evacuate them urgently to a lower altitude. Oxygen (if available) and a diuretic drug Frusemide (*Lasix*) may help to clear water from the lungs, but they are no substitute for rapid descent which has a miraculous effect. Those who have suffered once are likely to do so again, and should therefore beware.

Thrombosis: Persistent deep calf tenderness and slight fever and pain — more than muscular ache — may indicate a vein thrombosis. Women on the pill are especially at risk. You should rest, preferably with the legs bandaged and elevated, and start an antibiotic. This is a serious illness, so descend and seek medical advice.

Piles commonly trouble people at high altitude, probably due to raising the pressure inside the abdomen by overbreathing while carrying heavy loads. A haemorrhoidal suppository (*Anusol*) gives temporary relief.

Dry cough is eased by inhaling steam. Codeine Phosphate 15 mg. dampens it. In a violent bout of coughing, you can fracture a rib. The agony may make you think you have had a heart attack but the chances of this are slim.

Frostbite should not occur if you are clothed properly and take commonsense precautions. If you get very cold, rewarm the part quickly against warm flesh (someone else's if possible). Do *not* rub it or you will damage the skin and cause further wounding which may become infected.

Drugs which dilate the blood vessels (Vasodilators) have no specific action against frostbite although they make you feel a warm glow inside. This can be very dangerous as you are losing heat from the rest of your body and you may be tipped into exposure.

If a foot is frozen, it is better to walk on it back to a low camp where you can rapidly rewarm it in water 42–44° C. Thereafter the victim must be carried.

Women: When travelling or climbing, your periods may stop temporarily. This is nothing to worry about. Women on the pill are more at risk from thrombosis, and thrush.

Suggested Medical Kit

A prescription is needed for several items. You should ask your doctor to sign the entire list as a private prescription (i.e. it has to be paid for, as medical equipment to be taken abroad is not available on the NHS).

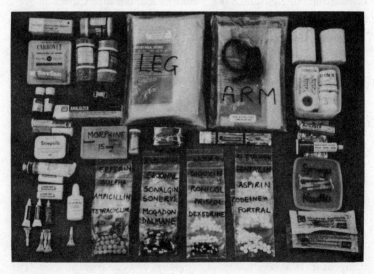

Leader's Kit (for 4–6 persons for 2 months)
Basic

Dressings	1	Plaster Dressing Strip 36"
	4	Anchor Dressings

Dressings	1	Zinc Oxide Plaster 1" × 5m
	1	Elastoplast 3" × 5m
	1	Steristrip ($^1/_4$" × 4")
	1	Bandages Crepe 3"
	1	Cotton 2"
	1	Triangular
	4	Gauze Squares Plain
	4	*Melolin* 4" × 4"
	4	*melolin* 2" × 2"
	2	*Jelonet* 4" × 4"
	1	Cotton Wool compressed
	1	Wound dressing No. 15
	1	Netelast (F) Head Dressing
Cleaning	1	Soap bar
		Gentian Violet (crystals)
	1	*Brolene* Antiseptic eye ointment
Instruments	1	Scissors blunt/sharp
	1	Forceps oblique end
	1	Scalpel blade (sterile)
	4	Safety pins
	2	Luggage labels
	1	Marker pencil

Medicines

Pain-killers (mild)	60	Aspirin
(moderate)	20	Pentazocine (*Fortral*)
(srong)	10	Pethidine 50 mg tab
Antibiotic	40	Co- Trimoxazole (*Septrin, Bactrim*)
Antihistamine	40	Promethazine (*Phenergan*) 25 mg
	20	Chlorpheniramine (*Piriton*) 4 mg
Sleeping	20	Nitrazepam (*Mogadon*)
	100	Water Purifying tablets
Diarrhoea	$^1/_2$lb	Kaolin powder
(and cough)	40	Codeine Phosphate 15 mg
	40	Diphenoxylate (*Lomotil*)
Constipation	10	*Senokot*
Indigestion	30	Magnesium Trisilicate
Salt	20	Salt tablets
Vitamins	40	Multivite
	40	Vit. C

Anti-worm	40 sach	Piperazine (*Pripsen*)
Eyes/Ears	1	Chloromycetin
Eyes	1	Amethocaine drops
	2	Homatropine drops
	2	Fluorescein papers
Nose	1	Otrivin Antistin spray
Throat	40	Hibitane lozenges
		Gentian Violet crystals
Teeth		Oil of Cloves
	1	gutta percha temporary filling
Skin	1	*Uvistat*
Sun creams, lip salves,	1	*Lipsyl*
Insect repellent, etc.	1	Flypel
	1	Calamine cream
	1	Methyl Salicylate & Iodex ointment
	25	Tinct Benzoin
	1 tin	Tinneafax powder (25G)
	10	*Anusol* suppositories
	1	Lorexane DDT powder
Diuretic	20	Frusemide (*Lasix*) 40 mg
Stimulant	4	Amphetamine (*Dexadrine*)

Individual Kit

Dressings	1	Plaster strip 12" × 2$\frac{1}{2}$"
	1	Zinc oxide 1" × 3m
	4	*Melolin* 2" × 2"
	1	Crepe Bandage 3"
	1	Razor Blade
	1	Luggage label
	1	Marker pencil
	10	*Fortral*
	20	Phenergan (25 mg)
Diarrhoea	20	Codeine Phosphate
Sun	1	tube
Uvistat		
	1	*Lipsyl*
Throat	40	Hibitane lozenges
Skin/Eyes/Ears	1	Chloromycetin
	100	**Water Purifying tablets**

Survival on Expeditions

John Ridgway

Small, lightly equipped and fast-moving expeditions tend to operate in a near survival situation all the time. I will list a few things I have learned under six main headings.

People

Survival really means the maintenance of life in adverse conditions, and for this the individual must be powerfully motivated to survive. Without the will, no amount of flesh is enough. As a guide, I would suggest three principles:

1. Self-reliance: Unless the individual is self-reliant, he will be unable to help others in the same dangerous predicament as himself. As a result, his thoughts will be turned in exclusively on himself, and he will not survive.

2. Positive thinking: "My water bottle is still half full". *Not*: "My water bottle is half empty."

3. Leaving people and things better than you found them. The survivor will probably need the help of the people around him; if he improves their morale, his chances are also improved. The few items of clothing and equipment possessed by the survivor may well hold the key to his survival, therefore every effort must be made to conserve and improvise.

It has been my experience that a team of friends works better than a group of strangers.

Food

Too much emphasis is put on this subject. In any really long distance project, a small team will be unable to carry all its own food. If you are operating in a place where local food is not available, then try a dehydrated diet with only two menus: curry one night, mince the next. We used this successfully in Patagonia. Any more than two menus and you will find yourself disliking various dishes which will therefore not get eaten. We supplemented our diet in Chile with fish we caught and ducks we shot.

If you are going down the Amazon for example, you will be able to eat the local food. In this case carry emergency rations on your belt and try to return home without touching them. Concentrate on sterilising the water and recooking all the food you are offered. This will kill the bugs.

Travel light, use your brains, and you will be surprised how far and fast you can move.

Clothing

To keep your spirits up, you must keep your body at its normal temperature. This can be achieved by wearing layers of clothing and putting them on or taking them off to suit. On our rowing trip, we had only one suit of oilskins each and one real change of clothing (we kept a new set for landing). We had no sleeping bag, only a space blanket each. The secret is to wash dirty clothes, as dirty clothing is a conductor of heat, not an insulator.

Medical

To keep fit, be sure to get plenty of sleep. Most mistakes are made because of tiredness. Sidestep serious illness by having a wide range of injections prior to leaving home. I have never had to use the comprehensive medical kits we have carried for anything but trivial irritations: but they seemed far from trivial at the time.

Preventive medicine is the thing to practise. Time spent in keeping clean will be amply rewarded by not falling sick. Never walk barefoot and jeopardise the success of the expedition by cutting yourself or catching hookworm through the soles of your feet. Save the calculated risk for the really important decisions. Even a cat only has nine lives — don't squander yours by taking unnecessary chances with your health.

Shelters

Most expeditions carry their own tents, but if these are destroyed, a little ingenuity will produce a satisfactory shelter in most climates. Before starting to build the shelter, consider the site and be clear which are the elements you need to shelter from: *cold, rain, sun* or *wind*. If possible, try to be close to drinking water and the source food — animal, vegetable, fish or fowl.

Jungle — Try to get off the ground. Ideally construct a hammock between two trees, with a sloping roof made from a waterproof sheet of

material stretched across a line tied between the same two trees but above the hammock.

Temperate Forest — Make a lean-to shelter from the available dead branches and leaves, or a fallen tree.

Snow — Snow-holes can be easily dug in a snow bank, but remember the entrance must be lower than the living chamber or the rising warm air will escape. Be sure to have a ventilating shaft with a stick down it to keep the air passage clear. An alternative to the snow-hole is a pit dug around the base of a tree and covered over with blocks of snow. In a long-term situation, an igloo is preferable, but in a survival emergency, dig the snowhole first and later progress to the igloo.

Treeless Mountainside — Make use of loose rocks to build the walls for a windbreak. Beware of rockfalls and avalanches.

Desert — Build a rock *sangar* and dig a pit to maximise the shade.

Navigation

Always carry a spare compass with the expedition for emergency. Without a compass, use the sun or the stars, bearing in mind that both are on the move. If possible, make your plan on high ground from where you can see much of your route. Rivers eventually reach the sea and will probably be crossed by a road on the way. Time spent in reconnaissance is seldom wasted, as I found in Chile when we carried all our boats and equipment for a week only to find the route impassable — so we had to carry it all back again.

A few days route-proving without gear would have saved us a lot of energy and me a red face.

Where energy is at a premium, accurate navigation may be the difference between life and death. Think hard before moving.

Summary

It is my view that survival depends mainly on morale. Once you give up trying to survive, then you are probably done for.

Trials of a Freelance Travel Writer

Christopher Portway

Most of the well-known travel writers are on the staff of newspapers and the more affluent magazines. A few free-lancers I know are commissioned by one such publication to supply a set number of travel articles per year but can still 'fill in' by writing occasionally for other markets. Well-known writers can ask and often get three times the fee I can prise out of a newspaper. These fees vary, for me, from around £40 to £80 for an 800-word article, while magazines will pay about the same for twice that number of words. American newspapers can cope with 2,000 words and pay well but there's a lot of competition. So you can see a struggling writer like me can hardly aspire to high living.

But I have no desire to change my status of 'freelance' for a staff position on a newspaper even if I get the chance. That would be going straight back to the nine-to-five category and donning a writing straitjacket into the bargain. I value my freedom even to the extent of being broke. Often I write for the smaller specialist magazine on subjects that interest me, even if I know I shall raise only the odd quid. But this is never wasted time for the more one's name appears in print, the better it becomes known and can command the attention of those Gods of Creation, the publisher and the editor. For this reason, I stick, mostly, to the name I was born with and don't hide behind a series of pseudonyms, each of which, in their turn, has to be laboriously made famous.

And on the stairway to fame comes the occasional invitation from travel or tourist office to spend a week here or a few days there. Very often it is to places from which I can raise little inspiration but I go, nevertheless, and I've yet to disappoint the hen that lays these golden eggs. There's always plenty to write about. In fact there lies the problem. It's not what to write that provides the difficulty but what to leave out. Different publications require different styles or expect a different aspect on a basic subject so it is important to study the various markets who buy the stuff. Occasionally one gets a break. In October 1973, my wife and I were invited to spend a week basking beneath the Menorcan sun (and making a study of that island). I got the resulting features into several top newspapers but not before the agency in question went bust. So desperately I searched for and found another running similar Menorcan holidays who benefited greatly from the last-minute free publicity. So much so in fact that my wife and I have been invited to sample one of *their* holidays!

More often, however, travel to places on which I choose to write is not an all-expenses-paid exercise. Frequently an airline, a railway or bus company provide a pass upon investigation of one's *bona fides* and occasionally I manage to talk a hotel into allowing special terms. But expenses still have a habit of creeping up towards or even past that which comes back in income in spite of all that can be claimed against tax. However, travel experience is never wasted and can frequently be drawn upon long after the event.

I don't think it's my job to tell you *how* to write a travel article. But I will suggest you start with a bang. Give the reader a *bonne bouche* before getting down to mundane details of hotel quality or beach density, which most editors deem a necessity to sell their newspapers. And keep the feature sharp and to the point. Editors don't want to know what you or I did, though opinions are accepted. And if you want to see your article in print, never run down a place. *You* may not like it, but others apparently do.

Submitting an article 'on spec' to an editor is a task for the amateur. I still do it, though I'm getting to know editors personally and so am gaining an idea of their whims and idiosyncrasies. Better still is to drop them a line or telephone them with an idea. You won't always get an answer but if you telephone enough times — and most newspapers accept transfer charge calls — you'll reach your man. It means spending a bomb on postage, particularly as some publications insist upon a stamped return-addressed envelope with the submission, but that's just one of the tribulations of travel writing.

So there you are. A few words of wisdom from an enthusiastic amateur. I'm just one step up the ladder and the rejections I keep receiving make slippery stair-carpeting. But I've been bitten by the bug and I shall persevere.

A Traveller's Guide to Photography

Rick Strange

Every year hundreds of expeditions set out all over the world, but it is only the larger sponsored ones that can afford to take a professional photographer along with them. And yet financially it is often the photographs, along with a well written report, that can make an expedition a success from the 'after sales' point of view.

Many people feel that they can walk into a camera store, buy a camera and walk out as a fully fledged photographer. Despite the fact that many modern cameras make the whole business of taking pictures remarkably easy, this really only applies to the technical side. It is still the person who holds the camera, frames the picture and pushes the button who makes a picture good or bad, saleable or non-saleable. After all, any camera, no matter how technically sophisticated, is only a tool, and is only as good as the person who is using it.

On many smaller expeditions that take place every year, the person who is 'in charge of the camera' will undoubtedly have a hundred and one other jobs to do as well, and often under difficult or hazardous conditions. It is therefore even more important that when a couple of seconds can be spared to take a picture, the photograph should be of the highest possible quality. To make the job of picture taking easier for the expedition photographer, the following 'simple rules' should be studied and where applicable practised.

First and most important is the selection of the camera itself. It must be robust, not too heavy, easy to use and reload. So without doubt it will be a single lens reflex (SLR) of the 35mm size with a standard 50mm lens. Nikon, Pentax, Canon and Leica are a few of the better known makes. They are expensive, this is true, but it is better to have a camera that continues to take pictures when you are half way up a mountain in the Andes rather than one that packs up just when you need it, even if it does cost more.

As well as the basic camera two additional lenses are a great asset. A wide angle lens of 28mm or 35mm and a telephoto lens of 135mm would be suitable. Obviously if bird photography is likely to be included, then a long telephoto of 400mm would be a useful, if a heavy asset. Some of the better known makes today incorporate a macro lens with the 50mm normal lens and though rather more expensive than the straightforward 50mm lens, they do permit extreme close-up shots of flowers and insects etc, as well as the standard pictures. Do remember to fit an ultra violet filter to each lens, not for technical reasons but simply to protect the lens.

Once the photographic equipment has been obtained it is essential for the photographer to get to know it. He must practise with it for several weeks before the expedition leaves, so that when it comes to the crunch he will know exactly what to do, instead of having to sit down with the instruction manual while the fantastic shot he was about to take vanishes for ever. Practise all the technical things so that they become second nature: focusing, changing lenses, setting exposure, changing film, following focus, lighting, using flash, close-ups, holding the camera correctly, framing, cleaning and the general care of the equipment. As soon as all of this is second nature it is possible to start being creative. It is astounding how picture quality seems to improve 100 per cent overnight, once a few simple rules are followed.

Film

On expeditions it is best to stick to just one basic general purpose film. Kodachrome 25 and 64, Ektachrome X or Agfachrome are all suitable films for the job, but once you have got used to one kind of film, stick to it, and life will be easier. Buy all the film you need before leaving, store it in as cool and dry a place in the expedition vehicle as you can find, and then go out and buy another 20 rolls, just in case. After all, it's better to have too much film than too little. If you are going to either very hot or very cold places, the film manufacturers will give you advice on storage, and the camera manufacturers will customise your camera equipment for these conditions.

There are three basic things that make a 'good' photograph: exposure, focus and composition. Before these are dealt with in detail, here are three other guidelines which will improve any picture.

Holding the Camera

Whatever the subject is and wherever a picture is taken, it is most important that camera shake is never permitted to spoil what might otherwise be a good shot. Hold the camera firmly with *both* hands,

Stripping may not improve the picture, but it's one way of beating the heat .

brace your arms against the side of your body or chest, and when actually shooting, squeeze the shutter as if it were the trigger of a rifle. Never jab or stab it. Perform the whole operation in slow motion and keep the camera up to your eye for at least a second after you have pushed the shutter. As well as bracing your arms it is often a very good idea to brace your legs, and even lean against any solid object which may be close at hand, like a tree or a wall. All this in effect turns your body into a tripod and ensures that no body movement will be transmitted to the camera. When shooting in low light conditions which necessitate a slow shutter speed, hold your breath when you push the shutter. This and the bracing positions already mentioned should reduce 'camera shake' to nil.

Being prepared for the unexpected

This applies to expedition photography more than any other kind, because of the very nature of expeditions. You never know exactly what is going to be round the next corner so it is of vital importance that the camera is ready for action all the time. Never put off reloading when the end of the film has been reached. Do it at once and mark the

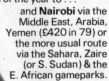

used film so that the pictures on it can be correctly identified. Of course in adverse weather conditions the camera should not be left lying around so that it might be damaged, but it should be ready to go, in its case, which must be near to hand.

Seeing, not just looking

This is really a subject all to itself. It might sound ridiculous, but it is surprising how few people really see! Without looking, tell yourself the colour of the tie the man next to you is wearing. What is the colour of the wallpaper in your office or sitting room? Things that you look at, touch or experience every day are registered by your brain, but only when you have trained yourself to observe are they consciously registered. Things that are so obvious that you do not notice them can ruin a photograph, or on the other hand make one that you had not realised was there. Telephone wires running through the middle of a picture ruin it, but most people do not even notice them when they push the shutter, because they have not 'seen them'. When viewing a picture you have taken, how often have you said, 'Oh I did not notice that was in the picture'? Teach yourself to SEE. Start consciously observing, by talking to yourself about what your eyes are looking at.

Focus, Exposure and Composition

Of these, *focus* is the easiest, but remarkably often neglected. In the heat of the moment the simple tracking in or out of the focus ring on the lens is forgotten. This will soon become second nature if it is practised. Just remember that what you see through the view finder is what the film will reproduce. Always make sure that the subject you are photographing is as sharp as it can be in the view finder.

Exposure is not quite so easy. Many modern SLR cameras have built-in exposure meters which read an average light as it falls on the whole subject contained in the view finder. It is very easy to let a bright sky affect the light reading so that the rest of the picture is underexposed. Many countries with a hot climate have white-painted houses. In a village scene, if an average light reading is taken, everything except the white houses will be underexposed. Conversely if a large dark object is part of the picture and the reading is taken off this, then everything else will be overexposed.

An exposure meter is only a simple computer and not a magic instrument for producing perfect pictures. The information it gives must be interpreted with an intelligent appreciation of the situation. The basic rule to follow is that the correct light reading is the one off the main subject of the picture. Thus in a village scene, the exposure reading should be taken from the people and the houses and not from the sky. A local character may be your subject (rather than the white wall he is leaning against): move in close and get your light reading from his face — don't let the brightness of the wall affect the reading.

If the subject is too far away for you to take a reading, use something near to you which is lighted in the same way and has the same tonal values. Several modern makes of cameras have spot reading light meters, which means that the light is read off a very small area in the middle of the frame. This is probably the most accurate type of meter, but again make sure that you take the reading off the subject.

When there are many different light values in a picture (e.g. bright sunlight and dark shadow), the best thing to do is to take a reading off both the light and the dark and then use an exposure which falls halfway between the two. If, however, you find yourself really in trouble because there are so many shades of light and dark and all the various degrees in between, find a nice section of a well lit neutral colour (preferably medium grey) and take your readings from this. The tarmac road ten yards in front of you often gives a very good neutral grey reading.

If you really are not sure what the exposure should be, try taking three pictures of the same subject, one at what you think is the right exposure, one at an f/stop above and another at an f/stop below. This way you can be sure that the picture is in the 'can'. After all, it is much cheaper to use more film and make sure of getting your picture than to have to go all the way back for another shot.

Composition is without a doubt the most difficult of the three basic rules, either to define or to teach. Generally it is something which is inborn or almost instinctive — people with a natural composition ability often become artists of one sort or another — but it can be learnt with practice. Although it is impossible to discuss composition very fully in an article of this length, here are a few practical suggestions which should help the expedition photographer to produce pictures of saleable quality.

The basic rule of composition is known as the Rule of Thirds. All this means is that if you divide any picture into thirds both horizontally and vertically, the point at which the thirds intersect are the optimum subject positions, with the lower right intersection point being the prime position.

Less technical, but just as important, is the policy of keeping your photographs simple. Don't try to say too much with one picture. After you have selected your subject, concentrate on it and don't let it become cluttered up with unnecessary objects. You can use the additional lenses you are carrying for selective composition. Don't just use the telephoto lens for distant subjects: use it for close subjects, cutting out the uninteresting foreground. Make sure that there are no trees 'growing' out of the top of peoples' heads, etc. — remember to see and not just look.

Use your picture to tell a story about the subject. Always start off with an orientation shot which places the subject in its environment — in other words, a long shot. Move in closer to show the subject in more detail, and finally get in really close to show extreme detail.

Always try to fill the view finder of your camera with the subject. Then you won't have to rehearse that all too common story, 'See those two black dots in the distance; well, that's the Landrover and our tent when we were halfway across the Sahara.' It might well be a beautiful shot of the desert, but if the subject is the expedition camp, then fill the frame with the expedition camp.

Good Luck and Good Shooting!

Check List

Camera body (2 if possible) 35mm type with built-in exposure meter and interchangeable lens

Normal macro lens for normal and close-up work

28mm. or 35mm wide angle lens

135mm telephoto lens

400mm telephoto lens (for bird and animal photography)

(All lenses fitted with UV filters to protect lens and dust caps for front and back)

Lightweight tripod

Set of jeweller's screwdrivers

Small pair of jeweller's pliers

Lens cleaning tissue and fluid

Antistatic cloth

Spare light meter

Cable release

Electronic flash and spare batteries and cables

Spare batteries for light meters

Strong camera case (aluminium)

Your estimate of film required (plus a reserve)

If going to extreme climates or conditions of high humidity, extreme cold or desert, have cameras customised by manufacturers and seek advice on film storage from film manufacturers.

Hints

Always hold your camera firmly with both hands and brace your arms against the sides of your body.

Squeeze the shutter gently ... never stab or jab it.

Take exposure readings from the main subject in the picture and don't let the sky, or bright or dark surroundings affect the reading.

Frame the subject carefully in the view finder making sure that extraneous objects do not spoil an otherwise good picture.

Fill the view finder with the subject. The amateur generally tends to stand too far back.

Selling Expedition Photography

John Douglas

A two-man canoe expedition up the Amazon ... a one-man trek through Afghanistan ... a full-scale assault on Everest involving a party of sixty ... a student group studying the fauna and flora of a remote Pacific island.

Question: What two features do these expeditions have in common?
Answer: They will all be short of money and they'll all be taking at least one camera.

The object of this article is to draw attention to the fact that these two features are not unrelated. Too few expeditions, whether they be on the grand scale or simply a student adventure, are aware that the camera can make a substantial contribution to much needed funds. When it is pointed out that a single picture may realise say £60, the hard-pressed expedition treasurer begins to see that he may be neglecting a very substantial source of revenue. While it is true that income from photography may not be received until some considerable time after the expedition has arrived home, it can be used to pay off debts — or perhaps to finance the next excursion.

If photography is to pay, then advance planning is essential. Too often planning is no more than quick decisions regarding types of camera, amount of film to be taken and who is to be responsible for this aspect of the expedition. Of course there *are* essential questions and something might first be said about their relevance to potential markets.

Unless sponsorship and technical assistance is received, a movie camera is certainly not worth taking on the average expedition. The production of a worthwhile expedition film is such an expensive, specialised and time-consuming matter that it is best forgotten. In order to satisfy television and other markets, a film must approach near-professional standards with all that that implies in editing, cutting, dubbing, titling and so on, to say nothing of filming techniques. Of course, if a film unit from, for example, a regional TV network can be persuaded to send along a crew, then some of the profit, as well as a fine record of the expedition's achievements, may accrue to the expedition. But for the average group this is unlikely. By all means allow members to take along a good 8mm movie camera but do not think of this as a source of income.

With still photography, the position is quite different. It *is* worthwhile investing in, or having on loan, a good range of equipment. It will probably be advisable to take perhaps three cameras, two 35mm SLRs and a larger format camera with an interchangeable back. If the latter is not available, then contrary to advice sometimes given, 35mm format is quite satisfactory for most markets except some calendar, postcard and advertising outlets.

A common planning argument is the old black and white/colour controversy. It is *not* true that mono reproduction from colour is unacceptable. Expertly processed, some 70–80 per cent of colour will reproduce satisfactorily in black and white. However conversion is more expensive and difficult than starting in the right medium and there are far more markets for mono than for colour. Although prices paid for black and while will be only some 50–60 per cent of those for colour, it is the larger market that makes it essential to take both sorts of film. A good plan is to take one-third fast black and white film and two-thirds colour reversal film. For formats larger than 35mm, take colour only. The reason for this imbalance is that it is easier to improve a sub-standard black and white during processing. To all intents and purposes, the quality of a colour picture is fixed once the shutter closes.

It is advisable to keep to one type of film with which you are familiar. Different colour film may reproduce with contrasting colour quality and spoil the effect of, say, an article illustrated with a sequence of colour pictures. Colour prints will not sell.

Little can be said here about the choice of a photographer for an expedition. So often the selection of personnel is determined by such a variety of factors that the individual skills of the group members are subordinate to other considerations. But if the expedition is to sell its photography, it is important that the photographer is experienced and skilled, and that he should be given ample time and scope to practise his art.

Before leaving, the photographer should contact possible outlets for his work. Magazines generally pay well for illustrations, especially if accompanied by an article. Such UK markets as *Expedition*, *Geographical*

Magazine, the colour supplements of Sunday newspapers or *Amateur Photographer* can be approached and, although they may not give a firm *yes*, their advice can be helpful. Specialist journals, assuming they are illustrated, may be approached if the work of the expedition is relevant but it should be remembered that the smaller circulation of such journals yields a lower rate of payment. It can be worthwhile to advertise the expedition in the hope of obtaining lucrative photography commissions, photography, but beware of copyright snags if film is provided free.

Overseas magazines such as the American *National Geographic* often pay exceptionally high rates but the market is tight. Much nearer home, local and national newspapers may take some pictures while the expedition is in progress. If the picture editor is approached, he may accept some black and white pictures if they can be sent back through a UK agent. If the expedition is regionally based, local papers will usually be quite enthusiastic, but it is important to agree a reasonable fee beforehand otherwise a payment of, say, £1 will hardly cover the costs involved. Local papers may also agree to take an illustrated story after the group has returned home but, again, it is important to ensure that adequate payment will be made for pictures published. When an expedition recruits nationally, there is the chance to exploit a number of newspaper outlets with 'local explorer' pictures.

It is not the purpose of this article to discuss techniques of photography but the photographer working with an expedition is well advised to seek guidance, before he leaves home, from others who have worked in the area. There can be problems of climate, customs and the like of which it is as well to be aware before starting out. Photography should be discussed at any planning meeting the expedition has with Embassy or High Commission staff.

Finally, one potentially contentious point *must* be settled before the first picture is taken. This is the matter of copyright ownership and the income received from the sale of photographs. It cannot be left to post-expedition arguments as to who bought which film and whether some photographs are *private* and others are expedition property. In law, copyright is vested in the owner of the film and *not* in the photographer. This can cause headaches if the expedition has no corporate identity in law. It might be best to get a lawyer to sort out an agreement. Certainly something should be in writing at least as far as the official photographer is concerned. One very satisfactory plan is to agree with the photographer that some form of licence shall be granted to the expedition. In any case, the golden rule is to be clear about the arrangements before any argument can start.

Once in the field, the photographer has two professional tasks. The first is to record the work and progress of the expedition. This is quite clearly his major role and in this he will be advised by the expedition leader. Secondly he should seek every opportunity to add to his photographic collections pictures which might have a market. This latter task is often most appropriately carried out prior to and after the expedition is properly under way. Thus the journey to and from the base position will often afford splendid opportunities for photography. Without increasing the overall cost it is sometimes possible for the photographer to make an earlier and more leisurely journey to the starting point of the expedition than the rest of the party.

Not unnaturally the question 'what sells?' will be asked. There is no simple answer except to say that at some time or other almost any technically good photograph may have a market. (Throughout, it is assumed that the photographer is able to produce high quality pictures. There is never a market for the out-of-focus, underexposed disaster!) Statements like, '*the photograph that sells best is the one that no one else has*' may not seem very helpful, yet this is the truth. It is no use building a collection which simply adds to an already saturated market. For example, an expedition passing through Agra will certainly visit the Taj Mahal — and photograph the splendid building. Yet the chances of selling such a photograph on an open market are dismal. It's all been done before, from every angle, in every light and mood. Perhaps a picture of the monument illuminated by a thunderstorm might be unusual enough to find a buyer but the best that can reasonably be hoped for is that the photographer will hit on a new angle or perhaps a human interest picture with the Taj as background.

On the other hand, a picture of village craftsmen at work might sell well, as will anything around which a story can be woven. Landscapes have a limited market but given exceptional conditions of light, then a good scenic picture might reap high rewards in the calendar or advertising markets. The golden rule is to know the markets well enough to foresee the needs. Sometimes the least obvious subjects are suddenly in demand.

Such was the case, for example, in 1976 during the raid on Entebbe Airport by Israeli forces. My own agency, *Geoslides*, was able to supply television with photographs of the old section of the airport and of the Kampala hospital just when they were needed. Yet who would expect a market for such subjects? Perhaps this is just another reason for carrying plenty of film. My own experience on expeditions is that I am constantly looking around for subjects. Certainly it is no use sitting back waiting for something to appear in the viewfinder. It is wise not to ignore the obvious, everyday scene. As I was preparing this article, *Geoslides* were asked for a photograph of a hailstorm in our Natal collection. Bad weather photographs sell well, so you should not always wait for brilliant sunshine.

One most important but easily overlooked point is the matter of record keeping. In the conditions experienced by many expeditions, this will not be easy, yet it cannot be emphasised too strongly that meticulous care must be taken to ensure that every picture is fully documented. It is true that certain photographs may be identified at a later date, for example macro-photography of plants, but no shot should be taken without some recording of at least its subject and location. It is usually best to number the films in advance and to have an identification tag on the camera which will indicate the film being exposed. A notebook can also be prepared in the days before the expedition leaves.

With the advertising market in mind, it is helpful to make sure that good photographs are taken which include the expedition's equipment. This may have already been agreed with suppliers. Less obviously, there is a market for photographs of proprietary brands of food, magazines, newspapers, items of clothing and equipment and so on in exotic or unusual settings.

If the expedition is to be away for a long time, it can be important to get some of the exposed film back home. There are dangers in this procedure because of the uncertainty of postal services but, provided some care is taken — perhaps with arrangements made through embassies — then there are advantages. Apart from the obvious problems involved in keeping exposed film in sub-optimum conditions, some preparatory work can be carried out by the expedition's agent. Of course if the film is sent home, it is essential that labelling and recording are foolproof.

Once the expedition has returned home, the serious business of selling begins. Topicality is a selling point, so there is no excuse for taking even a few days off, no matter how exhausted you may feel. Processing the film is clearly the first task, followed by cataloguing and the production of sample black and white enlargements. No one is going to buy if the goods are badly presented, so it is worth making sure that a portfolio of high quality mono enlargements and colour transparencies is prepared with a really professional appearance.

The first market to tackle will be local newspapers. Following up the advances made before the expedition set out is very important, no matter how lukewarm was the original response. It will be necessary for the photographer to work closely with whoever has the responsibility for the expedition's literary output. It often *looks* more professional if there is both a writer and a photographer to produce a magazine article, but it should be made clear to editors that a separate fee is expected for text and illustrations. This is invariably better than a lump sum or space-payment.

A direct source of income from photography can be slide shows for which the audience is charged. These are relatively easy to organise but must be prepared with slides of maps and perhaps an accompanying tape or live commentary. Incidentally, do not mix vertical and horizontal frames. It gives an untidy appearance to the show even when the screen actually accommodates the verticals. The bigger the screen the better. If these shows are to have a wide audience, it may be necessary to put the organisation into the hands of an agent.

A photographic exhibition can provide helpful publicity but it will probably raise little or no income in itself. Branch librarians are usually helpful in accommodating exhibitions and if these showings precede some other post-expedition event like a lecture or slide show, they can be indirect money spinners. For an exhibition, great care should be taken in making the display as professional as possible. Again, the bigger the enlargements the better. As far as photography is concerned, 'big is beautiful!' It is worth investing in a few really giant blow-ups.

Depending on the standing of the expedition, it can be a good plan to show some prints to the publicity department of the camera company or franchise agent whose equipment has been used, especially if you have made exclusive use of one company's products. The same may apply to the makers of the film that has been used.

If the expedition has not been too far off-the-beaten-track throughout its travels, then the firms may take photographs with which to illustrate brochures and posters. However, as with the calendar and postcard market, it must be pointed out that this is a specialist field, requiring not only particular sorts of photographs but pictures of a very high technical quality. This also applies to photographs used for advertising, although the suggestions made earlier regarding pictures of proprietary brands and expedition equipment leave this door slightly wider open than usual.

Whenever an original transparency or a negative is sent to or left with a publisher or agent, a signature must be obtained for it, a value placed on it should it be lost or damaged (anything between £50 and £100 per original), and a record kept of its location.

Lastly, when the cataloguing is complete, the expedition will wish to put the whole of its saleable photograph collection on the market. Now a decision must be reached on the thorny issue of whether or not to use an agency. Of course direct sale by the expedition would mean an almost 100 per cent profit, while agency sales will probably net only 50 per cent of the reproduction rights fees. But, as so often, it is the enlargement of the market, the professional expertise and marketing facilities of the agency, which are attractive. It is worth making enquiries of a number of agencies (see *The Writer's and Artist's Yearbook*) and finding a company which offers the sort of terms and assistance that satisfy the expedition's requirements. It is usually preferable to deal with a company which does not expect to hold the collection but simply calls for pictures when needed. This allows much greater freedom to the copyright owner as well as being a check on what is happening in the market. Some agencies, such as *Geoslides*, offer additional services to associate photographers in the way of help with the placing of literary as well as photographic material, and in the organisation of lecture services.

It may well be better to contact an agency before the expedition leaves. For a small consultancy fee, a good agency may be able to advise on the sort of pictures which sell well and on the level of reproduction fees which should be charged. There is nothing more annoying than selling rights for £5 and then finding that the market would have stood £25. Many amateurs sell their pictures for too low a fee and others assume that there is a set price irrespective of the use to which photographic material is put. In fact the market for photographic reproduction rights is something of a jungle and it may be better to gain professional advice rather than get lost. The same applies to locating markets. It is almost impossible for the inexperienced amateur to identify the likely markets for his work. There are thousands of possible outlets and a small fortune could be lost in trying to locate a buyer for a particular picture, no matter how high its quality.

An expedition of modest size and aims should expect to make a substantial profit from its photography, providing an effort is made along the lines indicated. In the case of a specialised and well-publicised expedition, it is not unknown for the whole of the cost of mounting the venture to be recouped from the sale of pictures. There are some simple points to remember. Don't treat the camera as a toy. Don't give the job of photography to a non-specialist. Don't put all those transparencies and negatives in the back of a drawer when you get home. As a money spinner, the camera may be the most important piece of equipment an expedition carries.

Overland and Adventure Trip Operators and Agents in the United Kingdom

Names are given here in abbreviated form. Full details may be found in the main list which follows this chart.

Firms offering:	Overland Tours Safaris and Treks	Other Camping Tours	Special Interest Tours	Tours in Britain and Europe	Middle East	Africa	Iceland/Greenland	Asia especially Indian Subcontinent	N. America	Central/S. America	Far East, Australasia	Information Services
Aardvark	*				*	*		*		*		
Abbott	*	*									*	
Abercrombie	*					*						
Adventure Africa	*					*						
Adventure Travel	*		*			*		*			*	*
Africanus	*					*						
Albert Tours	*							*				
Allen & Dunn	*					*		*				
Alta			*	*	*	*		*				
Amtrek	*								*			

Firms offering:	Overland Tours Safaris and Treks	Other Camping Tours	Special Interest Tours	Tours in Britain and Europe	Middle East	Africa	Iceland/Greenland	Asia especially Indian Subcontinent	N. America	Central/S. America	Far East, Australasia	Information Services
Argus			*									
Asian Greyhound	*							*				
Atrek	*		*			*						
A.U.S.												*
Bales	*					*		*				
Bennett	*						*					
Bill's		*		*								
Budget Bus	*							*				
Bustrek	*								*	*		
Butterfield	*							*				
Capricorn	*		*	*				*	*			
Contiki	*		*					*				
C.C.T.	*		*			*						
Cox & Kings			*				*	*				
Dick Phillips		*					*					
Encounter	*					*					*	
Eurasia	*		*	*				*				
European Express	*		*									
Exodus	*					*		*				

Firms offering:	Overland Tours Safaris and Treks	Other Camping Tours	Special Interest Tours	Tours in Britain and Europe	Middle East	Africa	Iceland/Greenland	Asia especially Indian Subcontinent	N. America	Central/S. America	Far East, Australasia	Information Services
Explorers		*	*			*	*	*	*	*		
Fairways			*					*				
Frontier			*									
G.A.A.	*					*						
Hann	*				*			*				
Highland			*	*								
Hughes	*		*			*		*		*		
Indian Railway								*				
Intertrek	*					*		*				
Kenworthy						*						
Maghreb	*					*						
Magic Bus			*					*				
Mistral	*					*						
Overlander Coaches	*							*				
Overlander Exp.	*					*		*	*	*	*	*
Penn	*		*	*	*	*	*	*	*	*		
Ramblers		*		*		*		*				
Regent		*		*			*					

Firms offering:	Overland Tours Safaris and Treks	Other Camping Tours	Special Interest Tours	Tours in Britain and Europe	Middle East	Africa	Iceland/Greenland	Asia especially Indian Subcontinent	N. America	Central/S. America	Far East, Australasia	Information Services
Sherpa	*	*						*				
Sundowners	*		*			*		*	*	*		
Tamar	*					*		*		*		
Tentrek	*			*	*	*						
Thomas Cook			*	*	*	*	*	*	*	*		*
Top Deck	*			*				*			*	
Top Kapi	*			*	*							
Tour East	*					*		*				
Trail Finders	*										*	*
Trans African	*					*						
Transit	*			*				*				
Trekamerica	*								*	*		
Twickenham			*	*	*	*			*	*	*	
West Himalayan	*							*				
WEXAS	*	*	*	*	*	*	*	*	*	*	*	

Overland and Adventure Trip Operators and Agents in the United Kingdom

Aardvark Expeditions Ltd
14 Coleridge Road
London N8
Tel. 01-340 7598
139 Forest Avenue
Aberdeen
Scotland

Jim and Moya Bothwell

South America round trip overland (by Mercedes vehicles and public transport), overland to Kathmandu, trips to the Middle East and North and East Africa. Camping.
About 16 weeks (S. America)

Abbott Travel
25 Sidney Street
Cambridge
Tel. 0223-51636

Branches in Grimsby and Sleaford.
Safaris in Borneo (Jorgen Bitsch Safari, escorted) and Mongolia.

Abercrombie & Kent (Europe) Ltd
4 Pont Street
London SW1X 9 EL
Tel. 01-235 3992/5753

Escorted safaris: off-the-beaten-track, specialist including trekking and saddle, gorilla tracking, ornithological, coast/ scuba diving, fishing, hunting and bird

watching; using own transport fleet or self-drive saloons; to East Africa especially.
Lodge or 'luxury' camping accommodation. 1–2 weeks.

Adventure Africa
34b High Street
Ramsbury
Wiltshire

Ken Edwards

West, North and East Africa, starting from London (flight to Tangier or Nairobi) or Nairobi and using 4 wheel drive truck for travel in Africa.
Camping/modest hotel/resthouse accommodation. 7–18 weeks.

Adventure Travel Shop and Pan Pacific
16a Soho Square
London W1V 5FB
Tel. 01-734 1072/3/4
01-437 5854
01-734 3094/5/6

Ivan Allen

Overland tour agents trans Asia, Africa and South America, coach to Australia and New Zealand.
Camping.
European tours: 4–9 weeks.
Skiing, winter treks, expeditions, safaris.

Africanus
15 Central Chambers
Cooks Alley
Stratford-upon-Avon
Warwickshire
Tel. 0789 740517

Dave Norris

*Chartered expeditions to Africa using
Land rovers and 4-wheel drive trucks.
Camping.
Self-drive expeditions for groups of
1–30 people by Safari Camp Services of
Nairobi.*

Albert Tours
The Bury
Buntingford
Hertfordshire
Tel. 02797 8321

*Overland London to India, using con-
verted bus (which provides accommodation).
5 weeks.*

Allen & Dunn Expeditions Ltd
19 St. Mary's Avenue
Norwood Green
Middlesex UB2 4LT
Tel. 01-574 5007

16a Soho Square
London W1V 5FB
Tel. 01-734 1072

Ivan Allen and Jonathan Dunn

*Fly/trekking tours, using Landrovers
and local transport, to Afghanistan, East
Africa, trans-Sahara, Morocco, Sudan,
southern Africa, Everest, Annapurna,
Little Tibet and Kashmir.
Camping/hotel accommodation.
Morocco — about 2 weeks.
Everest and Annapurna treks — $3^1/_2$
weeks.*

Alta Holidays Ltd
57 Victoria Street
London SW1H 0HG
Tel. 01-222 7632/4291

*Escorted interest tours including or-
nithology, photography, wildlife, in Asia,
North Africa, Middle East, Greece.*

Amtrek Overland
c/o Trail Finders Ltd
46–48 Earls Court Road
London W8 6EJ

*Details from Cantrek/Trail Finders,
Montreal and Trail Finders, Australia.
Mini-bus camping trips around Canada
and the USA. 9 weeks.*

Argus Travel Ltd
278–282 High Holborn
London WC1V 7ER
Tel. 01-242 9438/2797

Roy Featherstone

*Diving holiday in Truk Lagoon,
Micronesia (inc. flights, accommodation).
$2^1/_2$ weeks.*
Otherwise, a general travel agency.

Asian Greyhound Ltd
Head Office
15 Kings Road
Windsor
Berkshire
Tel. 95 69122/3/4

Norman Harria

A. G. Venture Centre
177 Kensington High Street
London W8
Tel. 01-937 6062/0072

Jo Ivosevic

*Overland London to India and Nepal
with connecting travel through the Far
East to Australia. Using coaches/buses
and avoiding 'tourist traps and sealed
roads' in groups of 32.
Camping. $8^1/_2$–$10^1/_2$ weeks.*

Atrek Travel Ltd
219a Kensington High Street
London W8
Tel. 01-937 4580/5761

Mervyn Hanna

Overland tours to Scandinavia, (including the Arctic Highway), USSR, Eastern and Southern Europe including Greece, Central Europe, Morocco, Algeria, Tunisia. Tours of all Europe as far as Asia Minor.
Groups of 18–28, aged under 35.
Camping.
6–11 weeks.

AUS Student Travel
Australian Union of Students Travel
117 Euston Road
London NW1 2SX
Tel. 01-387 0448

Bales Tours Ltd
16–17 Coventry Street
Piccadilly
London W1V 8 BL
Tel. 01-437 7992
      01-439 2478

Package tours round the world (30 days), Australia, New Zealand, Asia, Middle East, South America, Galapagos Islands, North America, Central America, Indian Ocean, Caribbean. Some self-catering. Escorted tours/treks to Annapurna Range foothills — 3 weeks; Everest — 3 weeks; East African safari — 3¹/₂ weeks.

Bennett Travel Bureau Ltd
229 Regent Street
London W1
Tel. 01-437 8223

Agents for Ulfar Jacobsen safaris in Iceland.

Bill's Coach Tours
65 Oxford Road
London W5
Tel. 01-741 0011

Bill Richmond

All Europe; Spain and Morocco; Scandinavia, Lapland and the Arctic Circle; Corsica, Sardinia and Italy; Turkey and Greece.
Camping.
3–6¹/₂ weeks.
Free trip for cook, selected after 'cook-in'.

Budget Bus
34 Oakleigh Park North
London N20
Tel. 01-445 8608

Emil and Wende Bryden

Overland tours to Asia.

Bustrek
Second Floor
167 Earls Court Road
London SW5 9RF
Tel. 01-373 3474

Agents:
Goway Travel Advisors, Canada
Atrek Travel Ltd, Sydney, Australia
Atrek Travel Ltd, Melbourne, Australia
Sundowners of London Travel Centre, Adelaide, Australia
Trail Finders Ltd, Sydney, Australia
Bustrek Australia, Melbourne, Australia
Latin World Travel, New Zealand
Kimbla Travel Pty. Ltd, South Africa
Going Places, Los Angeles, USA
Bus tours of North, Central and South America, in groups of 10.
Camping/modest hotel accommodation
4–12 weeks.

Butterfield, A.W. And R.
62 Victoria Walk
Horsforth
Leeds
Yorkshire
Tel. 0532 584744

Overland London to India and Nepal, using public transport, with guide, in groups of 15–35.
3–4 weeks.

Capricorn Travel and Tours Ltd
21 Ebury Bridge Road
London SW1W 8QX
Tel. 01-730 0657
Dick Cijfers

3 overland routes London to India, Kashmir and Nepal; Morocco, France and Spain, Middle East, Central Asia, trans-Indonesia, using coaches, in groups of 20–36.
Camping/modest hotel accommodation.
3–12¹/₂ weeks.
Associated with Sundowners Ltd

Contiki Travel Ltd
7 Rathbone Place
London W1
Tel. 01-637 2121

Tours of western and eastern Europe, including USSR (as far east as Moscow), Scandinavia, in groups of 40–45.
Camping.
3¹/₂–12 weeks.
Overland to Nepal, including visits to Greece and the Swat Valley, using coaches, in groups of up to 40, for 18–35-year-olds.
10¹/₂ weeks.

Continental Camping Tours (CCT)
139 Earls Court Road
London SW5
Tel. 01-370 1305/1044

Nine overland tours, to USSR, Africa, Greece, Turkey, 'at a leisurely pace', in groups of 27–40, using coaches.
Camping.
4¹/₂–9 weeks.

Cox and Kings Ltd
Vulcan House
46 Marshall Street
London W1V 2PA
Tel. 01-734 8291

Tours of Iceland for naturalists and geologists. Discovery tours of the Indian subcontinent (Sikkim and Bhutan, Maharajastan).
Hotel accommodation.
3¹/₂ weeks.

Dick Phillips
Whitehall House
Nenthead
Alston
Cumbria CA9 3 PS
Tel. 049-83 440

Information service.
Walking and motoring tours in Iceland, in escorted groups of 12–15 using where necessary chartered 4-wheel drive mountain bus.
Camping/hut accommodation.
12–20 days.
Agent for Ulfar Jacobsen
Hut/hostel accommodation, motor charters/car hire arranged.

Encounter Overland Ltd
Booking Office
271–280 Old Brompton Road
London SW5
Tel. 01-370 6845/6951/2
         01-373 7377
Head Office
Third Floor
1 Munro Terrace
London SW10
Tel. 01-352 2702/3

*Overland London to Johannesburg.
Long-range expeditions through Africa
and South America.
Camping.
14–16 weeks.
Overland London to Kathmandu, using
4-wheel drive vehicles, in groups of
19–28.
Camping.
10–11 weeks.*

Eurasia Overland Tours
The Broadway
Lamberhurst
Kent
Tel. 089 278 272

Trevor Bones

*Overland tours through Europe and
Middle East as far as Kathmandu.
Mostly camping.*

European Express
Hemisphere Holidays Ltd
80 King Street
Twickenham
Middlesex TW1 3SH
Tel. 01-891 0771

*Overland tours to Athens, Corfu, Spain,
France, Italy, in coaches, with guide.
Choice of hostel/camping/hotel accom-
modation.*

Exodus Expeditions
52 Earls Court Road
London SW5
Tel. 01-373 7895

*Overland trips to Asia, including Kur-
distan, the Dash-i-Lut, the Hindu Kush
or the Himalayas, using expedition vehicles, in groups of 25.
Camping.
10–12 weeks.
Overland trips to and in Africa.
Camping.
11–14 weeks.*

Explorers
(Explore Beyond Ltd)
1 Ludgate Circus Buildings
London EC4M 7LQ
Tel. 01-248 9082

*Escorted adventure holidays, mainly for
small groups of 6–12 people, using Landrovers or larger vehicles; to North,
Central and South America, Asia,
Africa.
Some camping.
1–48 weeks.*

Fairways & Swinford
18 St. George Street
London W1R 0EE
Tel. 01-629 6801

*One trip per year to Kashmir with Oleg
Polunin as guide, pony-trekking, riding,
fishing, walking, climbing and seeing rare
plants and birds. 3 weeks.*

Frontier Expeditions Ltd
37 High Street
Crawley
Sussex
Tel. 0293 31991/2

Barrie Payten and Laurie Smith

*Scandinavia, Lapland, USSR, the
Balkans, Eastern Europe, Greece,
France, Spain, Portugal, Turkey,
Morocco.
Tours of Central Europe and all Europe.*

Great African Adventure Co Ltd
233 Station Road
Leigh-on-Sea
Essex
Tel. 0702 73122

*Overland tours London to Capetown,
using an Amphibious DUKW.
Camping.
17 weeks.
Overland tours trans-Africa to Capetown, using a 4-wheel drive truck.
Air/overland tours London to Nairobi.*

Hann Overland
17 Stanhope Road
London SW16
Tel. 01-769 6659
Geoff Hann

Overland or air/overland tours through Asia, including Nepal, Turkey and the Middle East, in groups of 12–18, using mini-coaches. 4$\frac{1}{2}$–12$\frac{1}{2}$ weeks.

Highland Wildlife Enterprises
Cannich, Beauly
Inverness-shire IV4 7LY
Scotland
Tel. Cannich 327
John P.L. and Sorrel Lister-Kaye

Spring and summer daily outings from base to places of special natural historic interest; autumn and winter expeditions to wild and remote parts of the world; 'to provide informative recreation for those interested in the countryside', not necessarily experts.
Guest house accommodation at base.
Film location service, photographic information service, self-catering holiday cottages for letting.

Hughes Overland Ltd
Third Floor
Panton House
25 Haymarket
London SW1
Tel. 01-839 4267

Overland tours trans-Europe, trans-Siberia, in Africa, North, Central and South America, in groups of 10–24. 5–17 weeks.
Overland London to India and Nepal, Singapore and Sydney, using trucks or 'Asiaman' mini-coaches, in groups of 24. Camping/modest hotel accommodation. 13–18 weeks.
Minibus tours London to Europe, USSR, Asia and Africa. 3–4 weeks.
Jet-trek holidays to the Mediterranean.

Indian Railway Tours
c/o Trail Finders Ltd
46–48 Earls Court Road
London W8 6EJ
Tel. 01-937 9631

4-week tour of India from Delhi by rail.

Intertrek Expeditions Ltd
c/o Overlanders Expeditions Ltd
Third Floor
Panton House
25 Haymarket
London SW1
Tel. 01-839 4267

Overland London to India and Nepal, using 4-wheel drive vehicles; expeditions to other parts of Asia and to Africa; in groups of 20–24.
Camping/modest hotel accommodation. 10–11 weeks.
Overland London to Singapore, using 4-wheel drive vehicles, in groups of 22–24. 13 weeks.

Kenworthy, Trevor
c/o Trail Finders Ltd
46–48 Earls Court Road
London W8 6EJ

Conducted tours from Cairo to Nairobi by public transport (train and steamer) 4 weeks.

Long Haul Expeditions
See Tamar Travel Agents Ltd

Maghreb Safaris
c/o CBS Displays
8 St. Mary's Street
Wallingford
Oxon. OX10 oEL.
Tel. Wallingford 2230

Off-the-beaten-track, special interest, desert, mountain trekking, historical/archaeological expeditions in North and West Africa.
Camping/hotel accommodation.

Magic Bus
Head Office
Second Floor
24 Rokin
Amsterdam C
Netherlands
Tel. Amsterdam 212517/8

Second Floor
74 Shaftesbury Avenue
London W1
Tel. 01-439 0558/0729

London to Amsterdam, Athens, Barcelona, Paris, Delhi and many other destinations, by bus.

Mistral Safari
14 Cluny Crescent
Swanage
Dorset
Tel. Swanage 4629

Overland trips to the High Atlas Mountains of Morocco. 3 weeks.

Overlander Coaches
c/o Overlander Expeditions Ltd
Third Floor
Panton House
25 Haymarket
London SW1
Tel. 01-839 4267

Overland London to Delhi and Kathmandu, in groups of about 40, using coaches.
Modest hotel accommodation, 7–10$^1/_2$ weeks.

Overlander Expeditions Ltd
Four companies participating in programme:
Intertrek Expeditions, Hughes Overland, Overlander Coaches, Treasure Tours

Department TF
Third Floor
Panton House
25 Haymarket
London SW1
Tel. 01-839 4267

Main agents and branch offices in Auckland, Brisbane, Johannesburg, Melbourne, New York, Paris, Perth, Rotterdam, Stockholm, Sydney, Tokyo and Toronto.
Overland tours across Asia, Africa, North and Central America, South America, London to Kathmandu and vice versa; London to Sydney and vice versa; trans-Siberia, South-East Asia.

Penn Overland Tours Ltd
122 Knightsbridge
London SW1X 7PG
Tel. 01-589 0016

Offices in Amsterdam, Heidelberg, Berne, Lucerne, San Francisco, Cambridge (Mass.), Chicago, Toronto, Vancouver, Sydney, Melbourne, Perth, Adelaide, Brisbane, Auckland, Wellington, Christchurch.
Variety of 'action' and adventure trips, plus overland trips in Asia, North Africa and South America.

Ramblers Holidays Ltd
Ramblers' Association Services Ltd
Wings House
Bridge Road East
Welwyn Garden City
Herts
Tel. 070-73 31133

Unusual holidays, some for walkers and ramblers, to Kenya, the Annapurna region and other parts of Nepal, Western Anatolia and other parts of Turkey, India, Morocco, Madeira, Malta and many countries in western Europe.
Camping/hotel/rest house accommodation. 1–3 weeks.

Regent Holidays (IOW) Ltd
Regent House
66 Regent Street
Shanklin
Isle of Wight PO37 7AE
Tel. 098-386 4225/4212

13 Small Street
Bristol BS1 1DE
Avon
Tel. 0272-211711/2

Fly-drive holidays, hotel/hostel holidays, sea voyages to and around Iceland, Faroe Isles, Norway, the Westman Islands. High Country expeditions to the edge of the Arctic Circle.
Camping.
2 weeks.

Sherpa Expeditions

3 Bedford Road
London W4
Tel. 01-994 7668

Treks in Nepal and India; escorted groups of 12.
Camping.
3¹/₂ weeks.

Sundowners Ltd

8 Hogarth Place
London SW5
01-370 4317/8/4031
01-373 5623/1026

Various package tours (week-ends and short stays) to Europe and in Britain.
Overland London to Kathmandu, by 4 different routes, using first-class coaches, in groups of 36–40.
Camping/modest hotel accommodation.
6–10¹/₂ weeks.
6 different overland tours to Europe (including USSR) and North Africa, in groups of 40.
Camping
3–9 weeks.
Bustrek tours of South, Central and North America.
Camping/modest hotel accommodation.
4–12 weeks.

Tamar Travel Agents Ltd

(Long Haul Expeditions)
56 Bohun Grove
East Barnet
Hertfordshire EN4 8UB
Tel. 01-440 1582

Overland Nairobi to Johannesburg, using 4-wheel drive trucks.
Mostly camping.
6 weeks.
Overland round south South America, using powerful coach and local riverboats.
Camping.
17 weeks.
Overland to India and Nepal, using Landrover or larger vehicle.

Tentrek Expeditions Ltd

Tentrek House
Station Approach
Chislehurst
Kent BR7 5NW.
Tel. 01-467 9417/3473/9717

Overland expeditions to Morocco, Crete, Greece, Turkey, Iran, Scandinavia, using minibus.
Air/overland treks to Corfu, Greece, Turkey, in groups of 15.
Some camping.
2–6 weeks.

Thomas Cook & Son Ltd

Special Interest Group
Group Travel Service
Thorpe Wood
Peterborough
Cambridgeshire PE3 6SB
Tel. 0733 63200

London Head Office
45 Berkeley Street
London W1A 1EB
Tel. 01-449 4000

Manager: Ray Strickett.
Travel Co-ordinators: Roger Balsom and Paul Goodwin

Comprehensive service to travellers: currency, itineraries prepared, exchange facilities, passport renewal, visa service. Trips to various destinations.

Top Deck Travel
18 Dawes Road
London W6
Tel. 01-381 1388
    01-385 8032

Overland tours to Spain, Portugal, Turkey, Greece, Italy, Yugoslavia, USSR, Scandinania and Morocco, in groups of 20 or 34.
Camping.
6–7 weeks
Overland tours to Asia (Kathmandu), in groups of 18–20.
Camping.
7 or 9 weeks.
Overland tours to Nepal, Burma, Malaysia, Singapore and Australia, in groups of 20.
20 weeks.
All tours using converted double decker buses.

Topkapi Safari
48 Derwent Avenue
East Barnet
Hertfordshire
Tel. 01-361 0601

Overland tours as far as Asiatic Turkey.

Tour East
34 Oakleigh Park North
London N20
Tel. 01-445 8608

Overland London to Kathmandu — 11 weeks, to Delhi — 7 weeks, to Nairobi, trans-Sahara — 14 weeks.
A division of Budget Bus.

Trail Finders Ltd
46–48 Earls Court Road
London W8 6EJ
Tel. 01-937 9631/4569/3336/2429

Trail Finders agents overseas:
Trail Finders Ltd, Melbourne & Sydney, Australia.
Trail Finders & Co, Montreal & Edmonton, Canada
Trans-Himalayan Tour (P) Ltd, Nepal
Young Abroad Club, Japan
Skyline Travel Inc, USA.

Agents for many overland tours and expedition and holiday operators (e.g. Arena expeditions to Iceland).
Information service to travellers.

Trans African Expeditions Ltd
First Floor
165 Kensington High Street
London W8
Tel. 01-937 5694

Overland by 4-wheel drive truck London to Nairobi — 12 weeks, or London to Johannesburg — 15 weeks.
Camping.

Transit Travel Ltd
43 Kensington High Street
London W8 5ED
Tel. 01-937 6662
    01-937 8797 — coach hire
Ian M. Johnson

Tours of Western Europe including USSR and Morocco, using coaches, for 18–30 year-olds in groups of 42.
Camping.
3–9 weeks.
Overland London to Kathmandu, using luxury coach and trailermatic kitchen/baggage trailer (with fridge) in groups of 40–42.
Camping.
8 weeks.
Agents for Afro Ventures of South Africa.

Trekamerica Inc
62 Kenway Road
London SW5
Tel. 01-370 4013/2
    01-373 5858

Overland and air/overland tours in USA, Mexico and Central America, in groups of 13.
Camping.
3–6 weeks.

Twickenham Travel Ltd
22 Church Street
Twickenham
Middlesex TW1 3NW
Tel. 01-892 7606

378 Richmond Road
East Twickenham
Middlesex TW1 2DX
Tel. 01-891 0961

2 Chester Row
London SW1
Tel 01-730 5268/9

Tours and cruises, escorted, to South America, Galapagos Islands, Africa, Canada, Hawaii, Japan, Korea.
2–3 weeks.
Holidays in Europe, North Africa, Israel.
Aqua-Venture escorted holidays to Menorca, the Red Sea, Madagascar, Mauritius, including accommodation.
Personalised (package) holidays.
1–4 weeks.

West Himalayan Holidays Ltd
48 Conduit Street
London W1R 9FB
Tel. 01-437 5705

Treks in area from Simla to Lahoul, in own party or joining a group.

Wexas International
WEXAS
International Office
45 Brompton Road
Knightsbridge
London SW3

Wexas International Inc
Graybar Building, Suite 354
420 Lexington Avenue
New York
NY 10017
USA

The WEXAS Discoverers Programme of holidays for the adventurous of all ages is carefully arranged to give small congenial groups of 8–12 people the chance to visit some of the world's wild places while they still exist. Trips to 21 destinations. Available only to WEXAS members. For more details, see the 6- page WEXAS section in this handbook. It includes a WEXAS membership application form.

Overland and Adventure Trip Operators and Agents: Overseas

AUSTRALIA

Atrek Travel of London Ltd
332 Pitt Street
Sydney
NSW 2000
Tel. 61-9572

6 Flinders Way Arcade
238 Flinders Lane
Melbourne
Victoria 3000
Tel. 63-7231

Agents for
Bustrek tours of South, Central and North America.
Camping, modest hotel accommodation.
4–12 weeks.

Australian Pacific Camping Safaris
Australian Pacific
Seventh Floor
Network House
84 Pitt Street
Sydney
NSW 2000
Tel. 233 2744

First Floor
8a St. Andrews Street
Brighton
P.O. Box 81
Brighton
Victoria 3186
Tel. 92 8555

Booking office (Melbourne)
15 Degraves Street
corner Degraves Street and Mutual Arcade
Melbourne

Tours to various parts of, and around, Australia using coaches towing wagons with amenities. Starting from Sydney, Brisbane or New Zealand. Camping. 17–50 days.

Ausventure
Major Warwick Deacock
P.O. Box 54
Mosman
NSW 2088
Tel. 960 1677

Adventure expeditions to remote places in and around Australasia, e.g. New Guinea, New Hebrides, New Zealand, Fiji. Also abroad (in small groups) e.g. Annapurna, Everest areas; special interests catered for.
Agents for Mountain Travel, Nepal, Mountain Travel Inc, USA and Venture Treks Ltd, New Zealand.
Founded 1965.

Bustrek Australia
Second Floor, Room 4
247 Collins Street
Melbourne
Victoria 3000
Tel. 654 4916

Cogans
Corner Criterion and Liverpool
Streets
Hobart
Tasmania 7000
Tel. 34 3711

Agents for Australian Pacific Camping Safaris.

Fetco Travel
83 William Street
Second Floor
Melbourne
Victoria 3000
Tel. 624641

41 King William Street
Adelaide
S.A. 5000
Tel. 51-3503

Agents for Adventure International Club and Tours.

Great Adventure Travel Centre
147 Castlereagh Street
Sydney
NSW 2000
P.O. Box E126
St. James
Sydney
Tel. 26-2324/3269

Agents for Afro Ventures.

Koala Travel
28 Hindley Street
Adelaide
S.A. 5000
Tel. 51-3411

Agents for Australian Pacific Camping Safaris.

M.H. Travel
Third Floor
City Building
250 Edward Street
Brisbane
Queensland 4000
Tel. 229-5866

Agents for Continental Camping Travel.

Packhorse Adventures
P.O. Box 110
Wellington 2820
NSW

Q Tours
5 Henry Street
Fremantle
Western Australia 6160
Tel. 35-5811

305 Murray Street
Perth
Western Australia

Agents for Australian Pacific Camping Safaris.

Robert Paxton (Travel) Pty Ltd
90 Pitt Street
Sydney
NSW 2000
Tel. 233-3766

Agent for Adventure International Club and Tours.

Safari Land Tours
P.O. Box 110
Darwin
Northern Territory

Stewart Moffat Travel
Corner Elizabeth and Edward Streets
Brisbane
Queensland 4000
Tel. 21-3922

Agent for Adventure International Club and Tours.

Sundowners of London Travel Centre
129 First Floor
Adelaide Arcade
Adelaide
S.A. 5000
Tel. 223-1243/6619

Agents for The Sundowners Ltd., Capricorn Travel and Tours and The Overlanders.
Bustrek tours of South, Central and North America.
Camping, modest hotel accommodation. 4–12 weeks.

Sundowners of London Travel Centre
Shop 41
Block Place
317 Little Collins Street
Melbourne
Victoria 3000
Tel. 63-9566/7

Second Floor
Block Court
290 Collins Street
Melbourne
Victoria 3000
Tel. 63-8566

Agents for The Sundowners Ltd, Capricorn Travel and Tours and The Overlanders.

Sundowners of London Travel Centre
75 King Street
Sydney
NSW 2000
Tel. 25-4300/1553

Agents for The Sundowners Ltd, Capricorn Travel and Tours and The Overlanders.

Trail Finders Travel (Pty) Ltd
First Floor
15 Hunter Street
Sydney
NSW 2000
Tel. 233-1244

Shop 3
Manchester Lane
Melbourne
Victoria 3000
Tel. 63-8748

Agents for Trail Finders Ltd and Continental Camping Travel.
Agents (Sydney) for Bustrek tours of North, Central and South America.

Trans African Expeditions Ltd
147 Castlereagh Street
Sydney
NSW 2000

Agents for Trans African Expeditions Ltd (UK).

Victour
221 Queen Street
Brisbane
Queensland 4000
Tel. 21-4300

Agents for Australian Pacific Camping Safaris.

Travel-Time International Pty Ltd
766 Hay Street
Perth
Tel. 21-2911

428 Queen Street
Brisbane
Tel. 21-0577

Agents for The Overlanders programme (see Overlanders Expeditions Ltd).

V.U. (International) Pty Ltd
Second Floor
S.G.I.O. Building
815 Hay Street
Perth
Western Australia 6000
Tel. 21-8322

Agents for Continental Camping Travel.

Western International Travel Pty Ltd
430 Albany Highway
Victoria Park
Western Australia 6100
Tel. 61-9939

Agent for Adventure International Club and Tours.

BAHAMAS

Underwater Explorers Society
Box F-24337
Freeport
Lucaya

Diving courses and trips in the Bahamas.

BELGIUM

Explorado
Avenue Legrand 86
1050 Bruxelles
Tel. 02-648 22 69

Escorted tours to Africa (Omo region of Ethiopia, Sahara, Togo, Benin, Chad, Morocco), Asia (Iran, Indus valley, Kashmir, Himalayas, Central Soviet Asia, Afghanistan, Yemen, Indonesia), Central and North America (including Bahamas, New York), South America, Europe and USSR, in groups of about 8–15.
8–21 days.
Associated with Fédération Mondiale des Villes Jumelées.

Jerrycan Expédition
Avenue Legrand 86
1050 Bruxelles
Tel. 02-648 22 69

Escorted expeditions (using Landrovers and Ford-Saharas) to Greece, Iran and Turkey, the Yemen, Afghanistan, Mexico, the Amazon, Tierra del Fuego, Indonesia, Niger and Lake Chad, Togo and Benin, the Sahara; also Scotland and Provence.
Camping (2- and 6-man tents).

CANADA

Canadian Camping Tours
250a One Palliser Square
Calgary
Alberta T2G OP6

Hiking, sightseeing, canoeing holidays in Alaska, the Rockies, Alberta, Saskatchewan.
Camping in small groups.
12–22 days.

Canadian Mountain Holidays
Hans Gmoser
P.O. Box 1660
Banff
Alberta

Ski mountaineering and climbing trips, helicopter skiing holidays, with guides.

Canatrek
Box 1138
Banff
Alberta TOL OCO
Tel. (403) 762 2528

Backpacking, climbing and canoeing expeditions to the remote mountain regions of Greenland, Alaska, Western Canada, Baffin Island, Switzerland, Peru, Kashmir.

Canoe Arctic Inc
9 John Beck Crescent
Brampton
Ontario L6W 2T2

Wilderness trips to Arctic and sub-Arctic Canada.

Can-trek Overland Expeditions
6725 Somerled
Montreal
Quebec H4V IT7

Explorer Tours
640 Cathcart Street
Suite 307
Montreal
Quebec H33 IM3

Goway Travel Advisors
Suite 104
53 Yonge Street
Toronto 1
Tel. (416) 863 0799

Bustrek tours of North, Central and South America.
Camping, modest hotel accommodation.
4–12 weeks.
Agents for Capricorn Travel and Tours and The Overlanders.

Geo Expeditions
Kagawong
Ontario PoP 1JO
Tel. 705 282 2839

Director: D. Kirchgatter

Independent excursions from large farm serving as base camp or using wilderness camping facilities; or six-day kayak/canoe expeditions with others, camping; both in and around Manitoulin Island in northern Lake Huron.
Archaeological and snorkelling expedition by kayak along the Yucatan coast.

New Horizon Holidays Ltd
Suite 524
736 Granville Street
Vancouver 2
British Columbia
Tel. (604) 681 5291

Agent for Adventure International Club and Tours.

Northern Lights Alpine Recreation
Arnor Larson
399
Invermere
British Columbia VOA 1KO

Mountaineering weeks (from basic to advanced grades), alpine hiking treks, exploratory expeditions.

Trail Finders & Co
6725 Somerled Avenue
Montreal
Quebec H4V 1T7

9004 112th Street
Edmonton
Alberta TCZ 2C5

Agents for Trail Finders Ltd.

Western International Treks
9004 112 Street
Hub Mall
Edmonton
Alberta T6Z 2C5
Tel. 439 1222

Agents for Sundowners Ltd.

Western Outdoor Adventures Ltd
16115 32 Avenue
White Rock
British Columbia V4B 4Z57

Wilderness trips in Canada.

ECUADOR

Safari Ecuatorianos
Box A-122
Quito

Wildlife trips.

ETHIOPIA

Forsmark, Carl and Anya
P.O. Box 1811
Addis Ababa
Tel. 150659

Camping safaris in Omo, part of southern Ethiopia, at base on the Mui River.

FRANCE

Air Alliance
3 bis rue de Vaugirard
75006 Paris

Trips to out-of-the-way places.

Alliance Européene de l'air
4 rue de l'Echelle
75001 Paris

Worldwide trips to unusual places.

Assinter Voyages
154 Boulevard St. Germain
75006 Paris
Tel. 326 19 28
38 Rue Madame
75006 Paris
Tel. 544 45 87

Escorted tours to Greece, South and South East Asia, the Far East, Central and South America, the Caribbean, parts of Africa.
Hotel accommodation.
3-4 weeks.

Club Nord Sud
27 Rue Gay-Lussac
75005 Paris
Tel. 033 97 88

Expeditions to Morocco, Turkey, Crete, Lapland, North Cape. USSR, Scotland, USA, using mini-buses or Landrovers; small groups.

Découverte du Nouveau Monde
8 Rue Mabillon
75006 Paris
Tel. 325 17 45

Expeditions, self-drive tours, etc. in North and South America, especially Latin America (e.g. to the sources of the Orinoco, Venezuela, 17 days).

Explorator
5 Rue Cambaceres
75008 Paris

Unusual travel and camping expeditions to remote destinations.

Fédération Mondiale des Villes Jumelées
54 Rue des Ecoles
75005 Paris
Tel. 329 21 17

45 Cours Pasteur
33000 Bordeaux
Tel. (56) 91 71 07

Package tours to the Americas, Asia, the Mediterranean, Africa (e.g. Kenya safari) with guides.
Hotel accommodation, charter flights, etc. Associated with Explorado, Belgium; Jerrycan, Switzerland; Sotour, Luxembourg.

Jumbo
72 Rue Gay-Lussac
75005 Paris
Tel. 033 74 35

African tour specialists.

Jeunes Sans Frontières
7 Rue de la Banque
75002 Paris
Tel. 261 53 21

Expeditions and tours for young travellers aged 17 to 35, to parts of Europe, the Middle East, Far East, North and East Africa, the Americas, South East Asia, South Africa, USSR.

Le Raid — Expéditions
17 Rue d'Austerlitz
69004 Lyon
Tel. (78) 27 11 10

Migrator
25 Rue des Boulangers
75005 Paris
Tel. 033 05 19

Adventure expeditions: trekking, skiing, underwater, safaris; in West, Southwest and South Asia, Malaysia, Central America, Ecuador and Peru, Canada, Greenland, Iceland, the Sudan, trans-Sahara, Mali, South-west Africa, Austria, Spain, the Red Sea, the Atlantic Ocean, and a world circumnavigation in groups of about 12.
2 weeks–11 months.
Associated with Explore Beyond Ltd (UK) and Topastrek (Switzerland).

Nomade Expédition
68 rue de Vangirard
75006 Paris

Overland expeditions.

Nouvelles Frontières/ Touraventure
63 Avenue Denfert-Rochereau
75014 Paris
Tel. 325 57 51
     633 28 91
166 Boulevard du Montparnasse
75014 Paris
(Travel reference library at this branch)

Tours and treks to North, West, Central and East Africa, southern Europe, and West Indies, South-West and South-East Asia, North and South America, Iceland and Greenland, in small groups. 2–4 weeks.

Overland
11 Rue Vavin
75006 Paris

Passeport
68 Rue de Vaugirard
75006 Paris
Tel. 544 21 99/20 43
     548 16 69
110 Cours A. Briand
33000 Bordeaux
Tel. 91 37 52

Package holidays to islands of the Indian and Atlantic Oceans, to the Yemen, Ceylon, Thailand.
Flights at reduced rates on scheduled routes to all parts of the world.
Nomade Expéditions: tours/treks in Africa, the Yemen, Europe, USSR, using Landrovers or minibuses — small groups.
Nomade Expéditions: cruises.
Camping only.

Rivages Expéditions
330 Rue St. Jacques
75005 Paris
Tel. 325 43 99

Tours with guide in Europe, South-East Asia, Africa (safaris), Central and South Asia, USA, South America. 1–4 weeks.

Terres d'Aventure
5 Rue Saint Victor
75005 Paris
Tel. 033 63 51
     326 50 98

Adventure expeditions: trekking (in Morocco, on the Indian trail in Canada), mountain excursions (ascent of Mount Kilimanjaro), river-running (on the Grand Canyon and the Niger), sailing cruises, ski-touring (Canada), and other excursions in Lapland, Nepal, Thailand, Greece, West Africa, the Sahara, Algeria, the Air Mountains, Afghanistan.

ICELAND

Arena Tours
Hvassaleiti 26
Reykjavik

High-country expeditions for the layman.
Camping.
13 days.
Cross-country expeditions for organised groups.

Farfugladeild Reykjavikur
Laufásvegur 41
Reykjavik

Extensive programme of summer tours of Iceland.
Some camping.

Ulfar Jacobsen Tourist Bureau Ltd
P.O. Box 886
Austurstraeti 9
Reykjavik

Iceland 'safari' tours, using overland buses with kitchen-vans.
Camping.
12–13 days.
Trout-fishing and halibut deep-sea fishing excursions arranged.

INDIA

Baktoo, M.S.
P.O. Box 32
Srinagar
Kashmir
Tel. 3913

Houseboat and country house accommodation for hire. Sight-seeing, fishing, trekking , camping, hunting and off-the-beaten track excursions arranged.

JAPAN

Young Abroad Club
202 Sato Building
25 Daikyo-Cho
Shinjyuku-Ky
Tokyo 160

Agents for Trail Finders Ltd.

KENYA

Afrotrek Ltd
Box 40248
Nairobi

Motorcycle safaris in Africa, especially Kenya. Itineraries arranged for all types of rider.
1–4 weeks.

LUXEMBOURG

Sotour
20 Avenue Marie-Thérèse
Luxembourg City
Tel. 465 14

Associated with Fédération Mondiale des Villes Jumelées.

NEPAL

Annapurna Mountaineering and Trekking Pvt Ltd
P.O. Box 795
Darbarmarg
Kathmandu

Guides and equipment supplied to mountaineers and trekkers.

Manastrek
Durbar Marg
Kathmandu
P.O. Box 1519
Tel. 12422
12959

Agents for Sherpa Expeditions.

Mountain Travel
Maharajganj
P.O. Box 170
Kathmandu
Tel. 12808

Walking/trekking holidays in the mountains of Nepal for individuals, small groups or larger groups of up to 18 or so organised by clubs or travel agents; special interests catered for, e.g. photography, painting and sketching, bird watching.
Camping.
1–7 weeks or longer.
See also:
Mountain Travel Inc, USA
Sporthaus Schuster, West Germany
Ausventure, Australia
Thomas Cook & Son Ltd, UK
Eiselin Sport, Switzerland.

Sherpa Society
Ram Shah Path
Kathmandu

Equipment for rent and sale; assistance to trekkers and mountaineers.

Tiger Tops
P.O. Box 242
Kathmandu
Tel. 12706

Canoe trips, elephant-back/jungle excursions, river picnics, fishing, boating, Landrover excursions, short treks, nature walks, based at or near Tiger Tops Lodge in the Royal Chitwan National Park. Lodge or camping accommodation. 1–5 days.

Trans Himalayan Tour (P) Ltd
Bungalow No. 1
Seto Durbar
P.O. Box 283
Kathmandu
Tel. 13854
13871

Agents for Trail Finders Ltd. Trekking tours arranged in Nepal.

NEW ZEALAND

Latin World Travel
McKenzie and Willis Arcade
Colombo Street
Christchurch
Tel. 79481

Bustrek tours of North, Central and South America.
Camping, modest hotel accommodation. 4–12 weeks.

Sundowners of London Travel Centre
Suite 2
First Floor
50 High Street
Auckland 1
Tel. 372 003

Agents for The Sundowners Ltd.

Treasure Tours Ltd
First Floor
40–42 Willis Street
Wellington
Tel. 445 00

First Floor
338 Queen Street
Auckland 1
Tel. 364 592

Overland Sydney to London across Asia.
Escorted tours across USSR by Trans-Siberian Express; to Japan and Australia.
Expeditions through North, Central, and especially South America.
Founded 1969 — pioneers in the overland tour route Sydney to London.
One of the companies participating in The Overlanders programme (see Overlanders Expeditions Ltd).

United Travel Services
106 Albert Street
Auckland 1
Tel. 34039

Agent for Adventure International Club and Tours.

Venture Treks Ltd
Walter S. Romanes
71 Evelyn Road
Howick
Auckland
Tel. Howick 44844

Treks, with guide, to the Andes, Himalaya, Fiji, Indonesia and elsewhere, in small groups of up to 15.
14–35 days.
Treks/canoeing holidays in New Zealand, with guide.
Advice given to independent travellers, itineraries planned, leaders and equipment also supplied.
See also: Ausventure, Australia.

PERU

Peruvian Safaris SA
P.O. Box 10088
Lima

Wildlife safaris in Peru.

SINGAPORE

Holiday Tours and Travel (Pte) Ltd
Summer Centre
Second Floor
37 Somerset Road
Singapore 9
Tel. 370533

Agent for Adventure International Club and Tours.

Mas Travel Centre (Pte) Ltd
Suite 544
Tanglin Shopping Centre
Singapore 10
Tel. 235 4071/2

Agents for Sundowners Ltd.

SOUTH AFRICA

Afro Ventures
97a Main Street
P.O. Box 10848
Johannesburg 2000

Safaris to Botswana and Namibia, from Johannesburg; for small groups of young people, using a four-wheel drive vehicle. Camping. 11–18 days. UK general sales agents: Transit Travel.

Kimbla Travel Pty Ltd
50 Twist Street
Joubert Park
Johannesburg
Tel. 725 6525

Bustrek tours of North, Central and South America.
Camping, modest hotel accommodation.
4–12 weeks.

Tourist Centre Pty Ltd
64 Joubert Street
Johannesburg
Tel. 23 4701

Agents for The Overlanders.

Travel Rite (Pty) Ltd
P.O. Box 13011
Northmead
Benoi
Transvaal
Tel. 849 6633/6625
    54 3256/2453

Agents for The Sundowners Ltd and Capricorn Travel and Tours.

SWITZERLAND

Eiselin Sport
Max Eiselin
Obergrundstrasse 72
Lucerne

Agents for Mountain Travel, Nepal.

Jerrycan Expédition
53 Rue du Stand
1204 Geneva
Tel (022) 21 60 11

See Jerrycan, Belgium.
Associated with Fédération Mondiale des Villes Jumelées.

Topastrek
Reisebüro Topas AG
Hirschmattstrasse 36
6000 Lucerne
Tel. 041 23 53 69
    041 22 44 55

Programme of adventure expeditions as those of Migrator (France).

THAILAND

Rajata Tours
1/29–9 Soi Saladaeng
Silom Road
Bangkok
Tel. 233 1953

Agents for The Sundowners Ltd.

USA

Adventure Associates
150 SE Second Avenue
Suite 914
Miami
Florida 33131

Amazon trips.

Adventure Center
5540 College Avenue
Oakland
California 94618

Agents for Arena Tours, Iceland.

Adventures Unlimited
19 East 45th Street
New York
NY 10017

Amazon Safari Club Inc
R.D.1
Box 2
Elverson
Pennsylvania 19520
Tel. (215) 286 9041

President: John W. Abrams

Escorted tours for members, including 14-day tour of the Upper Amazon Basin, with guest lodge accommodation, and 21-day cruise to the Antarctic from Miami on an Argentine ship.

American River Touring Association
1016 Jackson Street
Oakland
California 94607

Non-profit organisation offering a variety of US whitewater trips.

Appalachian Mountain Club
5 Joy Street
Boston
Massachusetts 02108

Special excursions with experienced AMC leaders to destinations over 500 miles from home base and lasting over a week, including to Mount Everest Base Camp.

Archaeological Institute of America
260 West Broadway
Department EX
New York
NY 10013

'Journeys of Discovery':
Galapagos Islands, Peru and Bolivia, Egypt from the Nile, British Indies cruise, Yucatan Peninsula; with guides. In cooperation with the White Memorial Foundation.

Caribbean Schooner Cruises Inc
380 Lexington Avenue
New York
NY 10017

Doka Expeditions
2329 Sacramento Suite
San Francisco
California 94115

Unusual expeditions with scientific objectives, run entirely by members, to Central and South America, and Alaska. 6–14 weeks.

Earthwatch
10 Juniper Road
Box 127
Belmont
Massachusetts 02178

A non-profit-making organisation offering opportunities for people of all ages to join scientific research projects worldwide as unskilled volunteers paying their own way.
Earthwatch operates in conjunction with the Center for Field Research (same address) which helps fund scientific research in the field, especially in ecology and the natural sciences.

Eastern Mountain Sports Climbing School
Main Street
North Conway
New Hampshire 03860

Climbing and backpacking trips in North America and abroad.

Expedition Training Institute
P.O. Box 171
Prudential Center Station
Boston
Massachusetts 02199

Placement services for scientific research expeditions. Subsidies available.

Galice Raft Rental
14251 Galice Road
Merlin
Oregon 97532
Tel. (503) 467 8051

Nylon rafts for hire for half or full day trips down the Rogue River.

Going Places
611 South Kingsley Drive
Suite 208
Los Angeles
California 90005
Tel. (213) 385 0012

Bustrek tours of North, Central and South America.
Camping, modest hotel accommodation.
4–12 weeks.
Agents for Sundowners Ltd and Capricorn Travel and Tours.

Grand Canyon/Canyonlands Expeditions
P.O. Box 0
Kanab
Utah 84741
Tel. (801) 644 2691

River trips in Arizona, Utah and Colorado.
2–14 days.

Hans Ebenstein Travel Inc
55 West 42 Street
New York
NY 10036

Worldwide adventure and nature trips.

International Aquatic Adventures Inc
P.O. Box 1396
Ft. Collins
Colorado 80522

International Zoological Expeditions Inc
210 Washington Street
Sherborn
Massachusetts 01770
Tel. (617) 655 1461
President: Lau Magner

Tours/treks in Central America.
Camping or restaurant/lodge accommodation.
2–3 weeks.
Hire of 'island in the sun' to family or small group.

Islands in the Sun
2400 West Coast Highway
Suite 9
Newport Beach
California 92660

Sailing trips in the Pacific.

Lindblad Travel Inc
133 East 55th Street
New York
NY 10022

Comfortable tours/safaris to off-the-beaten-track places.
Mostly hotel accommodation.
Cruises in MS Lindblad Explorer.
Emphasis on wildlife and archaeology.
Intrepids Club for younger, more physical trips.

Lute Jerstad Adventures
9920 SW Terwilliger Boulevard
P.O. Box 19527
Portland
Oregon 97219
Tel. (503) 244 4364

Worldwide adventure excursions, special interest trips.

Joe McLean
Box 1774
Juneau
Alaska 99801
Tel. (907) 586 1374

Cruises aboard fully-equipped yacht in Glacier Bay, Alaska.
4 passengers and crew.

Middle Fork Trips
Stanley
Idaho

107-mile white water raft trip on the Middle Fork of the Salmon River which winds through the $1^1/_4$ million acre Idaho Primitive Area and here forms one of the deepest gorges in North America.

Mountain Travel Inc
1398 Solano Avenue
Albany
California 94706
Tel. (415) 527 8100

Unusual excursions and expeditions to wilderness areas throughout the world. Emphasis on back-packing and mountaineering.
See also: Sporthaus Schuster, W. Germany; Ausventure, Australia; Mountain Travel, Nepal; Eiselin Sport, Switzerland.

Nature Expeditions International
Box 1173
Los Altos
California 94022

Worldwide wildlife trips.

Northern Whitewater Expeditions Inc
P.O. Box 57
Rockwood
Maine 04478

Rafting trips on white water in the northeastern USA.

Oars Inc
Box 67
Angels Camp
California 95222

River rafting trips in the USA.

Oceanic Society
Building 240
Fort Mason
San Francisco
California 94123
Tel. (415) 441-5970
11 Prospect Street
Stamford
Connecticut 06901
Tel. (203) 327-0948

Organisers of Oceanic Expeditions, trips across oceans by sail. Trips suitable for learners and experienced sailors.

Odyssey Ltd
26 Hilltop Avenue
Berkeley Heights
NJ 07922

Wilderness trips.
Mountain backpacking trips in Canada, Alaska, Peru, Switzerland.

Outward Bound
165 W Putnam Avenue
Greenwich
Connecticut 66830

Wilderness courses.

Pearl's Freighter Tips
175 Great Neck Road
Suite 306
Great Neck
NY 11021

Specialists in arranging long or short freighter voyages throughout the world. No charge for the service.

Questers Tours and Travel Inc
257 Park Avenue South
New York
NY 10010

Worldwide nature tours.

See and Sea Travel Service
680 Beach Street
Suite 340
Wharfside
San Francisco 94109

Worldwide diving trips.

Sierra Club
530 Bush Street
San Francisco
California 94108

Wilderness trips in North America and overseas. Club members only.

Skyline Travel Inc
1754 East 86th Street
Indianapolis
Indiana 46240

Agents for Trail Finders Ltd.

Sobek Expeditions Inc
P.O. Box 67
Angels Camp
California 95222
Tel. (209) 736 2924

River expeditions: Omo River, Ethiopia, 2-4 weeks, Blue Nile, 2½ weeks, Venezuela (hike to the Angel Falls), New Zealand, New Guinea, Mexico. Fishing boat expeditions down the Sea of Cortez (offered in cooperation with Baja Expeditions Inc). 9 days.

University of California Berkeley Research Expeditions
c/o University Herbarium
Dept of Botany
University of California
Berkeley
California 94720
Tel. (415) 642-6586

Interested donors/participants are invited to join scientific research expeditions, mainly in the natural sciences. A non-profit organisation.

Wexas International Inc
Suite 354
Graybar Building
420 Lexington Avenue
New York
NY 10017

International Office
45 Brompton Road
Knightsbridge
London SW3

WEXAS International is the world's largest travel and exploration club, with

members in 83 countries. For more details on WEXAS, see the 6-page WEXAS section in this handbook. It includes a WEXAS membership form.

Whitewater Adventures
P.O. Box 1396
Ft. Collins
Colorado 80522

River rafting trips in the USA

White Water River Expeditions
Turlock
California

Excursions on the Colorado and other rivers under supervision of Henry and Grace Falmer.

Wilderness Company Inc
6505 Telegraph Avenue
Oakland
California 94609

River rafting trips in the USA.

Wilderness Expeditions Inc
230 Park Avenue
New York
NY 10017.

Wilderness Southeast
Route 3
Box 619
Savannah
Georgia 31405

Wilderness trips in the USA.

Windjammer Cruises
P.O. Box 120
Miami Beach
Florida 93139

Sailing cruises in the British Virgin Islands, the West Indies and the Bahamas.
Flexible routes and destinations (determined by the weather, and the Captain's preferences). 'Flagship', the

Fantome, at 282 feet the longest schooner in the world.

Worldwide River Expeditions
Salt Lake City
Utah 84115

River rafting trips in the USA.

WEST GERMANY

Lama Exp. Reisen GmbH KG
Frankfurt am Main
Kornmarkt
Tel. 0611 291629

Adventure expeditions e.g. to the Sudan.

Rotel-Tours
(Das Rollende Hotel)
Georg Höltl,
8391 Tittling/Passau

Tours in large touring buses with trailer articulated; thereto or in giant double-decker buses with built-in accommodation and kitchen facilities; Great Britain, Eire, many parts of Europe and the Mediterranean, including Scandinavia, USSR, Iceland, Africa, the Middle East, Central and South Asia, New Zealand, Australia, South and North America.
1–11¹/₂ weeks.

Sporthaus Schuster
Rosenstrasse 5–6
Munich

Agents for Mountain Travel, Nepal.

Expedition-oriented Organisations

Section A : United Kingdom

Aigas Field Centre
Beauly
Inverness-shire

Field studies centre concentrating on self-sufficiency. Small groups train by day and attend lectures in the evening. Courses last one week and run from March to October.

Archaeology Abroad Service
31/34 Gordon Square
London WC1

Aims to provide information about opportunities for British archaeologists and others based in Britain to take part in excavation and field work abroad.

Association of the Experiment in International Living
Otesaga
Upper Wyche
Malvern
Worcestershire WR14 4EN

Homestays with local families in various parts of the world including South America and East and West Africa. An ideal opportunity to come to terms with other cultures.

Auto Camping Club
5 Dunsfold Rise
Coulsdon
Surrey CR3 2ED

Services for the motorised camper.

Autombile Association
Fanum House
Leicester Square
London W1

The AA offers its route planning service to members. Routes through Africa and Asia can be made to order. Information on visas, inoculation and en route accommodation is also available to members. Six weeks should be allowed for preparation of route plans.

Brathay Exploration Group
Brathay Hall
Ambleside
Westmorland

Offers unique opportunities to young people for adventurous travel overseas and to isolated parts of the UK, each expedition combining definite fieldwork objectives with challenging physical activity.

British Antarctic Survey
2 All Saints Passage
Cambridge CB2 3LF

Recruits graduates and others for the British Antarctic Base.

British Girls' Exploring Society
c/o Miss M. Hayes
Outward Bound Mountain School
Penrith
Cumberland

Organises adventure and field research

expeditions for girls in the UK and over-seas.

British Sub-Aqua Club
70 Brompton Road
London SW3

The world's largest sub aqua club, with affiliates worldwide. Examining authority for divers in the UK. Extremely high standards. Interests cover sport, professional and scientific diving. Publishes Triton magazine monthly.

British Schools Exploring Society
Temple Chambers
Temple Avenue
London EC4

An old-established society which runs subsidised (in some cases) expeditions for senior schoolboys, generally to Iceland or Arctic Scandinavia.

Duke of Edinburgh's Award Scheme
2 Old Queen Street
London SW1

Offers youth courses in various fields of individual endeavour, including outdoor adventure activities, and Duke of Edinburgh's medals for those reaching various standards.

Egypt Exploration Society
2–3 Doughty Mews
London WC1

Concerned with archaeological research in Egypt.

Endeavour Training
Canal House
Drapers Fields
Coventry CV1 4LG

Outdoor adventure courses.

Field Studies Council
9 Devereux Court
Strand
London WC2

Support for certain field research expeditions.

Flying Doctors' Society of Africa
9 Upper Grosvenor Street
London W1X 9PA

Linked with the African Medical and Research Foundation, the Society provides medical services to the people of Africa through the East African Flying Doctors' Service. Members are offered the full flying doctor service themselves if they are seriously ill or injured in East Africa. For expeditions going to East Africa, membership of the Association could be most useful as a form of insurance.

Globetrotters Club
BCM
Roving
London WC1V 6XX

A small informal association of travellers from all over the world, linked by an interest in low-cost travel and the desire to study the cultures of other lands at first hand. Members share their personal experiences and detailed knowledge of local conditions. The club is small and personal and concentrates on attracting as new members only those 'non-tourists' with a genunine sympathy for the people in other lands. The club's newsletter Globe has been coming out regularly for thirty years. It is full of travel information, articles and diary notes. Members may advertise in it for information, travelling companions, etc. Globetrotters groups meet regularly for films and talks in London and southern California.

Guildford Travel Club
Miss J. Tubbs
Membership Secretary
'Cliffe End'
9 Ridgemount
Guildford
Surrey

Founded in 1966 with the aim of giving its members, limited to 250 in number, added interest and enjoyment in travel. Main meetings are held twice a month, with guest speakers, from October to April, and members' evenings in private homes, mainly for the showing of slides and the discussion of countries visited, during the year. A Sunday ramble is held once a month.

Iceland Information Unit
c/o E. A. Escritt
Losehill Hall
Peak National Park Study Centre
Castleton
via Sheffield S30 2WB
Tel. 0433 20714

Established by the Young Explorers' Trust, the Unit exists to improve communcation between past and present expeditions to Iceland. With a central working group and a body of consultants specialising in different fields of study, the Unit is building up a record of information useful to expeditions. (Inquiries should be accompanied by SAE).

John Ridgway School of Adventure
Ardmore
Rhiconich
By Lairg
Sutherland IV27 4RB
Tel. 097-182 229

Two week summer courses in north-west Scotland. Men and women 18-30. Expedition training, survival, hillwalking, canoeing, rock climbing and sailing. Also courses for children Easter and summer;

men and women 30-70, April-July and September.

Motor Caravanners' Club
29 Wimbledon Park Road
London SW18 5SJ

Services for motor caravanners.

National Association of Boys' Clubs
17 Bedford Square
London WC1

From time to time sends boys on adventure training courses.

National Association of Youth Clubs
30 Devonshire Street
London W1N 2AP

Arranges youth club expeditions and study tours from time to time.

Nature Conservancy
Attingham Park
Shrewsbury
Shropshire

Interest in certain expeditions in the natural sciences.

Outward Bound Trust
34 Broadway
London SW1H 0BQ

Offers residential courses for youth at the various Outward Bound Schools in the UK and overseas, giving boys and girls from all walks of life an opportunity for adventure training

Rover Company
Public Relations Department
The Rover Company
Solihull
Worcestershire.

Publishers of an invaluable 'Guide to Landrover Expeditions'. The company runs a three-day course on maintenance.

Royal Automobile Club
RAC Touring Services
P.O. Box 92
RAC House
Lansdowne Road
Croydon CR9 9DH

The RAC provides a foreign route planning service to members of the Club and draws up routes and itineraries on an individual basis. It also produces a number of touring publications useful to the motorist travelling overseas.

Sail Training Association
Bosham
Chichester
Sussex

Offers seamanship training courses for youth.

Schools' Hebridean Society
Chasefield Mews
Park Road
Bowden
Cheshire

Organises adventure and elementary field research expeditions for youth in the Hebrides.

Schooner 'Captain Scott'
Schooner Office
Achdalieu
Fort William
Inverness-shire

Provides youth training courses in seamanship aboard the schooner Captain Scott.

Royal Scottish Geographical Society
10 Randolph Crescent
Edinburgh EH3 7TU
Tel. 031–225 3330

Branches in Glasgow, Aberdeen, Dundee and Dunfermline. Various classes of membership. Extensive collection of books, maps and periodicals; lectures; RSGS publications.

Scott Polar Research Institute
Cambridge CB2 1ER

For information on polar regions.

Scout Association
25 Buckingham Palace Road
London SW1

Exchanges with scouts abroad, and study tours.

Survival International
36 Craven Street
London WC2N 5NG

Survival International is a non-religious, non-political, non-paternalistic organisation currently run by individuals who have mostly had direct personal experience of tribal life as anthropologists or in other professional capacities. Survival International works to help tribal peoples overcome the problems presented by steadily increasing contact and interaction with non-tribal members of the states within whose boundaries they live. To this end, Survival International engages in a number of activities and produces various publications. The funding of research projects that will assist endangered primitive cultures is a major concern. Funds are always needed to support the work of this charity, and donations are gratefully received. Subscriptions entitle donors to regular copies of News Report, *the SI publication.*

Trail Finders
48 Earls Court Road
London W8

Trail Finders offer an advisory service for those mounting their own long range expedition across Africa or India or beyond.

Robin Hanbury – Tenison of Survival International discusses problems facing the Cuna Indians.

WEXAS

International Office
45 Brompton Road
Knightsbridge
London SW3

Wexas International Inc.
Graybar Building, Suite 354
420 Lexington Avenue
New York N.Y. 10017 USA

The world's largest travel and exploration club, with members in 83 countries. For more details, see the 6–page WEXAS section in this handbook. It includes a WEXAS membership application form.

World Wildlife Fund

Founded by Sir Peter Scott in 1961, the World Wildlife Fund is the principal international body engaged in attempts to save the wildlife species threatened with extinction as a result of the human population explosion and the often adverse ecological effects of modern technology. The Fund has permanent appeals established in 25 countries, and to date more that $15,000,000 has flowed to over 1100 high priority conservation projects in some 70 countries.

Guy Mountfort, an International Trustee of the World Wildlife Fund, suggests ways in which expeditions can help the Fund: 'Many expeditions could, if they so wished, contribute valuable information to the World Wildlife Fund about endangered species which they may see on their travels. As animals become rarer, it is increasingly difficult to obtain reliable information as to their numbers or distribution. Where expeditions to little-known countries include a knowledgeable naturalist, the World Wildlife Fund would be delighted if he would report any sightings of such species, with appropriate details, map references and altitude. Existing information on all endangered mammals, birds and reptiles, with their last-reported status and distribution, is available in the IUCN Red Books of Endangered Species, which can be consulted either at the WWF headquarters at 1110 Morges, Switzerland, or the offices of the British National Appeal at 29 Greville Street, London EC1. As these are classified by country, it would not be difficult to compile a list referring to the region which the expedition plans to visit.

Nearly all countries now have conservation laws which prohibit the collecting of endangered species of wildlife. Permits are, however, usually obtainable to collect for bona fide scientific purposes. If an expedition intends to collect specimens, members should first make quite sure that adequate series are not already available in the leading museums. Every additional specimen taken, whether it be of a rare species of mammal, bird, orchid or butterfly, hastens the final extinction of the species. And bear in mind that in some cases the entire surviving world population may be restricted to a single small locality, or a tiny island. A photographic record might help conservation, whereas collecting mught put the species at risk'.

The beautifully reticulated design of the leopard's coat is one of the main reasons why the survival of this beautiful cat is so threatened.

Section B: Overseas

American Adventurers' Association

Suite 404
5200 University Way N.E.
Seattle
Washington 98105
USA
Tel. (206) 523 2980

President: Bob Citron

Founded in 1977 to become a clearing house for information on adventure travel opportunities available to the general public, to establish an adventure trip booking service, to publish a monthly magazine Adventure Travel *and to publish an* Annual Guide to Adventure Travel, *a 500 page directory listing the numbers, types, geographical areas with brief descriptions of the thousands of adventure trips offered throughout the world. Three different types of membership are offered: for organisations, individuals and students. The AAA's publications are not related to* Adventure Travel USA *published by Adventure Guides Inc.*

Australian Youth Hostels Association

383 George Street
Sydney
New South Wales 2000
Australia

92 hostels in Australia. Handbook available for members.

Calgary Explorers' Club

c/o Department of Geography
University of Calgary
2920 24 Avenue N.W.
Calgary
Alberta T2N 1N4
Canada

Club President: David Werrett

Founded in 1973 and by January 1977 had organised and mounted two expeditions, to South America and South East Asia, mainly with the object of introducing near beginners to the simple skills of moving and working in tropical areas. Two-month expeditions to Taiwan and the Philippines and to some of the less well-known parts of the South Pacific were planned for 1977 and 1978 respectively.

The Explorers Club

46 East 70th Street
New York
NY 10021
USA

This old established club keeps in touch with expeditions worldwide and organises lecture evenings in New York. Branches throughout the USA and in London c/o Egerton Sykes, 14 Montpellier Villas, Brighton, Sussex.

Foyer International d'Accueil de Paris

30 Rue Cabanis
75014 Paris
France
Tel. 707-25-69

Holds discussion 'forums' for the exchange of information between travellers.

Guilde Européenne du Raid

15 quai de Conti
75006 Paris
France
Tel. 033-52-53

Promotes adventure in remote parts of the world. It organises meetings, conferences, lectures, film evenings and permanent exhibitions, and a small number of organised tours/treks. Since 1971 it has made annual grants under the heading

Dotation Nationale de l'Aventure to responsible but adventurous expeditions having a definite goal, usually those mounted by individuals or small groups. Other grants and donations in money or kind are available through the Guilde, as are also the advice of experts, access to documents, discounts and benefits from associated bodies, and help with the safe-keeping and sale of expedition reports and photos. The Guilde has recently established its Ecole de l'Aventure at Saint-Pé-de-Bigorre in the Hautes-Pyrénées, along the lines of the Outward Bound Schools. It aims to encourage character development through the pursuit of outdoor activities, to permit the emergence of individual potential and team spirit and to foster the growth of necessary human qualities in young people aged between 18 and about 30. The main part of the course lasts 26 days and the follow-up course a week. Each intake may number up to 120. Activities pursued include swimming, kayaking, caving, climbing, orienteering, survival, foot and ski touring, mountain rescue and safety, photography.

National Geographic Society
17th and M Streets NW
Washington DC 20036
USA

The Society's aim is to pursue and promulgate geographic knowledge and to promote research and exploration. The Society publishes the National Geographic Magazine, and occasionally sponsors high-powered expeditions. Articles may be sold to the magazine but the standards required (particularly for photographs) are very high.

Overland Club
Third Floor
Queens Arcade
Auckland 1
New Zealand

Secretary:
Miss Ruth Dornauf
Flat 5
63 Church Street
Northcote
Auckland 9
New Zealand

Holds meetings twice a month.

**South American Explorers'
Club**
Casilla 3714
Lima 1
Peru

Non-profit-making exploration club. Membership $25. Magazine 'The South American Explorer'.

Travel Wise Club
444 Robson Street
Vancouver
British Columbia
Canada

A club for low-budget travellers, with aims similar to those of the Globetrotters Club.

Wexas International Inc.
Graybar Building, Suite 354
420 Lexington Avenue
New York
NY 10017
USA

WEXAS International
45 Brompton Road
Knightsbridge
London SW3
England

The world's largest travel and exploration club, with members in 83 countries. For more details on WEXAS services see the 6-page WEXAS section in this handbook. It includes a WEXAS membership application form.

Directory of Services

Section A: United Kingdom

AWARDS
Winston Churchill Memorial Trust
10 Queen Street
Mayfair
London W1X 7PD
Tel. 01–629 0091

Awards of Travelling Fellowships sometimes offered to individuals undertaking exploration or expeditions which will 'produce results of worthwhile significance'. There are no age limits, nor any academic or professional requirements, but candidates must be citizens of the UK. A Fellowship lasts on average three months. In 1976 there were 3,209 applications for Travelling Fellowships and 106 awards made.

BOATS

Avon Inflatables Ltd
Dafen
Llanelli
Dyfed
Wales
Tel. 055–42 59171

Pioneered the use of inflatables in both Britain and the USA. They make dinghies, sports boats, life rafts, river runners and accessories such as life jackets.

The Canoe Centre (Twickenham) Ltd
18 Beauchamp Road
Twickenham
Middlesex
Tel. 01–892 8979

Factory:
Marsh Lane,
Crediton,
Devon.
Tel. 0363–23295

Sell slalom, racing, touring, surf, folding kayaks; down-river boats; accessories.

BOOKSELLERS

BAS Overseas Publications
50 Sheen Lane
London SW14 8LP
General sales agents for a wide range of British, American and European timetables, hotel directories, etc.

Compendium Bookshop
240 Camden High Street
London NW1

A useful source of travel books that are difficult to obtain elsewhere.

Roger Lascelles
3 Holland Park Mansions
16 Holland Park Gardens
London W14 8DY
Tel. 01–603 8489

Travel and cartographic publisher. Maps, guides and narrative books on travel,

*especially Asia and Europe. Sells Africa
for the Hitchhiker (£3.90) and Latin
America for the Hitchiker (£3.90).*
Please send stamped addressed
envelope with inquiries.

John O'Reilly
100 The Broadway
Leigh-on-Sea SS9 1AB
Tel. 0702–710474

*Sells mountain and polar books: second
hand, single copies, first editions etc. and
issues catalogues.*

Snowden Smith Books
41 Godfrey Street
London SW3 3SX
Tel. 01–352 6756

*Sells books on travel and anthropology,
especially first editions, and issues a
catalogue.*

YHA Services
29 John Adam Street
London WC2N 6JE
Tel. 01–839 1722

*Sell guides and books on climbing and
caving and a leaflet 'Books of Interest to
Hostellers'*

CURRENCY INFORMATION

Bank of England
(Foreign Department)
Threadneedle Street
London EC2
Tel. 01–601 4444

CUSTOMS INFORMATION

HM Customs
Kings Beam House
Mark Lane
London EC3
Tel. 01–283 8911

EQUIPMENT : CAMPING

Adventure Tents
Aireworth Road
Keighley
West Yorkshire BD21 4DN

Tent manufacturers.

Blacks of Greenock
22–24 Gray's Inn Road
London WC1

Port Glasgow
Renfrewshire PA14 5XN
Scotland

Ruxley Corner
Sidcup
Kent DA14 5AQ

*Have tents and camping equipment for
hire from centres in Aberdeen,
Birmingham, Bristol, Edinburgh,
Fareham, Hull, Leicester, Leeds,
Liverpool, London (3 centres),
Nottingham, Stoke on Trent, Swansea
and Wolverhampton. They supply
lightweight, patrol, frame, mountain and
touring tents, camp furniture, kitchin kits,
stoves and lamps, clothing and
accessories, convertible, specialist and
summer-weight sleeping bags.*

Camp Trails International Ltd
Waterford Industrial Estate
Waterford, Eire
Tel. Waterford 32469

*Supply all-weather packs, bags and
frames of tough nylon with waterproof
urethane coating, 'designed' by experts'
and field tested. Free catalogue and guide
to European Long-Distance Foot-trails.*

Cli-pon Insect Screens Ltd
495 Ipswich Road
Trading Estate
Slough
Berkshire

Insect screens for vehicles and tents.

Laurence Corner
62–64 Hampstead Road
London NW1

*Suppliers of high quality government
surplus clothing (camping, outdoor,
protective) and newly manufactured
protective and outdoor wear for shooting,
climbing, fishing, rambling, walking,
motoring or flying. At the 'Jean Centre',
a few doors from the main store, jeans,
shirts, jackets and other sportswear are
sold. The firm also stocks sleeping bags,
canteens, rucksacks and tents. Mail order
service. Catalogue available.*

Overland Camping Services
232–8 Norwood Road
Tulse Hill
London SE27 9AS
Tel. 01–670 7789

*Manufacture, supply hire and repair
tents for expeditions, safaris and camping
tour operators.*

Raclet Ltd and **The Camping
Centre**
24 Lonsdale Road
Kilburn
London NW6 RD

*Supply tents and camping accessories,
including the Campcase: an Antler
suitcase with essentials for camping
packed into it — including a Raclet tent
with awning, airbeds and sleeping bags,
cooker, billies, plates, pump, wash bowl,
water carrier, mugs, cutlery, salt and
pepper, clothes hanger clip, stools, night
light — altogether weighing 43¹/₂ lb.*

Roy Ryder Ltd
St. Oswalds Road
Gloucester
Tel. 045–33116

*Can supply the new Stormryder Tent
System, tested on Everest in 1976 by the
Army Mountaineering Association team.*

**Tarpaulin & Tent
Manufacturing Co**
Head Office
101–3 Brixton Hill
London SW2
Tel. 01–674 0121/3
(Catalogue available from Head Office)

137 Clapham High Street
London SW4
Tel. 01–720 5451

19 Wimbledon Bridge
London SW19
Tel. 01–946 9600
(accessories only)

*Suppliers to commercial and private
expeditions of all kinds of tent from the
marquee to the 2-man, of camp beds, air
beds, stoves, mosquito nets, sand ladders,
jerricans (water and petrol), wire ropes
and slings, towing chains, all types of
ropes and tarpaulins. They also repair
tents.*

Vango (Scotland) Ltd
47 Colvend Street
Glasgow G40 4DH
Tel. 041–556 7621

*Have stockists in other parts of the UK
and are manufacturers of Vango Force
Ten Tents (supplied to the 1975 Everest
South West Face Expedition) and of the
recently developed Force Ten
Microweights. Also suppliers of
rucksacks.*

**EQUIPMENT : CAMP
KITCHEN**

Dudley Hill Engineering Co Ltd
300 Goswell Road
London EC1V 7LU
Tel. 01–837 2828

*Manufacture Jet Gaz appliances for
cooking, lighting, heating, including
blowlamps, a fondue set, table stove,*

express percolator, barbecue set; also
containers. Spare parts are available in
over 30 countries from Europe to the Far
East.

Electrolux Ltd
Luton
Bedfordshire

*Make Camping Box refrigerators;
portable, top-openings: can be operated
by 220–240 volt mains electricity or by a
12 volt car battery.*

Europleasure Gas Ltd
Curtis Road
Dorking
Surrey RH4 1XA

*Manufacture EPI gas butane-fuelled
leisure appliances which operate from
almost any available butane fuel and
which may be obtained from good
camping, leisure and hardware stores.
They include a picnic stove, 'backpacker'
stove, lantern, heater, blowlamp and
converter units.*

Globe Trotter portable stove

*Made by Camping Gas, it is very small
and light, measuring 3¾ ins. in height and
4½ ins. in width and weighing 16 oz.
Unfolded it reveals 2 half-litre
saucepans, single burner and windshield,
cartridge holder and detachable handle. It
takes under 4 minutes to boil half a pint
of water. The stove operates for 1½ hours
from a Camping Gaz GT cartridge.*

EQUIPMENT: EXPEDITION FOOD

L. & I. Equipment
14 Bromborough Road
Bebington
Merseyside
Tel. 051 645 7577

*Supply to the trade only Turblokken
emergency rations for survival kits.*

Ranch House Meals
Direct Foods Ltd
Bedford Road
Petersfield
Hampshire GU32 3LT

*Supply lightweight packets of meals
which take under 10 minutes to prepare.*

Ravel Meals
Alexa Products
23 Oxendon Road
Arthingworth
Market Harborough
Leicestershire LE16 8LA

*Manufacture complete, extra-large,
lightweight, tasty meals for campers and
backpackers. The meals only need 5
minutes cooking.*

EQUIPMENT: GENERAL

Berghaus
34 Dean Street
Newcastle-upon-Tyne NE1 LPG
Tel. Newcastle 23561

*Sell boots, equipment and clothing for the
outdoor enthusiast.*

Bridon Fibres & Plastics Ltd
Condercum House
171 West Road
Newcastle upon Tyne NE99 1AE

Anchor & Hope Lane
Charlton
London SE7

*Manufacture ropes, including the
'Dynamic' (3-strand nylon) and the
'Dynaflex' (Kernmantel). Suppliers to
the 1975 British Everest South West
Face Expedition.*

Chilecrest Ltd

155–7 Pitshanger Lane
Ealing
London W5

Manufacture the Milograph: a thermometer-type route mileage calculator, suitable for use with maps ranging in scale from 0.1 to 40 miles to the inch. It is supplied with a plastic slipcase, instruction leaflet and mile/kilometre conversion table.

Expedition Supplies Ltd

280 Old Brompton Road
Earls Court
London SW5
Tel. 01–370 6677

Suppliers of camping and expedition, travel and outdoor wear, sheepskins and ski equipment, cameras, binoculars, etc.

Field & Trek (Equipment) Ltd

25 Kings Road
Brentwood
Essex
Tel. 22–1259

Field & Trek Ltd offers WEXAS members discounts of 15% off the list price plus VAT on most leading makes of expedition equipment including tents, rucksacks, boots, waterproof clothing, sleeping bags and mountaineering gear. Large mail order department. Expedition bulk orders entitled to additional discount. Ask for special quotation. Send for free comprehensive price list.

Gardenwork

Ell
The Dell
Catherine de Barnes
Solihull
West Midlands

Manufacture 100 different types of gardening machettes, some of which have often been used on expeditions, e.g. Crocodile Brand Machettes.

Karrimor International Ltd

Avenue Parade
Accrington
Lancs

Manufacture mountaineering and outdoor pursuits equipment, including sacs, frames, tents, overboots, gaiters, Karrimats. They have supplied equipment to the International Everest Expedition of 1971, the 1972 (British) Everest South West Face Expedition, the Japanese Ladies Everest Expedition of 1975, the Japanese South West Face Everest Expedition and the Army Mountaineering Association Everest Expedition 1976.

Pindisports

14 Holborn
London EC1
Tel. 01–242 3278

1098 Whitgift Centre
Croydon
Surrey
Tel. 01–688 2667

373 Uxbridge Road
London W3
Tel. 01–992 6641
(this branch handles all mail orders)

27 Martineau Square
Birmingham
Tel. 021–236 9383

5 Welsh Back
Bristol
Avon
Tel. 0272–211577

Provided some equipment for the 1972 Everest South West Face Expedition and the 1970 Annapurna South Face Expedition and are suppliers to the John Ridgway Adventure School at Ardmore. They supply equipment for hill-walking, rockclimbing, big-wall climbing, alpinism, expeditions, shelter and survival; also guide books and magazines.

Pindi Contracts
373–5 Uxbridge Road
Acton
London W3
Tel. 01–992 6641
Manager : Martin Penstone

*The contract division of Pindisports,
suppliers of gear to bona fide bulk buyers
such as Education Authorities,
expeditions — but not to individuals.*

Polywarm Products Ltd
Quay Road
Rutherglen
Glasgow
Scotland G73 1RS

Electronic House
Churchfield Road
Weybridge
Surrey KT13 8DH

*Manufacture a selection of lightweight
and compact specialist sleeping bags
suitable for the mountaineer and hiker,
including conventional and mummy-
shaped bags, made of washable man-
made fibres and stitched by a special
process that prevents the filling from
moving. The sleeping bags are all
guaranteed for 12 months. The firm also
manufactures the Insul Vest, thermal
waistcoat.*

Scientific Exploration Society
Home Farm
Mildenhall
Marlborough
Wiltshire
Tel. 06725 2994

*Has on the premises an Explorers' Shop,
which sells maps, handbooks, certain
other books on exploration, philatelic
covers, autographs, photos, and some
expedition equipment.*

Travel and Sports Centre
405 Strand
London WC2
Tel. 01–240 1788

*Sells camping equipment, especially
clothing, at discount prices.*

Ultimate Equipment
The Butts
Warkworth
Morpeth
Northumbria NE65 0SP

c/o Royal Robbins
Mountain Paraphernalia
906 Durant Street
Modesto
California
USA

*Sell clothing, climber's helmets,
lightweight tents, waterproof jackets.*

EQUIPMENT: MOUNTAINEERING

G. & H. Products
Blackburn Road
Bristall
Batley
Yorks

*Supply gear to mountaineering
expeditions.*

YHA Services
29 John Adam Street
London WC2N 6JE

35 Cannon Street
Birmingham B2 5EE

36–38 Fountain Street
Manchester M2 2BE

*Supply lightweight tents and equipment
for overland travel, mountaineering and
caving, also weatherproof clothing and a
good selection of boots.*

EQUIPMENT: PHOTOGRAPHIC

Agfa Gaevert Ltd
20 Piccadilly
London W1
Tel. 01–734 4854

Bulk film supplies.

Kodak Ltd
PO Box 66
Kodak House
Station Road
Hemel Hempstead
Hertfordshire HP1 1JU
Tel: 0442 61122
Enquiries to: Rita Osborn, PR
Division, ex. 221

Supply a limited number of films on trade terms to expeditions having the support of the Royal Geographical Society or a similar authority, provided that purchases are made in bulk, that one order is placed at a minimum value of £50 and that delivery at an address in the UK (excluding docks and airports) is accepted.

Olympus Optical Co (UK) Ltd
2–3 Honduras Street
(enquiries: Department E)
London EC1Y OTX

Manufacture cameras, including the ultra small and light Olympus OM1.

John Piercy Ltd
34a Bryanston Street
London W1
Tel. 01–723 1487

Film processing. Discount for professionals. Same day service for Ektachrome.

EQUIPMENT: SUB-AQUA

Marine Unit Technology Ltd
3 Friars Lane
Richmond
Surrey
Tel. 01–940 3682

Manufacturers of a still underwater camera with a built-in electronic flash which allows divers with no photographic knowledge to take high-quality pictures underwater.

EQUIPMENT: WATER FILTERS
Safari (Water Treatment) Ltd
28 The Spain
Petersfield
Hampshire

Manufacture a wide range of lightweight water purifiers which guarantee to remove all harmful and offensive elements from water from any non-salt water source.

EXPEDITION CONSULTANTS

David Hodgson
24 Longfield House
Uxbridge Road
London W5

A former Fleet Street editor, journalist, author and explorer, with a great deal of experience in publishing and international syndication. He offers free professional advice to expeditions on the sale of publication rights.

Quest 4 Ltd
Aston Wold
Peterborough PE8 5LZ
Cambridgeshire
Tel. 083–22–2614

Expedition consultants who organise and advise expeditions to remote places, including in the past numerous expeditions to North Africa with such varied objectives as collecting for museums, ballooning, observing a total eclipse of the sun, filming and anthropological and wildlife research. Quest 4 undertake planning and preparation in all aspects of an expedition : vehicles, route notes, equipment, etc.

Special Travel
Christopher Portway
Jasan
White Ash Green
Halstead
Essex
Tel. Halstead 2603

This travel consultancy aims to assist the individual or group with the planning of a mainly overland holiday or journey, outside the scope of a package tour, to suit individual whims and requirements. It specialises in giving advice on surface transport and particularly railway journeys of the world, arranging regimental association battlefield tours, helping with individual expeditions and offering, from personal experience, hints and suggestions that will make a dream travel project cheaper and more attainable than you think. For more details contact writer and novelist Christopher Portway, sending an SAE.

Trail Finders (Services) Ltd
46–48 Earls Court Road
London W8 6EJ

Provides information for the private overlander and a booking service for those making reservations on commercial overland services. Covers Asian overland routes in particular, but also the Americas.

FILM HIRE

British Sub-Aqua Club Film Library
Guild Sound and Vision Ltd
Sponsored Sales Division
85–129 Oundle Road
Peterborough PE2 9EY
Tel. 0733–63122

The British Sub-Aqua Club have established a library of underwater films.

Concord Films Council Ltd
201 Felixstowe Road
Ipswich
Suffolk

Offer for hire 16 mm films, including films from the Granada Television series 'Disappearing World' concerning the survival of minority cultures.

Explorer Films
58 Stratford Road
Bromsgrove
Worcs
Tel. 0527 3566

Expedition films, some of them made by the Brathay exploration groups.

Fauna Preservation Society Wildlife Library
Films Officer
FPS
c/o Zoological Society
Regent's Park
London NW1 4RY
Tel. 01–586 0872

Offer a selection of wildlife films for hire.

The Royal Anthropological Institute

36 Craven Street
London WC2N 5NG
Tel. 01-930 6328

Have a collection of over 70 anthropological films, showing for the most part how people live in non-industrialised societies, and including the entire Granada Television series 'Disappearing World'. Distribution in the UK only by the Scottish Central Film Library, 16 Woodside Terrace, Glasgow G3 7XN. Tel. 041-332 9988. List of films from the SCFL or the RAI.

FREIGHT

Michael Gibbons & Co Ltd

25 Great Windmill Street
London W1V 7PH
Tel. 01437 2866/8

Also at London (City), Heathrow Airport, Southampton, Liverpool and Dover. Supply of tea chests, shipment of baggage, private cars overseas. Storage. Free estimates.

Neale and Wilkinson Ltd

78 Broadway
Stratford
London E15 1BR

Thor Transport Ltd

Caverswall Lane
Blythe Bridge
Stoke on Trent
Staffordshire
Tel. 07818-5115

Offer a freight service overland to Asia.

INSURANCE

Aaron Insurance Consultants

61 Whitefield Road
New Duston
Nortbampton

Life insurance for expedition members.

Bray, Gill and Wrightson Ltd

Kingston Bridge House
Church Lane
Kingston-upon-Thames
Surrey
Tel. 977 8888

Vehicle insurance

British Mountaineering Council

Crawford House
Precinct Centre
Booth Street East
Manchester M13 9RZ

Offers a comprehensive mountaineering insurance scheme, details of which may be obtained by sending an SAE to Fred Smith.

Campbell Irvine Ltd

48 Earls Court Road
London W8 6EJ
Tel. 01-937 9903

Insurance brokers who offer motor (accidental damage, fire and theft, third party liability, carnet indemnity, marine transit) insurance to overseas travellers.

Mitchell Cotts

(Insurance Dept)
283 Camomile Street
London EC3
Tel. 01-283 1234

Vehicle insurance.

Norwich Union Insurance Group
(MAC Dept)
PO Box 2
7 Surrey Street
Norwich NOR 9IA

Expedition insurance.

Royal Insurance Company Ltd
48 St James's Street
London SW1
Tel. 01–493 7151

Vehicle insurance and indemnity carnets.

Slugocki Norman & Co Ltd
48 Earls Court Road
London W8 6EJ
Tel. 01–937 6981

Insurance brokers who can arrange vehicle insurance for long-distance travel abroad, including insurance carnets.

Travellers' Insurance Association Ltd
82 Pall Mall
London SW1Y 5HQ
Tel. 01–930 5276

Insurance for overland expeditions.

W.E. Found & Co Ltd
Boundary House
7 Jewry Street
London EC3 2HH
Tel. 01–709 9051

Can arrange insurance cover for carnets to travel overland by vehicle.

West Mercia Insurance Brokers
High Street
Wombourne
nr. Wolverhampton WV5 9DN
Ph. 09077–2661/4705

Provide insurance for mountaineers, including personal accident, life, equipment and expedition insurance.

WEXAS
International Office
45 Brompton Road
Knightsbridge
London SW3

WEXAS International Inc.
Graybar Building
Suite 354
420 Lexington Avenue
New York
New York 10017
USA

Personal travel insurance (accident, medical, cancellation, luggage and personal money) available to members. Membership £ 8.75 (£12 from family membership). Competitive premium rates. WEXAS does not handle expedition insurance. See 6-page section on WEXAS in this handbook for more details. It contains a WEXAS membership application form.

LANGUAGE LEARNING
The World of Learning Ltd
359 Upper Richmond Road West
London SW14 8QN
Tel. 01–878 4314

Offer a means of learning French, German, Spanish, Italian, Russian, or Afrikaans to speakers of English or other languages, called programmed instruction language learning ('pill'), which involves an average of 24 hours study at home from a cassette, tape or LP record.

LOW COST AIR TRAVEL
Wexas
International Office
45 Brompton Road
Knightsbridge
London SW3

WEXAS International Inc
Graybar Building
Suite 354
420 Lexington Avenue
New York
New York 10017
USA

WEXAS, Europe's largest travel club (members in 83 countries), offers reliable low cost flights to over 150 worldwide destinations. Most flights are on the scheduled services of large international airlines. Savings through WEXAS may be as high as 50 per cent. For more details on WEXAS, see the 6 page WEXAS section in this handbook. It includes a WEXAS membership application form.

LOW COST BUS TRAVEL
Asian Rover

Available from Trail Finders Ltd., 46–48 Earls Court Road, London W8 6EJ. Tel. 01–937 9631. London to Delhi by public transport, for the independent traveller. Valid for any period between 21 and 365 days.

MAPS
Cook Hammond and Kell Ltd
22 Caxton Street
London SW1

Map retailers

Edward Stanford Ltd
12 Long Acre
London WC2

Map publishers and sellers.

Foyles Travel Department
1st Floor North Building
212 Charing Cross Road
London WC2

Map department.

The Map House
54 Beauchamp Place
London SW3

Wide selection of maps and travel books.

The Map Shop
A.T. Aykinson & Partner
4 Court Street
Upton-on-Severn
Worcestershire
Tel. 06846 3146

Sell Ordnance Survey, Michelin, Geographia, Philips, A to Z publications, HMSO guides, etc. Send 15p stamp for catalogue with prices.

Roger Lascelles, Cartographic and Travel Publisher
3 Holland Park Mansions
16 Holland Park Gardens
London W14 8DY
Tel. 01–603 8489

Sells maps, guides and narrative books on travel; especially useful for Asia and Europe. Please send SAE with inquiries.

Sherratt and Hughes
17 St Ann's Square
Manchester 2

Retailers of maps.

MEDICAL CARE

The Flying Doctors' Society of Africa
9 Upper Grosvenor Street
London W1X 9PA

Exists to provide financial backing for the East African Flying Doctor Services (part of the African and Medical Research Foundation). Members are guaranteed free air transport if injured or taken seriously ill while on safari in East Africa. Temporary membership is available for tourists or visitors to East

Africa, and confers the same benefits. There is also an annual lottery based on membership card numbers, for which the prize is a round trip by air to Africa or from Africa to Europe. The Society depends upon subscriptions and donations.

Slaney's
40A Church Road
Richmond-upon-Thames
Surrey TW10 6LN
Tel. 01–940 8634

Suppliers of first-aid essentials, especially for expeditions, including snake sera, tropical and marine supplies, foil blankets.

The Young Explorers' Trust
c/o Royal Geographical Society
1 Kensington Gore
London SW7 2AR

YET has a card index of medically qualified people, some with, some without, expedition experience, who may be available to offer their services to expeditions. Those wishing to be placed on the register may write to the Executive Officer with details of their experience and preferences. Expedition organisers wishing to consult the list may do so through membership of the YET and by application to the Executive Officer. The list is not for general distribution.

VACCINATION CENTRES
British Airways Medical Centre
Victoria
London SW1
Tel. 01–834 2323

West London Vaccination Centre
53 Great Cumberland Place
London W1

OVERLAND INFORMATION CENTRES
Overland Mart
Trail Finders Ltd.
46–48 Earls Court Road
London W8 6EJ

A display board permanently on view on which travellers or expedition organisers can advertise for companions, vehicles, etc.

PICTURE LIBRARIES

Alan Hutchinson Library
2 Logan Mews
London W8 6QP
Tel. 01–373 4830

Collect first-class transparencies, expedition photos, specialising in Third World subjects; sell single shots and article illustrations to book publishers, magazines, newspapers, advertising agencies, large companies, schools, universities, etc, both in the UK and abroad.

Bruce Coleman Colour Picture Library
16a/17a Windsor Street
Uxbridge
Middlesex UB8 1AB

15 East 36th Street
New York
NY 10016
USA

Established in 1959, represents a small number of well-known photographers including Chris Bonington, specialises in wildlife, geography, anthropology, archaeology, science. Literature available on the agency's requirements and terms of business on receipt of SAE.

Geoslides Photographic Library
4 Christian Fields
London SW16

Collect photos taken by travellers, especially in Africa, Asia, the Arctic and sub-Arctic, sell reproduction rights to publishers in a wide field, especially educational and publish free leaflets (send SAE): 'Services for Freelance Lecturers and Resource Centres' and 'Services for Publishers'.

John Moss
6 Queen's Terrace
Windsor
Berkshire

Specialist in African photographs taken by himself.

Nigel Press Associates
167 Coldharbour Lane
London SE5 9PA
Tel. 01-274 1705

Offer a free service to bona fide expeditions for the acquisition and interpretation of satellite photography, of which they have a large holding covering most parts of the world. Satellite photographs can be used to produce accurate maps at scales between 1 : 1 Million and 1 : 200,000 or even larger.

Paul Popper Ltd
24 Bridge Lane
Fleet Street
London EC4Y 8DR
Tel. 01-353 9665

Historical photo library including Scott's Antarctic Expedition 1910–12.

Picturepoint Ltd
7 Cromwell Place
London SW7

Robert Harding Associates Picture Library
5 Botts Mews
Chepstow Road
London W2
Tel. 01-229 2234

Represent many expedition photographers, collect 35 mm or $2^1/_4$ in. square transparencies of exceptional quality on geographical, anthropological, botanical or zoological subjects and sell reproduction rights in photos of remote areas.

ROUTE PLANNING
International road information may be obtained from :

The Royal Automobile Club
Foreign Touring Department
P.O. Box 92
Croydon
Surrey

The Automobile Association
Overseas Operations (Routes)
The Marlborough Building
383 Holloway Road
London N7

TRAVEL BOOK CLUBS

Foyles Travel Book Club
119 Charing Cross Road
London WC2

TRAVELLER'S CHEQUES
Thomas Cook Ltd
45 Berkeley Street
London W1A 1EB
and all branches

Can provide traveller's cheques in several major currencies. Recognised and accepted worldwide as are American Express traveller's cheques. On both, you pay a 1 per cent charge, mainly to ensure against loss of the cheques. Cooks publish a brochure entitled Offices Worldwide *which list all their offices. Very useful, expecially as Cooks are very handy for obtaining difficult rail bookings overseas.*

VEHICLES
Four by Four Ltd
Twickenham Road
Feltham
Middlesex
Tel. 01–894 1211

Have Landrovers for hire (over 200 at any one time), mostly equipped for camping.

Fram Expeditions Ltd
John Hamilton
69 Ledi Drive
Bearsden
Glasgow G61 4JN
Tel. 041–942 6254.

A small but reliable organisation which hires out Diesel Landrovers for expeditions. Founded in 1953 by Stan Whitehead. Fram now has four 12-seater station wagons available, three in Birmingham and one in Glasgow. The service is intended to be neither a charity nor profit-making, but merely self-supporting. Fram does not organise expeditions, but hires out vehicles to ready-made expeditions.

Harvey Hudson
Woodford
London E18 1AS
Tel. 01–989 6644

Landrover specialists, suppliers of new and used vehicles to expeditions.

Land-Roving Ltd
30 Sidbury
Worcester
Tel. 0905–26988
Landrovers for sale and hire.

Matador Motor Caravans
Matador Service Station
Boston Road
Hanwell
London W7
Tel. 01–529 9061

Sell used Volkswagen motor caravans, used British and continental motor-homes, service Volkswagens and operate a tourist 'buy-back' scheme.

Roverhire
12 Seagrave Road
London SW6
Tel. 01–385 5291

Landrover for sale and hire

Vantage Motor Co
88 the Avenue
Highams Park
London E4
Tel. 01–527 6512

Provide coaches for contract hire to India.

Varu Garages of Amsterdam and Varu Garage
13 Sussex Mansions
Old Brompton Road
London SW7
Tel. 01–584 2938

Offer secondhand vehicles, mostly already converted for camping, for sale. Buyers may purchase through the London office from a current stock list, collect the vehicle in Amsterdam and receive, into the bargain, a free ticket from London to Amsterdam.

Rover Company Ltd
Solihull
Warwickshire
Tel. 021–743 4242

Manufacturers of Landrovers. Purchase must be through authorised dealers, however. No second hand vehicles are available from the Rover Company, or vehicles for hire. The company's PR department publishes a very useful Guide to Landrover Expeditions.

Windmill Motor Caravans
106–112 Windmill Road
Brentford
Essex
Tel. 01–568 2199

Sell new and used motor caravans and accessories, operate a tourist 'buy-back' scheme.

VEHICLE : OUTFITTING
Companies specialising in equipping or converting 4-wheel drive vehicles for overland use:

Alpinair Ltd
Alpine House
Honeypot Lane
London NW9 9RU
Tel. 01–204 3393

Vehicle air-conditioning suppliers and fitters.

Brownchurch (Components) Ltd
Attention: Chris Wood
308–310 Hare Row
off Cambridge Heath Road
London W2
Tel 01–729 33606

Cover all Landrover needs for trips anywhere, including the fitting of jerricans and holders, sand ladders, pump and light guards, crash bars, winches, water purifying plants, suspension seats, roof racks (custom-made if necessary), overdrive units. They also supply new vehicles and offer a service, maintenance and spares service for Land and Range Rovers.

Carawagon International Ltd
Attention: Mr. Forsyth
Thames Street
Sunbury-on-Thames
Middlesex TW16 5QR
Tel 76–85205

Land- and Range Rovers only.

Dunlop Ltd
Dunlop House
Ryder Street
London SW1
Tel. 01–930 6700

Information on Dunlop special purpose tyres.

Ever Ready Co Ltd
Ever Ready House
High Road
London N20
Tel. 01–446 1313

Information on Ever Ready batteries.

Fairey Winches
South Station Yard
Whitchurch Road
Tavistock PL19 9DR
Tel. 0822–4101

Supply winches suitable for use with expedition overland vehicles.

Firemaster Ltd
Friendly Place
Lewisham Road
London SE13
Tel. 01–692 6231

Vehicle fire extinguishers, an essential for all overland trips.

FLM Pandcraft
Attention: Mr. Fry
32–35 The Arches
Broughton Street
London SW8.
Tel. 01–662 2080

J.C. Salt & Co
Attention: Malcolm Chaplin
27 Speedwell Road
Hay Mill
Birmingham 25
Tel. 021–772 7675

Michelin Tyre Co Ltd
81 Fulham Road
London SW3
Tel. 01–5891460

Special purpose tyres.

Monorep Ltd
Poplar Avenue
Norwood Green
Southall
Middlesex UB 2 4PN
Tel. 01–574 0722

Vehicle air-conditioning suppliers and fitters.

Stevenson Motors
Cannon Lane
Tunbridge Wells
Kent
Tel 0892 64444
Contact: Paul Bowman

TVC Sales Ltd
13 Sussex Mansions
Old Brompton Road
London SW7 3JZ
Tel. 01–584 2938

Quality roof tents (for 2) and baggage trailers. A long wheelbase Landrover can accommodate 2 roof tents (4 people).

Yachts International Ltd
Marine Centre
Beckett's Wharf
Lower Teddington Road
Kingston-upon-Thames
Surrey KT1 4ER
Tel. 01–943 0161

Fridges supplied and fitted for boats and vehicles.

WEATHER INFORMATION

Meteorological Office (International)
Bracknell
Berkshire
Tel. 0344 20242 ex 2297

Land Rovers fitted with TVC Air-Campers.

Section B: Overseas

BOATS (JET & INFLATABLE)

Berkeley Pump Co
829 Bancroft Way
Berkeley
California 94710
USA

Manufacturers of Berkeley Jet Drive Boats.

C.W.F. Hamilton & Co Ltd
Head Office:
Lunns Road
Middleton
Christchurch
New Zealand

Branches:
Takapuna
Auckland 9
New Zealand

4a Lake Tekapo
Fairlie
New Zealand

437 Hutt Road
Petone
Wellington
New Zealand

Jet Propulsion Division
Box 709
Christchurch
New Zealand
Tel. 44-179

U.K. Headquarters:
Hamilton Jets (UK)
Osborne House
Osborne Road
New Milton
Hampshire
Tel. 0425-616 789

The world's largest manufacturers of marine jet propulsion units. They make cabin cruisers, runabouts, sports and ski boats, jet rescue craft, oyster boats, jet barges, river ambulances, fishing dories.

Zodiac of North America Inc
11 Lee Street
Annapolis
Maryland 21401
USA
Tel. (301) 268 2009

Manufacturers of Zodiac Inflatable Boats.

BOOKSHOPS

AMC Books
5 Joy Street
Boston
Massachusetts 02108
USA

Sell mountain and river guides, guides to country walks, canoeing and white water guides, books on mountaineering and adventure and survival guides.

L'Astrolabe
46 Rue de Provence
75009 Paris
France
Tel. 285-42-95

Sells travel books.

Librairie Ulysse
35 rue Saint Louis en l'Ile
75004 Paris
France
Tel. 325-17-35

Sells geographical, travel and guide books.

Rocky Mountain Books
c/o Gillean Daffern
106 Wimbledon Crescent
Calgary
Alberta T3C 3JI Canada
Tel. (403) 246 5262

New and used books on climbing and mountains. List available.

EQUIPMENT: CAMP KITCHEN

Camping Gaz International
ADG 15
rue de Chateaubriand 75
Paris 8
France

Butane gas camping equipment.

EQUIPMENT: GENERAL

Naval Undersea Research and Development Center
San Diego
California 92132
USA

Have developed a large bag of thin, strong, very light material with inflatable collars at the top which will completely conceal a 'castaway' at sea and serve as a shark screen. The bag can also be used as a sleeping bag, pup tent, lean-to, stretcher or solar still.

EQUIPMENT: WATER FILTERS

Beam Trading N.V.
Langstraat 52 Gel. A.
2200 Borgerhout
Belgium

Agents for portable water purifying filters manufactured by Pollution Control Products, Inc, USA.

Katadyn France
39 Avenue des Piliers
94210 La Varenne
France
Tel. 283-67-87

Deutsche Katadyn GmbH
8 München 21
Schaufeleinstrasse 20
W. Germany
Tel. 089-575673

HITCH-HIKING

Organisations which put hitch-hikers in touch with drivers include:

Provoya
14 Rue du Faubourg St. Denis
75010 Paris
France
Tel. 770-64-13

SOS Voyages
12 Rue de Nice
69008 Lyon
France
Tel. 72-73-80

Travel-Mate of Australia
496 Newcastle Street
West Perth
Western Australia 6005
Tel. 28-6685
Charges a registration fee to put drivers and prospective passengers in Perth for the eastern or northern states in touch with each other.

Viastop
144 Avenue Pierre Brossolette
10000 Troyes
France
Tel. 72-17-01

INSURANCE

WEXAS International Inc
Suite 354, Graybar Building
420 Lexington Avenue
New York
NY 10017
USA

International Office
45 Brompton Road
Knightsbridge
London SW3

Personal travel insurance (accident, medical, cancellation, baggage) available to members. Competitive premium rates.

WEXAS does not handle expedition insurance. For more details on WEXAS, see the 6-page WEXAS section in this handbook. It contains a WEXAS membership application form.

LOW COST AIR TRAVEL

WEXAS International Inc
(see previous entry for addresses)

WEXAS, the largest club of its kind in the world, specialises in low cost air travel to and from London and New York.
The WEXAS Flight Programme covers over 150 worldwide destinations at special low cost rates for members. For more details, see the 6-page WEXAS section in this handbook. It contains a WEXAS membership application form.

LOW COST FREIGHTER TRAVEL

Pearl's Freighter Tips
175 Great Neck Road
Suite 306
Great Neck
NY 11021
USA

This organisation helps plan and book worldwide freighter trips. No charge for their services.

LOW COST BUS TRAVEL

Nord Norge Bussen
Kongensgate 66
Narvik
Norway

A Norwegian-based bus service operating a service along the Arctic Highway.

LOW COST RAIL TRAVEL

Amerailpass
Associacion Latina-Americana de Ferrocarriles
Paracas 50
Buenos Aires
Argentina

Permits unlimited travel over 30,000 miles of railways in 6 South American countries.

Austrailpass

Permits travel on 27,000 miles of railways throughout Australia. Different rates are available for 14 and 21 days, 1, 2 and 3 months.

Indian Railway Travel-as-you-like Tickets

Valid for 21 days. Purchasable with foreign currency only.

New Zealand Rail Pass

Gives 14 days or unlimited travel on all railways and bus routes and on the ferry between Wellington and Picton, between June 1 and November 30. Extensions may be purchased at a daily rate, up to a maximum of 28 days.

MAPS

Travel Centers of the World
P.O. Box 1673
Hollywood
California 90028
USA

Calogue available containing details of 6,000 maps. This catalogue is not free.

PICTURE LIBRARIES

Black Star Inc
450 Park Avenue South
New York
NY 10016
USA

Rapho Agency
8 Rue d'Alger
75001 Paris
France

Sidoc Photothèque
15 quai de Conti
75006 Paris
France
Tel. 637-30-49

Unusual travel features and pictures for sale, especially overland. Reasonable rates.

TRAVEL BOOK CLUBS

Explorers Book Club
Riverside
New Jersey 08075
USA

VEHICLES: OUTFITTING

Maloja Tyres
Ave Appia 1211
Geneva
Switzerland
Tel. 346 061
Special purpose tyres.

Zebco Consumer Division
Brunswick Corporation
PO Box 270
Tulsa
Oklahoma 74101
USA

The Travelers 4000 is a flameless catalytic heater using disposable cartridges. Write for a spare 'pad' unit and adapt it for bottle-fed gas.

VISAS

Visas International
6331 Hollywood Boulevard
Hollywood
California 90028
USA

Provide up-to-date-visa information.

Personal Accounts of Expeditions and Travels Off the Beaten Track: A Useful Selection

Across the Top of the World
by Wally Herbert
Pub. Longmans, London & Harlow,
1969 and G.P. Putnam's Sons,
New York

*The British Trans-Arctic Expedition of
1968–9.*

African Sanctus
A Story of Travel and Music
by David Fanshawe
Pub. Collins, London

*Nine years' travel in the Middle East
and east Africa, recording and
experimenting with local music. Personal
account, with notes, letters, doodles.*

All Out for Everest
by Michael Montgomery
Pub. Paul Elek, London

*Lively account of journey on the well-
trodden overland trek route to Everest.*

Alone on the Blue Nile
by Kuno Steuben
Pub. Robert Hale, London, 1973

*German author's adventures whilst
descending the river alone.*

**Backpacking in Alps and
Pyrenees**
by Showell Styles
Pub. Gollancz, London

*Description of mountain treks in the
Bernese Oberland, the Central Pyrenees
and the Penine Alps, based on author's
holidays there.*

The Circumnavigators
Small Boat Voyages of Modern
Times
by Donald Holm
Pub. Angus & Robertson, London,
1975

*Brief accounts of the voyages of some of
the best and most representative
circumnavigators, from Slocum to Blyth.
Appendices, including one on ideas on
constructing the ideal cruising boat.*

Cockleshell Journey
by John Ridgway
Pub. Hodder & Stoughton, London,
1974

*Journey by author, wife and two others
in engine-powered rubber dinghies in
Tierra del Fuego; and the first crossing of
the Gran Campo Nevada icecap.*

Coming down the Zambezi
by Bernard Venables
Pub. Constable, London

*Anecdotes, descriptions and reflections of
trip by air, in boat and on foot down
river.*

Crying Drums
by Lt.-Col. Lionel Gregory

Pub. Allen & Unwin, London

The Comex expeditions.

Cucumber Sandwiches in the Andes
by John Ure

Pub. Constable, London, 1973

Crossing on horseback of a remote pass between Chile and Argentina. With historical perspective.

Daffodil and Golden Eagle
The saga of Two Balloons
Crossing the Sahara
by Jonathan Yeatman

Photos by Jon Gardey

Pub. Aidan Ellis, UK, 1972

The Dancing Waiters
by Joseph Hone

Pub. Hamish Hamilton, London

Various leisurely, voluntary — and allegedly preposterously expensive — journeys in different parts of the world, by BBC producer and broadcaster sponsored by the BBC and several UN agencies.

Delhi is Far Away
by John Wiles

Pub. Elek, London

Travel in the Indian subcontinent from the southernmost tip, Cape Cormorin, to Delhi, on foot, on crowded buses and in third-class railway carriages; with descriptions of the land and the people.

Dirtroads
by Mary Cole

Pub. Gill & MacMillan, Dublin

Vivid account by young Irish girl of trekking around Lake Rudolph and of

teaching at a remote school in Kenya.

Everest: The Hard Way
by Chris Bonington

Pub. Hodder & Stoughton, London, 1976

British Everest South West Face Expedition 1975. 81 pp. of appendices testifying to the massive effort of planning involved.

Fatu-Hiva
by Thor Heyerdahl

Pub. George Allen & Unwin, London

Escapist sojourn, hardly idyllic but eventful and educational, in the Marquesas in the mid-1930s with first wife Liv. Source of Heyerdahl's inspiration for the Kon-Tiki voyage.

The Fearful Void
by Geoffrey Moorhouse

Pub. Hodder & Stoughton, London, 1974

Two thousand mile crossing with camels of the Sahara between Mauritania and Tamanrasset, Algeria, via Timbuctoo; and simultaneously the study of one man's confrontation with fear.

Flight of the Kiwi
by Cliff Tait

Pub. Ure Smith, Sydney, and Whitcombe & Tombs, Christchurch, 1970

Around the world solo in a tiny single-engined plane.

Francis Chichester
by Anita Leslie

Pub. Hodder & Stoughton with Hutchinson, London, 1975

Biography.

Full Tilt
Dervla Murphy
Pub. John Murray, London, 1965

Cycling journey from Eire to India by author alone.

A Giant among Rivers
by Richard Snailham
Pub. Hutchinson, London, 1976

Official account of the Zaïre River Expedition of 1974–5, told mainly from the vantage point of the river party. Various appendices, including one on the scientific results.

The Grand Trunk Road
by John Miles
Pub. Elek, London, 1972

Travels on the Indian subcontinent.

Guide Vécu des Voyages Sauvages
by Muriel Dechavanne
Pub. Editions Stock

Stories of journeys told by twelve French travellers, all students or ex-students (all under 25), who used independent means and stayed away from established routes and campsites.

Half a Dozen of the Other
by Sebastian Snow
Pub. Hodder & Stoughton, London, 1972

Six adventures in South America.

Half Way Round
Bicycle ride from England to Australia
by Colin Martin
from:
Overland Mail Order
3 Bedford Road
London W4

The Hundred Days of Darien
by Russell Braddon
Pub. Collins, London, 1974

The British Trans-Americas Expedition, 1971–2: first vehicle crossing of the Darien Gap of Panama and Colombia.

I Chose to Climb
by Chris Bonington
Pub. Gollancz, London, 1966

Autobiographical account of early career in climbing.

In the Steps of Stanley
by John Blashford-Snell
Pub. Hutchinson, London

The Zaïre River Expedition 1974–5. Account based on the leader's log. Historical perspective provided by extracts from H.M. Stanley's diaries.

The Next Horizon
by Chris Bonington
Pub. Gallancz, London, 1973

Autobiography II.

Nothing Venture, Nothing Win
by Sir Edmund Hillary
Pub. Hodder & Stoughton, London, 1975

Autobiography of an explorer, best known for the 1953 conquest of Everest, but who has continued to explore ever since, mainly in Asia.

On a Shoestring to Coorg
An Experience of South India
Pub. John Murray, London, 1976

Experiences travelling by boat and bus in southern India with five-year-old daughter.

On Top of the World
by Sheila Scott

Pub. Hodder & Stoughton, London, 1973

Autobiography, including account of equator-to-equator flight in light plane over the North Pole.

A Pattern of Peoples
by Robin Hanbury-Tenison

Pub. Angus & Robertson, UK

Three months spent making a survey of the indigenous peoples of Indonesia — nine different tribes in Sumatra, Borneo, Celebes, Ceram and Irian Jaya — and studying their problems as minority groups.

A Peak in Darien
by Freya Stark

Pub. John Murray, London, 1976

The latest collection of essays from this great travel writer, full of personal, philosophical and descriptive insights.

A Question of Survival
by Robin Hanbury-Tenison

Pub. Angus & Robertson, London, 1973

Account of visit to Brazil, where author found that the survival of the Indian culture was being jeopardised by the Government's quest for progress.

Rahui
by Colin Iles

Pub. Elek, UK

Account by ex-paratrooper and motorcycle racer of voyage in cutter Clarinda from Europe to New Zealand via Atlantic and Pacific, where he married Rahui from the Cook Islands and whence they sailed together 5,000 miles to Fiji, the New Hebrides, the Solomons, New Guinea and Australia.

The Reindeer People
by Marie Herbert

Hodder & Stoughton, London

The Lapps, with whom author spent part of 1975 in Arctic Scandinavia, travelling in their annual migration from the Finmark plateau to the coast.

The Rucksack Man
by Sebastian Snow

Pub. Hodder & Stoughton, London, 1976

Story of the planning for, and execution of, Snow's long walk from Ushuaia in Tierra del Fuego to Costa Rica in 1973-4.

Rule of Thumb
by Paul Coppersmith

Pub. Simon & Schuster, New York, 1973

Entertaining anecdotes and useful information, based on four years' travel in Europe, north Africa and the East.

Sailing to Timbuctoo
by John Marriner

Pub. William Kimber, London 1974

Journey by sea and land along Algeria's Barbary coast and to Timbuctoo. With historical background.

Seven League Boots
The Story of My Seven-Year Hitch-Hike round the World
by Wendy Myers

Pub. Hodder & Stoughton, London, 1969

A South Sea Spell
by June Knox-Mawer
Drawings by Pearl Binder

Pub. John Murray, London

Tales of magic, spirits, spells, legends and

historical stories, based on author's twelve years living in Fiji and Travelling in the South Seas.

A Talent for Trouble
by Capt. Sir Ranulph Fiennes
Pub. Hodder & Stoughton, London, 1970

Adventure autobiography.

Theirs is the Glory
by Chay Blyth
Pub. Hodder & Stoughton, London

Round the World Yacht Race, 27,570 miles, in which Blyth with a crew of paratroopers was first over the finishing line in 144 days.

Through Persia in Disguise
by Sarah Hobson
Pub. John Murray, London, 1973

Travels studying Islamic art, design and way of life by author disguised as a boy.

Wai-Wai
Through the Forests North of the Amazon
by Nicholas Guppy
Pub. John Murray, London

Plant collecting expedition, which also provided the opportunity for its members to meet untouched tribes and explore virgin country.

Where the Indus is Young
A Winter in Baltistan
by Dervla Murphy
Pub. John Murray, London, 1977

Travels in Baltistan or Little Tibet in the Karakoram, with daughter Rachel, aged 6, on pony and on foot, seeing no other westerners and surviving on a staple diet of apricots.

Where the Trails Run Out
by John Blashford-Snell
Pub. Hutchinson, London

Autobiographical experiences on expeditions in Africa, on the Dahlak Islands, in Darien and elsewhere.

With Love .... Siri and Ebba
by Siri Fraser and
Ebba Pederson
from:
Nicholas Saunders
65 Edith Grove
London SW10
and:
BIT Information and Help Service
146 Great Western Road London
W11

Letters home from two young girls travelling in Africa. Pub. 1973.

World Understanding on Two Wheels
by Paul R. Pratt
Pub. 1976
Alemar-Phoenix Publishing House Inc.
927 Quezon Boulevard Extension
Quezon City

Motorcycle journeys in Canada, USA, Mexico and Central America 1961–3, then between 1966 and 1975, the longest continuous journey in motorcycle history, through Mexico, Central America, the USA, the Far East, USSR and South East Asia. By a Yorkshire-born electronics engineer who has lived both in Britain and the USA. With tips on costs, climate, altitude, crossing frontiers, etc.

Useful Books

ADVENTURE EDUCATION

Adventure Education and Outdoor Pursuits
by Colin Mortlock

Pub. 1973

Available from the author:
Old Fisherbroak
Old Lake Road
Ambleside
Cumbria

from:
Frank Davies
Compston Corner
Ambleside
Cumbria

and from:
Joe Brown
Menai Hall
Llanberis
Caerns

The Character-Training Industry
by Howard J. Parker, Kenneth Roberts, Graham E. White

Pub. David & Charles, UK, 1974

CAMPING, BACKPACKING, HOSTELLING AND MOTOR CARAVANNING

Camping
by Department of Education and Science

Pub. Her Majesty's Stationery Office, 1970

Camping and Hill Trekking
by P. F. Williams

Pub. Pelham Books, London

Handbook of Camping and Caravanning

Pub. The Camping Club of Great Britain, London

International Youth Hostel Federation Handbook
Vol 1: Europe and the Mediterranean; Vol 2: Africa, America, Asia, Australasia

Pub. IYHF, 1973
Midland Bank Chambers
Howardsgate
Welwyn Garden City Herts

also from:
Youth Hostels Association
29 John Adam Street
London WC2

Guide to youth hostelling principles and regulations, and lists of all youth hostels in the areas named with notes on their amenities, location, costs, etc.

Knapsacking Abroad
by Herb and Judy Klinger

Pub. Feffer & Simons

from: Stackpole Books
Harrisburg
Pa 17105
USA

Motor Caravanning
A Complete Guide
by Henry Myhill

Pub. Ward Lock, London

*Guide to acquiring and utilising a
motorised home, with much practical and
also some delightful anecdotal material.*

CAVING

American Caves and Caving
Techniques, Pleasures and Safeguards
of Modern Cave Exploration
by William R. Halliday MD

Pub. Harper & Row, New York, 1974

*Discusses types of caves, clothing, gear
and techniques, dangers from wind, water
and animals, food, communication,
medical aid and rescue procedures.
Drawings and photos.*

Surveying Caves
by Bryan Ellis

Pub. 1976 British Cave Research
Assoc.
Calderbrook Road
Littleborough OL15 9ND
Lancs

COUNTRY BY COUNTRY
LOW COST TRAVEL GUIDES

All of Mexico and Guatemala at Low Cost
Pub. Harian Publications
203 Thomas Street
Greenlawn NY 11740
USA

Arthur Frommer Guides
India — Spain & Morocco —
Israel — Turkey —
Mexico & Guatemala
... on $10 a Day

Pub. Arthur Frommer Inc.
70 Fifth Avenue
NY 10011
USA

UK Distributors:
Roger Lascelles
3 Holland Park Mansions
16 Holland Park Gardens
London W14 8DY
England

Caribbean Island Hopping
A Handbook for the Independent
Traveller
by Frank Bellamy

Pub. Wilton House Gentry, London,
1977, £5.95

*Detailed itineraries, prices, etc, for the
traveller on a budget.*

Central America Travel Guide
from:
Cliff Cross
P.O. Box 301
North Palm Springs
California
USA
Pub. 1973

Fodor Guides
Country Guides

Pub. Hodder & Stoughton, USA and
London

Guides to all parts of the world.

Freighter Days
How to Travel by freighter

Pub. Harian Publications
203 Thomas Street
Greenlawn
New York 11740
USA

*Life aboard a passenger-carrying
freighter.*

The Freighter Travel Manual
by Bradford Angier

*Destinations, routes, times and
advantages of sailings by freighter, an
inexpensive way to reach remote spots.*

Guide to the East
by Satyadas

Pub. 1973
Alchemy
253 Portobello Road
London W11

Short personal guide, based on one man's journey along the 'Hippy Trail' from England to India. Helpful though limited.

Guide to the Peruvian Andes —
Part 1: Yuraq Janka
The Cordilleras Blanca and Rosko
by John F. Ricker

Pub. 1976
The Alpine Club of Canada
Box 1206,
Banff
Alberta
Canada TOL OCO

General geographical, mountaineering and reference guidebook, useful for any party planning a trip or expedition to the area. With notes on mountain routes, history, climate, geology, conservation, glaciation and language. Maps and illustrations.

How to Travel Without Being Rich
by Norman D. Ford, with the assistance of Richard Leavitt and Raymond P. Quin

Pub. 1972
Harian Publications
203 Thomas Street
Greenlawn
NY 11740
USA

Where to go on a budget, and the best ways of travelling, by ship, rail, bus or aeroplane.

Indonesia and Papua New Guinea
by Bill Dalton

Pub. Lonely Planet Publications
P.O. Box 88
South Yarra
Victoria 3141
Autstralia

from:
Roger Lascelles
3 Holland Park Mansions
16 Holland Park Gardens
London W14 8DY

Guide to all the major islands.

Into India
by John Keay

Pub. John Murray, London, 1973

An area by area coverage of modern India and Indian life, to introduce the country to the intending traveller or to help the experienced traveller to interpret what he has seen.

Island Hopping
by Maurice Taylor with Trail Finders

Pub. Wilton House Gentry, London, £5.95

A guide to travel at leisure and on the cheap through Thailand, Malaysia, Indonesia, including Sumatra, Java and Bali, Timor and on to Darwin. With town plans and very detailed recommendations on where to find bargains in lodging or food in many tiny, out-of-the-way places where independent travellers may find themselves.

Mexico and Central America
A Handbook for the Independent Traveller by Frank Bellamy

Pub. Wilton House Gentry, London, 1977, £5.95

Practical details, routes and maps, and a section on the culture of the countries described.

The Nile Journey
by Trevor Kenworthy

from:
Trail Finders (Services) Ltd
46–48 Earls Court Road
London W8 6EJ

Information on the journey down the Nile by public transport, with details of train and steamer fares, costings, equipment, connecting air travel, visas. Also advice on health, food, drink, sightseeing, souvenirs. Sketch maps of major towns en route.

The 1977 South American Handbook
Ed. John Brooks

Pub. 1976, 53rd annual edn.
Trade & Travel Publications Ltd
The Mendip Press
Parsonage Lane
Bath BA1 1EN

Covers cost of living, climate, clothing, health, language, sights, accommodation, restaurants, motoring, currency, the economy, transport to and around South America.

Pacific Paradise on a Low Budget
How Two Toured Hong Kong, Japan, the Fiji Islands, Tonga, American Samoa, Western Samoa, by Charles and Carolyn Planck

Pub. Acropolis Books Ltd, Washington DC, 1973

A 'how-to-do-it' book full of travel tips and hints for the independent traveller rather than for the 'tourist' by retired couple aged 76 and 63, in comfort but at the low cost of $30 per day for two for all expenses.

The People's Guide to Mexico, Guatemala and Belize
by Carl Franz

Pub. 1974, 2nd edn.

Tips on how to behave towards officials, dress to adopt on crossing borders, acceptable hairstyles, information on disclosing or revealing profession or length of stay, bribery, what to do if charged with some offence.

Safari
(East Africa and its National Parks.)
by Derek Townsend

Pub. George Allen & Unwin, London

Seeing the World via Today's Best Buys in Travel
Pub. Harian Publications
203 Thomas Street
Greenlawn
New York
NY 11740
USA

Hotels, things to see and do, tips on places throughout the world.

South American Survival
by Maurice Taylor

Pub. 1975
Trail Finders Ltd
46–48 Earls Court Road
London W8 6EJ

1977 expanded edn. from Wilton House Gentry, London £5.95

Full details on (including Amazonas), regional differences, statistics, sketch maps of countries, regions and towns.

South-East Asia on a Shoestring
by Tony Wheeler

Pub. Lonely Planet Publications
P.O. Box 88
South Yarra
Victoria 3141
Australia

1977 revised edn. from:
Roger Lascelles
3 Holland Park Mansions
16 Holland Park Gardens
London W14 8DY

Guide for the budget traveller, with practicial, and some background, information, on 8 south-east Asian countries.

South Sea Journey
by George Woodcock

Pub. Faber, London.

Factual information (not illustrated) about the Gilbert and Ellice Islands, Samoa and Fiji, the Solomons, New Caledonia and the New Hebrides, and forecasts of their economic future. Based on author's tour while film-making for the Canadian Broadcasting Corporation

Student Guide to Asia
Ed. David Jenkins

Pub. Australian Union of Students

from:
Roger Lascelles
3 Holland Park Mansions
16 Holland Park Gardens
London W14 8DY

Useful low-cost guide for students and other budget travellers visiting any of 24 countries in southern and eastern Asia. Visa requirements, health requirements, currency, transport, accommodation, food and sights.

Today's Outstanding Buys in Freighter Travel
by Norman Ford

Pub. Harian Publications
203 Thomas Street
Greenlawn
New York
NY 11740
USA

A selection of the world's outstanding passenger-carring freighters.

Travellers' Guide to Africa
Eds. Colin Legum and Richard Synge

Pub. Wheatsheaf House
Carmelite Street
London EC4

Rather 'glossy', but good background on each country.

Travellers' Guide to East Africa
(includes Ethiopia)

Travellers' Guide to Southern Africa
(includes S. W. Africa — Namibia)

Travellers' Guide to the Caribbean

Pub. Thornton Cox, London

First two available from:
Trail Finders (Services) Ltd
46–48 Earls Court Road
London W8 6EJ

Game parks, sights to see, places to stay and eat. Background on history, culture, society. For short-term holidaymakers seeking average diversions and comforts.

A Traveller's Notes on Indonesia
by Bill Dalton

Pub. 1973 Moon Publications
73 Darghan Street
Glebe
NSW
Australia

From Compendium Books

Excellent booklet giving costs, places to stay, travel routes, including some off-the-beaten-track.

Travel Routes Around the World

The Traveller's Directory to passenger-carrying freighters and liners.

By Fredric E. Tyarks

Eds. Norman D. Ford and M. Drouet

Pub. Harian Publications
203 Thomas Street
Greenlawn
New York
NY 11740
USA

700 freighter lines sailing from almost every port in the world, their destinations, prices, accommodation, tips on what to take.

Utopia is an Island

Pub. Harian Publications
203 Thomas Street
Greenlawn
New York
NY 11740
USA

Fifty islands paradises a car can reach and a hundred others.

The World's Wild Places

Alaska
The Amazon
The American North Woods
The Andes
Australian Outback
Borneo
Caribbean Isles
Central American Jungles
Florida's Everglades
The Grand Canyon
The Great Barrier Reef
The Great Rift Valley
Hawaii
The Himalayas
Lapland
New England Wilds
New Guinea
The Rocky Mountains
The Sahara
Sierra Madre
Soviet Deserts and Mountains
Wilderness Europe

Pub. Time-Life International Ltd
London, 1975

Inquiries to:
Time-Life Books
c/o Time and Life Building
New Bond Street
London W1Y 0AA
Tel: 01-499 4080

All volumes illustrated.

DESERT TRAVEL

Algeria and the Sahara

by Valerie and Jon Stevens

Pub. Constable, London, 1977

Cruising the Sahara

by Gerard Morgan-Grenville

Pub. David and Charles, Devon

Detailed reference book on every aspect of desert planning and travel.

Sahara

by John Julius Norwich

Pub. Longmans, London and Harlow

The Sahara is Yours

A Handbook for Desert Travellers by Jon Stevens

Pub. Constable, London

A Simple Method of Navigating in Deserts

by D. N. Hall

Pub. in Geographical Journal, Vol. 133, Pt. 2, June 1967

The Tuareg
by Ken and Julie Slavin
Pub. Wilton House Gentry, London,
1975

*Well documented and illustrated book on
the nomadic tribe of the Sahara.*

EXPEDITION AND TRAVEL PHOTOGRAPHY

Camera Underwater
by Horace E. Dobbs

3rd edn. 1976

from:
Horace Dobbs Underwater
Photographic Services
'Dolphin'
Parklands
North Ferriby
Humberside HU14 3ET

How to Earn £5,000 a Year with Your Camera
by David Hodgson

from:
Airfairs Ltd
21–23 Balham Hill
London SW12 9DY

*For the freelance photographer and
photojournalist.*

Photography on Expeditions
by D. H. O. John
Pub. Focal Press, London

Picture Researcher's Handbook
An International Guide to Picture
Sources and How to Use Them
by Hilary and Mary Evans and
Andra Nelki

from:
Mary Evans Picture Library
Tranquil Vale
Blackheath
London SE3 0BU

or:
Saturday Ventures
Samuel Smiles House
11 Granville Park
London SE13 7DY

*Detailed information about the scope,
procedure, hours, rates, etc. of each
archive. General information also on
copyright, etc.*

Travel Photography
Time/Life Library of Photography.

Inquiries to:
Time-Life Books
c/o Time and Life Building
New Bond Street
London W1Y 0AA
Tel. 01–499 4080

What You Must Know When You Travel With a Camera

Pub. Harian Publications
203 Thomas Street
Greenlawn
New York
NY 11740
USA

Wildlife Photography
A Field Guide
by Eric Hosking and John Gooders

Pub. Arrow Books, London, 1977

*Paperback. Covers cinematography, bird,
zoo, studio and safari photography.
Information on cameras and equipment.*

EXPEDITION PLANNING

The Young Explorers' Trust Expedition Equipment Guide
from:
Young Explorers' Trust
c/o Royal Geographical Society
1 Kensington Gore
London SW7 2AR

Covers personal equipment, footwear, sleeping bags, carrying gear, tentage, cooking equipment, home-made equipment, sources of general, specialist and material suppliers, with information on costs and quantities, manufacture and maintenance. Very suitable for any novice expeditioner, as also for the ordinary camper, hiker, walker or even do-it-yourself enthusiast. Limited number of copies on general sale.

The Young Explorers' Trust Expedition Food and Rations Planning Manual

from:
Young Explorers' Trust
c/o Royal Geographical Society
1 Kensington Gore
London SW7 2AR

Covers basic nutrition, practical hints on food preparations, packing, suggested lists, emergency rations. Written for organisers of expeditions abroad composed of young people, but invaluable for many other expedition or even holiday organisers. Limited number of copies on general sale.

Expedition Guide
by John Disley
Pub. The Duke of Edinburgh's Award Scheme, London

Early edn. features designs for making tents, packframes and sleeping bags.

The Expedition Organiser's Guide
by John Blashford-Snell and Richard Snailham

from:
Home Farm
Mildenhall
Marlborough
Wiltshire

Includes list of facilities for training and assessment, recommended books, notes on equipment, etc.

Expedition Pamphlets

1. Land Navigation for Travellers and Small Expeditions.
2. Hints for Travelling Divers.
3. The Collection of Place Names by Small Expeditions.
4. Air Photographs for Small Expeditions.
5. Cave Surveying for Expeditions .
6. Electronic Calculators for Expedition Surveyors.
7. Advice for Small Expeditions to Forested Regions.
8. Survey Methods for Small Expeditions.

50p each

From:
Royal Geographical Society
Publications Department
1 Kensington Gore
London SW7 2AR

Expeditions: The Experts' Way
Eds. John Blashford-Snell and Alistair Ballantine.

Pub. Faber & Faber, London, 1977

Includes: Expedition Planning and Logistics (Kelvin Kent), Expedition Health and Medicine (Peter Steele), Jungle Exploration (John Blashford-Snell), Desert and Bush Exploration (David Hall), The Polar Regions (Wally Herbert), Underwater Exploration (Christopher Roads), Ocean Sailing (Chay Blyth), River and White Water Exploration (Roger Chapman), Caving (Russell Gurnee), Mountains (Malcolm Slesser), Kit & Equipment (Kelvin Kent); with bibliography and biographical notes on the editors and contributors.

Field Studies

Pub. Griffin & George Ltd
285 Ealing Road
Wembley
Middlesex HAo 1HJ

*Catalogue. Clear and interesting,
includes articles on the use of equipment
and examples of field study projects.*

Handbook for Expeditions

Pub. Brathay Exploration Group
Brathay Hall
Ambleside
Westmorland LA22 oHP

*Includes chapter on medicine and
prevention of illness, list of recommended
books, list of contents of standard
camping unit, useful addresses, including
firms in the U.K. selling expedition
equipment and clothing.*

Leaflets

A Suggested List of Clothing and
Equipment for One Month's
Independent Travel; Safety on
Expeditions; Expedition Tents;
Principles of selection; Choosing
cookers for expedition use.

Pub. Young Explorers' Trust,
c/o Royal Geographical Society
1 Kensington Gore
London SW7 2AR

For YET members only.

Survey Methods for Small Expeditions

Pub. Royal Geographical Society
1 Kensington Gore
London SW7 2AR

EXPEDITION AND TRAVEL SOURCE BOOKS

The adventurer's Guide

by Jack Wheeler

from: The Explorers Book Club
Riverside
New Jersey 08075
USA

*A 'how-to' book by mountaineer,
explorer and long-distance swimmer.*

Atlas of Discovery

by Gail Roberts

Pub. Aldus Books, Jupiter Books,
London, 1973

Explorers Source Book

Ed. Al Perrin

Pub 1972 Explorers Ltd
2107 Grant Avenue
Wilmington 19809
Delaware
USA

*Advice, addresses, etc. on training,
equipment, books and maps, governing
bodies; by type of activity, e.g. canoeing,
climbing, backpacking.*

Guide de l'Aventure et du Voyage

Pub. Guilde Européenne du Raid,
15 Quai de Conti
75006 Paris
France

*Comprehensive alphabetical reference
work giving advice, information and
addresses covering the range of adventure
and travel in France. Items include:
insurance, hitch-hiking services, green
cards, map sources, grants, adventure
schools, libraries, books and guides, air
transport, international driving licences,
photography, health, vehicle servicing.*

Hints to Travellers

Pub. Royal Geographical Society,
London, 1930; reprinted 1947

*An impressive fund of information, some
of it outdated but much still relevant.
Especially useful on selecting personal
equipment.*

Traveller's Survival Kit — Europe

from:
Overland Mail Order
3 Bedford Road
London W4

and:
Trail Finders (Services) Ltd
46–48 Earls Court Road
London W8 6EJ

*Paperback. Contains much useful
information. Concise, easy-reference
format.*

World Atlas of Exploration

Ed Eric Newby

Pub. Mitchell Beazley, London

*Compendium of history of exploration of
individual areas, compiled by well-
travelled author. Comprehensive yet
compact, readable.*

EXPLORER BIOGRAPHIES

The Challengers

by Ingrid Cranfield

Pub. Weidenfeld and Nicolson 1977

*Thoroughly documented account of the
achievements of outstanding British and
Commonwealth explorers and travellers
since the Second World War. Covers off-
the-beaten-track sporting activities (e.g.
gliding and caving) as well as epic
journeys, outstanding personalities (such
as Eric Shipton) and major achievements
(such as the 1953 conquest of Everest).*

FUND-RAISING FOR EXPEDITIONS

Directory of Grant-Making Trusts

Pub. Charities Aid Fund of the
National Council of Social Services

Educational Charities

Pub. National Union of Students,
London

GUIDES TO ADVENTURE TRIPS

Adventure Travel USA

(formerly 'Adventure Trip Guide')
Ed. Pat Dickerman

Pub. Adventure Guides Inc
36 East 57th Street
New York
NY 10022
USA

*Covers outfitters, services, trip organisers,
for all kinds of adventure travel.
Arranged by mode of travel, e.g. on foot,
on horseback, by boat, and, within each
category, by type, e.g. 'on foot' includes
backpacking and hiking, mountaineering
and rock climbing, walking with
packstock. Also list by state (alphabetical
within each) of outfitters, holiday
organisers, etc.*

The New York Times Guide to Adventure, Travel and Study, USA

For High School and College
Students
by Howard S. and Beatrice L.
Rowland

Pub. Quadrangle Book Co./New
York Times,
New York, 1975

*Discusses criteria for selecting a
programme and the opportunities*

available including adventure holidays and trips, paid work and work camps, volunteer work, the arts and special interests, sport, study. With appendix on various relevant organisations, e.g. Sierra Club, American and Canadian YHAs, etc.

Sport and Adventure Holidays
Ed. Hilary Sewell

Pub. Central Bureau for Educational Visits and Exchanges, London, 1976

Details on activity holidays in Britain and abroad, ranging from go-karting and canal cruising to trekking, mountaineering and overland expeditions in Asia, Australia, Africa or the Americas. Bibliography.

HITCHHIKING

Africa for the Hitchhiker
from:
Roger Lascelles
3 Holland Park Mansions
16 Holland Park Gardens
London W14 8DY

Available in the USA from:
Information Exchange
T.E.J. 22
West Monroe Street
Chicago
Illinois 60603

Detailed advice for budget travellers, though some areas (e.g. Malagasy Republic) receive shallow treatment. Translated from Danish original.

Asia for the Hitchhiker
Out of print, but possible revised edition in 1978. If so, obtainable from:
Roger Lascelles
3 Holland Park Mansions
16 Holland Park Gardens
London W14 8DY

Available in the USA from:
Information Exchange
T.E.J. 22
West Monroe Street
Chicago
Ill 60603

Latin America for the Hitchhiker
from:
Roger Lascelles
3 Holland Park Mansions
16 Holland Park Gardens
London W14 8DY

Available in the USA from:
Information Exchange
T.E.J. 22
West Monroe Street
Chicago
Illinois 60603

Detailed advice for budget travellers. Translated from Danish original.

ICELAND

Check-List of Principal Books on Iceland and Faroe
by Dick Phillips

Pub. 1975

from the author:
Whitehall House
Nenthead
Alston
Cumbria CA9 3PS

Paperback. Bibliography of over 240 books in English, excluding saga translation and specialised sceintific publications.

Iceland in a Nutshell
by Peter Kidson

Pub. Ferotahandbaekur sf.
Reykjavik
Iceland

from:
Dick Phillips
Whitehall House
Nenthead
Alston
Cumbria CA9 3PS

Complete guidebook for the independent traveller.

Iceland: Notes for Expeditions

Pub. the Iceland Unit
86 Dovedale Crescent
Buxton SK17 9BQ
Derbyshire

Free (on receipt of SAE).

Iceland Road Guide

Ed. O. Hálfdanarson

Pub. Orn & Orlygur h.f., Reykjavik

from:
Dick Phillips
Whitehall House
Nenthead
Alston
Cumbria CA9 3PS

English edn. of Icelandic work. 1975. Describes notable features and historic sites accessible from virtually all roads passable by normal cars. With road maps and street plans.

LANGUAGE LEARNING

Swahili for Travellers

Berlitz

Pub. Johnston & Bacon, London

Introduction to the lingua franca of some 35 million people in East Africa and the quasi-international language for the rest of Africa. Also travel tips.

LOW COST TRAVEL

Charter Flight Directory

by Jens Jurgen

Pub. Travel Information Bureau
P.O. Box 668
Kings Park
New York
NY 11754
USA

Paperback. Gives tips on special air fares, ways of obtaining stopovers, of getting airlines to pay for accommodation, of transferring tickets, or joining charter flights, etc. Also includes many addresses of airlines, operators, etc.

Air Travel Bargains

Ed. Jim Woodman

P.O. Box 987
Coconut Grove
Miami
Florida 33133
USA

What is WEXAS?

Pub. (twice a year) by WEXAS
International Ltd
45 Brompton Road
Knightsbridge
London SW3 1DE

and:
WEXAS International Inc
Graybar Building, Suite 354
420 Lexington Avenue
New York
NY 10017
USA

This catalogue of low cost flights to over 150 worldwide destinations is constantly updated and is published in September and March each year. A Stop Press supplement is also normally published in November. Available free to anyone in any country on request. Possibly the best way to keep up to date on what is going

on in the low cost scheduled and charter
airfare jungle. For more details on
WEXAS, see the 6–page WEXAS
section in this handbook. It contains a
WEXAS membership application form.

World's Best Travel Bargains
Start in London
by Arthur Latchford

Pub. Joyer Publications
Box 707
Corona del Mar
California 92625
USA

MEDICINE & FIRST AID FOR
EXPLORERS & TRAVELLERS

Emergency Dentistry
by Dr David Watt

Pub. Clausen Publications
115 St. Mary's Road
Weybridge KT13 9QA
Surrey

*Useful especially for larger expeditions.
'Intended for those who must treat the
occasional dental patient'.*

New Essential First Aid
by A. W. Gardner and
P. J. Roylance

Pub. Pan Books, London, 1972

Expedition Medicine
A Planning Guide
by R. N. Illingworth

Pub. 1976
Brathay Exploration Group
Brathay Hall
Ambleside
Cumbria

*Main sections: medical planning, the
prevention of disease, medical equipment;
bibliography.*

Expedition Travel & Your
Health
by P. R. Steele

Pub. University of Bristol,
Bristol, 1974

Exploration Medicine
Eds. O. G. Edholm and
A. L. Bacharach

Pub. John Wright & Sons Ltd
Bristol, 1965

First Aid
St. John Ambulance, St. Andrew's
Ambulance Association, and British
Red Cross Society.

3rd edn. 1972

Preservation of Personal Health
in Warm Climates
Pub. 1971 (7th edn.)
Ross Institute of Tropical Hygiene
London School of Hygiene and
Tropical Medicine
Keppel Street
Gower Street
London WC1E 7HT

The Traveller's Health Guide
by Dr Anthony C. Turner

2nd edn. 1977

from:
Roger Lascelles
3 Holland Park Mansions
16 Holland Park Gardens
London W14 8DY

*Paperback by the Senior Overseas
Medical Officer of British Airways
Medical Services and Hon. Associate
Physician and Lecturer at the Hospital
for Tropical Diseases, London.
Invaluable for visitors to Africa, Asia or
Latin America.*

Travel Medicine
Handbook for Practitioners
by Dr. Anthony C. Turner

Pub. Churchill Livingstone,
Edinburgh, 1975

MOUNTAINEERING

Encyclopedia of Mountaineering
by Walt Unsworth

Pub. Robert Hale, London

Survey of the world's climbing areas; micro-biographies of mountaineers past and present; techniques and equipment, with emphasis on safety.

Modern Mountaineering
by Showell Styles

Pub. Faber, London.

Mountaineering
by Alan Blackshaw

Pub. Penguin, Harmondsworth

from:
Mountain Leadership Training
Board
Crawford House
Precinct Centre
Booth Street East
Manchester M13 9RZ

Mountain Leadership
by Eric Langmuir

Pub. 1969,
Mountain Leadership Training
Board
Crawford House
Precinct Centre
Booth Street East
Manchester M13 9RZ

Official MLTB handbook. Useful section on personal equipment.

The Mountain Year Book No. 1

Pub. 1976
Holmes McDougall Ltd
36 Tay Street
Perth PH1 5TT

Reference book containing lists, addresses, news, notes on equipment and conservation, etc.

A Short Manual of Mountaineering Training
by W. C. Burns

Pub. Mountaineering Association

MOUNTAIN RESCUE AND FIRST AID

Accidental Hypothermia
by D. Maclean and
D. Emslie-Smith

Pub. Blackwell Scientific
Publications, Oxford, 1976

Don't Die on the Mountain
by Dan Allen

Available in the USA from:
Appalachian Mountain Club
5 Joy Street
Boston
Massachusetts 02108

Hazards in Mountaineering

Pub. Paulcke and Dumler

from:
Pindisports (various branches in the
UK)

International Mountain Rescue Handbook
by Hamish McInnes

Pub. Constable, London

Medical Care for Mountain Climbers
by P. R. Steele

Pub. 1976
Heinemann Medical Books
23 Bedford Square
London WC1B 3HT

From publishers, booksellers and equipment shops

Survival manual aimed at the climber or inexperienced doctor in the first throes of a mountain accident or emergency.

Medicine for Mountaineering
Ed. J. A. Wilkinson

Pub. 1967 The Mountaineers
719 Pike Street
Seattle,
Washington 98101
USA

Mountaineering First Aid
by Dick Mitchell

Pub. 1972
The Mountaineers
719 Pike Street
Seattle
Washington 98101
USA

Mountain Hypothermia

Pub. 1972
British Mountaineering Council

Available from:
Mountain Leadership Training
Board
Crawford House
Precinct Centre
Booth Street East
Manchester M13 9RZ

Mountain Medicine
Clinical Study of Cold and High
Altitude
by Michael P. Ward

Pub. Crosby Lockwood Staples,
London 1975

Ellis Brigham Mail Order Dept.,
Wellington Place,
Liverpool Road,
Manchester M3 8BL.

By a consultant surgeon and teacher in clinical surgery, and experienced Himalayan mountaineer. Illustrated.

Mountain Medicine and Physiology
Eds. C. R. A. Clark, M. P. Ward,
and E. S. Williams

Pub. 1975
Alpine Club
74 South Audley Street
London W1

Proceedings of a symposium in February, 1975.

Mountain Rescue and Cave Rescue

Pub. Mountain Rescue Committee
9 Milldale Avenue
Temple Meads
Buxton
Derbyshire

and from:
Mountain Leadership Training
Board
Crawford House
Precinct Centre
Booth Street East
Manchester M13 9RZ

Mountain Rescue Training
Handbook for RAF Moutain Rescue
Team

Pub. HMSO, London.

Mountain Safety, Basic Precautions
Pub. Castle Douglas, Scotland;
Climber & Ramber

Leaflet

Safety on Mountains
Mountain Hypothermia
Moutain Code

Booklets and leaflets from:
Moutain Leadership Training Board
Crawford House
Precinct Centre
Booth Street East
Manchester M13 9RZ

Safety on Mountains *is aimed at
young people who are just becoming
interested in hill walking and climbing.
Useful for leaders and others involved in
training*

Safety on the Hills

Pub. Scout Association
The Programme and Training Dept
25 Buckingham Palace Road
London SW1W 0PY

From above or the Scout Shop

MOUNTAIN TOURING

Mountain Touring Holidays in Norway

Pub. Nortrabooks (Norwegian
Travel Association), Oslo

from:
Norwegian National Tourist Office
20 Pall Mall
London SW1Y 5NE

High Level Route
by Eric Roberts

from the author:
9 St. Peter's Square
Ruthin LL15 1DH
Glwyd
North Wales

*Guidebook to the most famous ski-tour
in the Alps, involving the traverse of 11
glacier passes from Chamonix to Saas
Fee via Zermatt. Also covers alternative
itineraries, a survey of ski-
mountaineering in that part of the Alps,
and the history of the route, its facilities,
dangers, etc. Illustrated.*

Stubai Alps
by Eric Roberts

from the author:
9 St. Peter's Square
Ruthin LL15 1DH
Glwyd, North Wales

*Climbing and walking guidebook to this
important Austrian region near
Innsbruck, containing peaks up to 3,500
m., an area recognised as ideal for Alpine
novices. Covers routes, tours, valley
information, the hut system and a
technical grading of climbs.*

NEPAL

Exploring Nepal
by Stan Armington

Pub. La Siesta Press
*Handbook for the trekker, both on an
independent trip and on an organised
tour, though orientated more towards the
latter, pointing out the advantages and
disadvantages of both. Comprehensive
and accurate.*

An Introduction to Nepal
by Stan Armington

from:
Trail Finders (Services) Ltd
46–48 Earls Court Road
London W8 6EJ

*Written for overland travellers with a
week or two to spend in Nepal. What to
do, where to stay.*

Nepal — a Traveller's Guide
by Prakash A. Raj

Pub. Lonely Planet Publications
P.O. Box 88
South Yarra
Australia
Victoria 3141

from:
Roger Lascelles
3 Holland Park Mansions
16 Holland Park Gardens
London W14 8DY

*History, culture, festivals, things to do
and see, places to stay and eat.*

Nepal Namaste
from:
Overland Mail Order
3 Bedford Road
London W4

*Concise, entertaining guide, with hints,
addresses, places of interest.*

Trekking in the Himalayas
by Stan Armington

Pub. Lonely Planet Publications
P.O. Box 88
South Yarra
Victoria 3141
Australia

from:
Roger Lascelles
3 Holland Park Mansions
16 Holland Park Gardens
London W14 8DY

OVERLAND GUIDES

Across Asia on the Cheap
A complete guide to making the
overland trip with minimum cost
and hassles
by Tony Wheeler

Pub. 2nd edn. 1975
Lonely Planet Publications
P.O. Box 88
South Yarra
Victoria 3141
Australia

from:
Roger Lascelles
3 Holland Park Mansions
16 Holland Park Gardens
London W14 8DY

*Pocket guide for travellers between
Australia or New Zealand and Europe,
with advice on bargains, what to avoid,
and some background information on the
countries concerned.*

Africa on Wheels
A Scrounger's Guide to Motoring in
Africa
by John J. Byrne

Pub. Patrick Stephens and
Haessner Publications, USA, 1973

*Practical information and anecdotes on
security, documents, food etc., based on
author's journey from Casablanca to
Capetown in eight months.*

The Arctic Highway
by John Douglas

from:
Geoslides Photographic Library
4 Christian Fields
London SW16

*A full description of north Norway's
famous road to the Arctic, with details of
the northern road system and a discussion
of the environment and history.*

Cairo to Nairobi
A Handbook for the Independent
Traveller
by Trevor Kenworthy

Pub. Wilton House Gentry, London,
1977, £5.95

*Details on transport and accommodation,
etc., for the traveller with limited time at
his disposal.*

Digging in the East
Vaisnava Pilgrimage Guide of
Eurasia and Overland Guide to India
by Christos E. Raftis

Pub. privately by the author,
London, 1975

form:
Roger Lascelles
3 Holland Park Mansions
16 Holland Park Gardens
London W14 8DY

Guide to Western Asia — Overland Route
by E. M. Wheeler

Pub. Youth Hostels Assoc.
29 John Adam Street
London WC2

Journey to Kathmandu
by Michael H. G. Baker

Pub. David & Charles, UK, 1974
from:
Trail Finders (Services) Ltd
46–48 Earls Court Road
London W8 6EJ

Account of 3-month journey to and back from Kathmandu on a limited budget, in three 4-wheel drive Bedford trucks named Faith, Hope and Charity.

Kathmandu by Truck
A modern narrative of a journey of a lifetime
by Barbara Lamplugh

from:
Roger Lascelles
3 Holland Park Mansions
16 Holland Park Gardens
London W14 8DY

Personal narrative of 3-month overland journey in 1976 by Bedford truck with one of the English overland companies.

Latin American Motoring
by Jonathan Hewat

Pub. Wilton House Gentry,
London, 1977, £5.95

Detailed route instructions, information on how to get to Latin America from Europe, Australia and North America, maps and town plans, hints on accommodation.

Latin American Travel Guide including the Pan American Highway Guide

Pub. Compsco Publishing Co
663 Fifth Avenue
New York
NY 10022
USA

Prepared in co-operation with the Pan American Union and the American Automobile Association. Covers Mexico, Central and South America, includes profile chart of the Pan American Highway, 14-page mileage table. Facts and figures, not a guide to tourist attractions.

Mexican Journey
by Frank Bellamy

from:
Trail Finders Ltd
46–48 Earls Court Road
London W8 6EJ

For the overland traveller going independently through Mexico, using public transport. Covers details of connecting economy air flights.

Morocco by Car
by Leslie Keating

Pub. 1972
from Kenneth Mason
13 Homewell
Havant
Hampshire

Routes, useful tips for planning.

The New Grand Tour
by Frederick Alderson

from:
Trail Finders Ltd
46–48 Earls Court Road
London W8 6EJ

Travelling today through Europe, Asia Minor, India and Nepal.

Overland
by Peter Fraenkel
Pub. David & Charles, UK

Indispensable, money-saving guide to planning, preparation, equipment, vehicle modification, etc., (but not routes) by author with 100,000 miles of overland experience in Africa, Asia and Europe.

Overland and Beyond
Advice for Overland Travellers
by Theresa and Jonathan Hewat
Pub. Gulliver Press
25 Lloyd Baker Street
London WC1
from:
106 West Street
Corfe Castle
Dorset
and other distributors.

Planning, equipment and the other essentials of overland travel, based on author's 3-year trip around the world in a Volkswagen Campervan.

Overland through Central and South America
Overland through Africa
Overland to India and Australia
Pub. BIT Information and Help Service
146 Great Western Road
London W11

'Underground' guides intended to counter-balance glossy literature on the overland routes. With information on accommodation, visas, contacts, how to find work, special hazards (including health), police using 'heavy' methods, transport, tour operator firms offering medical insurance, sources of vaccinations; recommended reading.

Overland to India
by Douglas Brown
Pub. Outerbridge & Drenstfrey, UK, 1971

Pre-Departure Handbook Trans-Africa
from:
Trail Finders Ltd
46–48 Earls Court Road
London W8 6EJ

Deals with vehicle type and modification, tools and spares, camping and cooking equipment, medical, immigration and health requirements, visas, carnets de passage, insurance, estimate of total budget, photography.

Tips für Tips
by F. von Engel
Pub. 1973
from:
31 Celle
Stauffenbergstrasse 9
W. Germany

Booklet on overland journey by vehicle from Germany to India and beyond; with facts, figures and costs.

Trans-Africa Motoring
by Colin McElduff
Pub. Wilton House Gentry, London, 1975, £5.95

Equipment, visas health regulations and other details in Part 1. All major routes of Continent, with condition, facilities, maps, etc., in Part II. Author an experienced traveller himself, Head of the Foreign Routes Department of the RAC.

Trans African Route Report
from:
Trail Finders (Services) Ltd
46–48 Earls Court Road
London W8 6EJ

Detailed descriptions of the recommended routes and common alternatives, with mileage, estimated driving time, formalities, ferries, hotels, campsites, fuel and water points, points of special interest and sketch maps. Sections on cross country driving, navigation and camping.

Trans-Asia Motoring
by Colin McElduff

Pub. Wilton House Gentry, London, 1976, £5.95

For travellers between Istanbul and Bangladesh. Main sections cover preparation, individual countries, conditions and facilities along the main routes. Information also on ferries and ships, campsites, entry and customs regulations.

Die Traumstrasse der Welt
by Ludmilla Tuting

Pub. 1974

from:
58 Hagen
Hassleyerstrasse 4
W. Germany

Guide based on journey by Volkswagen bus through South, Central and North America.

Two Wheel Travel
Bicycle Camping and Touring
by Peter Tobey

Pub. 1973
Dell Books
Dag Hammarskjold Plaza
New York
NY 10017
USA

Vagabonding in Europe and North Africa
by Ed Buryn

Pub. Random House, New York, 1973

Guide based on personal experiences; intimate and informal style but with practical information, e.g. recommended reading, clubs, useful associations, home-stay programmes, etc.

Walking, Hiking and Backpacking
by Anthony Greenbank

Pub. Constable, London, 1977

West of Centre
by Ray Ericksen

Pub. Heinemann, London, 1972

Travels in a Landrover in the western half of Australia.

SAILING

The Longest Race
by Bob Fisher and Peter Cook

Pub. Stanford Maritime Ltd

Two yachting journalists' account of the Round the World Race 1973. Notes on life on board, analysis of boats and gear, navigation, communication, medical care.

Sailing
by Robin Knox-Johnston

Pub. Collins International Library, 1977

SEA CANOEING

Sea Canoeing
by Derek Hutchinson

Pub. A. & C. Black, London, 1976

Covers technique, equipment, weather, navigation, etc. Good bibliography.

SOCIOLOGY OF TRAVEL AND TOURISM

The Golden Hordes
International Tourism and the Pleasure Periphery
by Louis Turner and John Ash
Pub. Constable, London

An examination of the consequences of mass package tourism, with recommendations for preventing damage to cultures and localities.

SUB-AQUA

British Sub-Aqua Club Diving Manual
Pub. The British Sub-Aqua Club
70 Brompton Road
London SW3 1HE

An indispensable guide for all amateur divers in the UK training with the BS-AC.

British Sub-Aqua Club Snorkeling Manual
Pub. The British Sub-Aqua Club
70 Brompton Road
London SW3 1HE

Conquest of the Underwater World
by Hans Hass
Pub. David & Charles, UK

Hass' own underwater adventures, including his work in popularising underwater swimming using Draeger's closed-circuit rebreathing apparatus. Account of other underwater activities and phenomena, including saturation diving, monsters of the deep, archaeology, mining the sea bed.

Dive, Dive, Dive
by David Hodgson
Pub. William Luscombe

Survey by photojournalist of underwater activity including training, equipment, marine biology, wreck hunting and conservation.

The Goldon Sea
by Joseph E. Brown
Pub. Cassell, London

Chronicle of the search for artefacts and other archaeological remains, especially treasure, and of other underwater activities.

The Master Diver and Underwater Sportsman
by T. A. Hampton
Pub. David & Charles, London

Sports Illustrated Skin Diving and Snorkeling
by Barry Allen
Pub. J. B. Lippincott,
Philadelphia, 1973
Authorised British edn.
revised by George Cherry:
*Black's Picture Sports:
Skin Diving & Snorkeling*
Pub. A. & C. Black, London, 1976

Useful bibliography.

Underwater Medicine
by Stanley Miles
Pub. Staples Press, London, 1969
3rd. edn. (o/p)

The Water Safety Code
Pub. Royal Society for the Prevention of Accidents
52 Grosvenor Gardens
London SW1

SURVIVAL

Jungle Survival
Desert Survival
Sea Survival
Snow Survival
Survival against the Elements
Pub. Ministry of Defence, London

Booklets not usually available to the
general public, but readers may be able to
obtain copies if they have any contacts in
the Services. All have useful information
on first aid, possible sources of injury,
illness or danger.

Stay Alive in the Desert
by Dr K. E. N. Melville

Pub. new edn. 1977
Roger Lascelles
3 Holland Park Mansions
16 Holland Park Gardens
London W14 8DY

Available from the author:
Laws House
nr. Duns
Berwickshire

or from:
Trail Finders Ltd
46–48 Earls Court Road
London W8 6EY

Deals with the hazards of desert driving,
including advice on equipping the vehicle,
procedure if stuck or stranded,
precautions when driving, against ill-
health or accidents. Also covers health
and hygiene. By author with seven years'
experience as a doctor in Libya.

Survival in Cold Water
The Physiology and Treatment of
Immersion Hypothermia and of
Drowning
by W. R. Keatings

Pub. Blackwell Scientific
Publications,
Oxford, 1969

VEHICLES

Fitness for the Motorist
Pub. Letts Guides, UK

Four Wheel Drive Handbook
Pub. USA, 4th edn.

from:
Overland Mail Orders
3 Bedford Road
London W4

For beginners.

A Guide to Landrover
Expeditions
Pub. The Rover Co. Ltd
Solihull
Warwickshire

Free booklets.

How to Keep your VW Alive
Pub. John Muir Publications
Box 613
Santa Fe
New Mexico 87501
USA

Passport to Shell
Pub. Shell International
Petroleum Co
Shell Centre
London SE1 7NA

Useful data on various countries and
addresses of Shell agencies around the
world.

Periodicals

ABC AIR/RAIL EUROPE

ABC Travel Guides Ltd
Oldhill
London Road
Dunstable LU6 3EB
Beds.

**ABC GUIDE TO
INTERNATIONAL TRAVEL**

Ed: J. Frank Holt

ABC Travel Guides Ltd
Oldhill
London Road
Dunstable LU6 3EB
Beds.

Subscriptions
30–40 Bowling Green Lane
London EC1R 0NE

Consulates, journey times, baggage
charges, taxes, temperature and
humidity charts, WHO maps of
spread of diseases, etc.

ABC RAIL GUIDE

ABC Travel Guides Ltd
Oldhill
London Road
Dunstable LU6 3EB
Beds.

ABC SHIPPING GUIDE

ABC Travel Guides Ltd Oldhill
London Road
Dunstable LU6 3EB
Beds.

Details of fares, sailing dates,
company addresses, for passenger
shipping lines all over the world.

**ABC WORLD AIRWAYS
GUIDE**

ABC Travel Guides Ltd
Oldhill
London Road
Dunstable LU6 3EB
Beds.

ACTIONS

Ed: Hugues Toussaint

Guilde Européenne du Raid
15 Quai de Conti
75006 Paris
France

Reports on grants made by the
Guilde, forthcoming events,
organised tours, classified
advertisements.

**AMC (APPALACHIAN
MOUNTAIN CLUB) TIMES**

Appalachian Mountain Club
5 Joy Street
Boston
Massachusetts 02108
USA

Newspaper. Club business, outings
calendar.

APPALACHIA

Ed: W. Kent Olson

Appalachian Mountain Club

5 Joy Street
Boston
Massachusetts 02108
USA

International notes on recent climbs, articles on parts of the Appalachians, book reviews, poems.

APPALACHIA BULLETIN

Appalachian Mountain Club

5 Joy Street
Boston
Massachusetts 02108
USA

Dedicated to the advancement and understanding of the self-propelled recreation ethic. It features editorial opinions, readers' letters as well as current articles and news items in the general field of conservation and pedestrian recreation.

BACKPACKER

Backpacker Inc.

65 Adams Street
Bedford Hills
N.Y. 10507
USA

BALLOONING

Journal of the Balloon Federation of America.

Editorial office
2516 Hiawatha Drive
N.E. Albuquerque
New Mexico 87112
USA

Subscriptions
Ballooning
P.O. Box 2592
Columbus
Ohio 43216
USA

News, articles on flights, technical questions, rallies and races, helpful hints. Classified advertisements.

BCRA (BRITISH CAVE RESEARCH ASSOCIATION) BULLETIN

BCRA

Geology Department
Trent Polytechnic
Nottingham
England

News items of interest to speleologists around the world, including book reviews, details of the Association's meetings, conferences and symposiums, plus short scientific and technical articles.

CAMPING

Ed: Barry Williams

Caravan Publications Ltd

Link House
Dingwall Avenue
Croydon CR9 2TA
Surrey
England

CAMPING & CARAVANNING

Magazine of the Camping Club of Great Britain and Ireland

Camping Club of Great Britain and Ireland Ltd

11 Lower Grosvenor Place
London SW1W 0EY
England

CANOEING

Canoeing Press

The Chapel
19 Main Street
Hemington
Derby DE7 2RB
England

CHALET CLUB WAYS

Garrison Publications Inc.
9800 S. Sepulveda Boulevard
Suite 520
Los Angeles
California 90045
USA

Magazine of the Chalet Club, 116
East 30th Street, New York, NY
10016, USA.

CLIMBER & RAMBLER

Official magazine of the British
Mountaineering Council.

36 Tay Street
Perth PH1 5TT
Scotland

Editorial office
16 Briarfield Road
Worsley
Manchester M28 4GQ
England

CRAGS

Ed: Geoff Birtles

Dark Peak Ltd
34 Folds Crescent
Sheffield S8 0EQ
England

EXPEDITION

The International Exploration and
Travel Magazine

Ed: Kathy Lambert

Published by:
WEXAS
45 Brompton Road
Knightsbridge
London SW3 1DE
England

and

WEXAS International Inc
Suite 354
Graybar Building
420 Lexington Avenue
New York
New York 10017
USA

Established 1970. Sent regularly to
all members of WEXAS throughout
the world. Photofeatures in colour
and black and white on travels and
expeditions. High standard of
photography and writing. Letters to
the Editor, controversial editorials,
classified ads (people looking for
expeditions to join, expeditions
recruiting members etc.), display ads
by suppliers of expedition goods and
services, latest news on travel,
expeditions and overland, book
reviews. Available only to WEXAS
members. For more details on
WEXAS, see the 6-page WEXAS
section in this handbook. It contains
a WEXAS membership application
form.

EXPLORERS JOURNAL

Official quarterly of the Explorers
Club.

The Explorers Club
46 East 70th Street
New York
NY 10021
USA

Established 1902.
Articles on scientific discoveries,
expeditions, ornithology,
personalities and many other
branches of exploration.
Reviews. Embraces space
exploration.

FREIGHTER TRAVEL NEWS

P.O. Box 504
Newport
Oregon 97365
USA

Fortnightly newsletter on freighter
routes and bargains worldwide.

GEO

Gruner & Jahr AG & Co
Warburgstrasse 50
2000 Hamburg 36
West Germany

Editorial office
Warburgstrasse 45
2000 Hamburg 36
West Germany

Subscriptions
Postfach 111629
2000 Hamburg 11
West Germany

Travel and places (but not academic
issues) in the style of the *National
Geographic Magazine*

THE GEOGRAPHICAL MAGAZINE

1 Kensington Gore
London SW7 2AR
England

Articles, notes, news, reviews,
classified advertisements.

GLOBE

Newsletter of the Globetrotters Club

The Globetrotters Club
BCM/Roving
London WC1V 6XX
England

Travel information. Articles on
individual experiences, tips, news of
'members on the move', mutual aid
column for members.

INTERNATIONAL EXPLORERS

Journal of the International Explorers
Society.

International Explorers Society
3132 Ponce de Leon Boulevard
Coral Gables
Florida 33134
USA

THE INTREPIDS MAGAZINE

The Intrepids Club Inc.
133 East 55th Street
New York
NY 10022
USA

JET BOATING

Official journal of the New Zealand
Jet Boat Association.

**New Zealand Jet Boat
Association**
Box 659
Christchurch
New Zealand

Subscriptions
Box 339
Christchurch

JOYER TRAVEL REPORT

'The newsletter that brings you the
bargains in travel — in the USA and
around the world'.

Phillips Publishing Inc.
Editorial Office
8401 Connecticut Avenue
Washington DC 20015
USA

Subscriptions
Box 707
Corona del Mar
California 92625
USA

MARIAH
'The quarterly journal of wilderness exploration'.

Mariah Publications Corporation
3401 West Division Street,
Chicago
Illinois 60651,
U.S.A.

NATIONAL GEOGRAPHIC MAGAZINE

Published by the National Geographic Society, Washington DC, USA

This long-established magazine is familiar to many people. Noted for the quality of its photography, articles cover travel and expeditions and many other fields.

PARTIR

32 rue du Pont Louis Philippe
75004 Paris,
France.

Articles on places and expeditions; travel tips, including how to reach places mentioned in text. Designed mainly for independent travellers overlanding on a tight budget. Publication tends to be sporadic and subscriptions unreliable.

PRACTICAL CAMPER

Haymarket Publishing Ltd.
Gillow House,
5 Winsley Street,
Oxford Circus,
London W1A 2HG,
UK

Subscriptions
34 Foubert's Place,
London W1,
England

Articles on sites, attractions, lightweight equipment, practical tips, buyer's guide, advertisements.

QUEST/77
Published bi-monthly by the Ambassador International Cultural Foundation.

Subscriptions:
P.O. Box 3700
Greenwich
Connecticut 06830
USA

Dedicated to the pursuit of excellence, each issue of *Quest/77* is devoted in part to outstanding achievements in exploration. Well edited and luxuriously designed. High-quality photography.

RUCKSACK
Journal of the Ramblers' Association

The Ramblers' Association
14 Crawford Mews,
London W1H 1PT
England

SCOTTISH GEOGRAPHICAL MAGAZINE

Royal Scottish Geographical Society
10 Randolph Crescent,
off Queensferry Street,
Edinburgh EH3 7TU,
Scotland.

Articles, notes, reviews, some with special relevance to Scotland.

SIERRA CLUB BULLETIN
Official magazine of the Sierra Club

Sierra Club
530 Bush Street,
San Francisco,
California 94108,
USA

Articles on geography, conservation, urban development, history etc. List of Sierra Club books (guides, handbooks, 'exhibit format' books). Advertisements (suppliers, adventure holiday organisers).

THE SOUTH AMERICAN EXPLORER
Official journal of the South American Explorers' Club

South American Explorers' Club
Casilla 3714,
Lima 1,
Peru.

Sections include area field guides, news, club activities, book reviews, an equipment directory, classified advertisments, letters. Plus four full-length articles.

TRAVELLERS' DIRECTORY

c/o Peter Kacalanos,
5102 39th Avenue,
Woodside,
N.Y. 11377,
USA

Puts travellers in touch with each other. Nominal fee charged to be placed on and receive list.

TRITON
The magazine of the British Sub-Aqua Club

Eaton/Williams Publications
40 Grays Inn Road,
London WC1X 8LR,
England

WILDERNESS CAMPING
Official magazine of the American Youth Hostels and U.S. Canoe Association

1597 Union Street,
Shenectady,
New York,
N.Y. 12309,
U.S.A.

YHA HOSTELLING NEWS

The Youth Hostels Association (England and Wales)
Trevelyan House,
St. Albans,
Herts. AL1 2DY,
England

News, forthcoming events, advertisements, including classified.

Maps

Asian Highway Series

Published by Bridgestone Tire Co Ltd, Tokyo, Japan.

Free. Worth obtaining.

Asia Overland

From:
Roger Lascalles,
3 Holland Park Mansions,
16 Holland Park Gardens,
London W1A 8DY.

and other good stockists.

Full colour 30" × 40" map for road travellers between Istanbul and Burma. With current information on the western Asian Highway network, distance chart, currency table, petrol and diesel points, climatic maps, medical and repair services.

Ethiopian Airlines map of Ethiopia

From offices of Ethiopian Airlines.

Free.

General Maps

Maps originally published in the *Geographical Journal* and maps published separately by the Society from:
Royal Geographical Society
Publications Dept.
1 Kensington Gore
London SW7 2AR.

Iceland

From:
Dick Phillips,
Whitehall House,
Nenthead,
Alston,
Cumbria CA9 3PS.

At scales of between 1:750,000 and 1:25,00 (general maps) and thematic or specialised maps held in stock or usually obtainable by special order.

Embassies, High Commissions and Consulates in London

The Consulates are closed on English public holidays and on the national holidays observed in their own country.

	Telephone
Afghanistan: 31 Princes Gate, SW7	01–589 8891
Algeria: 8 Hyde Park Gate, SW7 5EW	01–584 9502
Argentine: 53 Hans Place, SW1X 0LB	01–584 1701
Australia: Australia House, Strand, WC2B 4LA	01–836 2435
Austria: 18 Belgrave Mews West, SW1X 8HU	01–235 3731/4
Bahrein: 98 Gloucester Road, SW7	01–370 5132/3
Bangladesh: 28 Queen's Gate, SW7	01–584 0081
Belgium: 103 Eaton Square, SW1W 9AB	01–235 5422
Bolivia: 106 Eccleston Mews, SW1X 8AQ	01–235 4255
Brazil: 6 Deanery Street, W1Y 5LH	01–499 7441
Bulgaria: 12 Queen's Gate Gardens, SW7 5NA	01–584 9400
Burma: 19a Charles Street, W1X 8ER	01–499 8841
Canada: Macdonald House, 1 Grosvenor Square, W1X 9LA	01–629 9492
Chile: 12 Devonshire Street, W1N 2DS	01–580 1023
China: 31 Portland Place, W1N 3AH	01–636 5637
Colombia: Suite 10, 140 Park Lane, W1Y 3DF	01–493 4565
Cuba: 57 Kensington Court, W8 5oQ	01–937 8226
Cyprus: 93 Park Street, W1Y 4ET	01–499 8272
Czechoslovakia: 28 Kensington Palace Gardens, W8 4QY	01–727 3966/7
Denmark: 67 Pont Street, SW1X 0BQ	01–584 0102
Ecuador: 3 Hans Crescent, SW1X 0LN	01–584 2648
Egypt: 19 Kensington Palace Gardens, W8 4QQ	01–229 8818/9
Ethiopia: 17 Princes Gate, SW7 1PZ	01–589 7212
Finland: 38 Chesham Place, SW1	01–235 9531
France: 24 Rutland Gate, SW7 1BB	01–584 9628
Germany (East): 34 Belgrave Square, SW1X 8QB	01–235 4465
Germany (West): 6 Rutland Gate, SW7 1AZ (Visas)	01–584 1271
Ghana: 38 Queen's Gate, SW7 5HT	01–584 6311
Greece: 1a Holland Park, W11 3TP	01–727 8040
Hungary: 35b Eaton Place SW1X 8BY	01–235 4462
Iceland: 1 Eaton Terrace, SW1W 8EY	01–730 5131
India: India House, Aldwych, WC2B 49A	01–836 8484
Indonesia: 38 Grosvenor Square, W1X 9AD	01–499 7661
Iran: 50 Kensington Court, W8 5DD	01–937 5225/8
Ireland: 17 Grosvenor Place, SW1X 7HR	01–235 2171

Israel: 15 Old Court Place, W8 4QB 01–937 8050
Italy: 38 Eaton Place, SW1X 8AN 01–235 4831
Jamaica: 20/2 Mount Row, W1Y 5DA 01–499 8600
Japan: 43–46 Grosvenor Street, W1X 0BA 01–493 6030
Jordan: 6 Upper Phillimore Gardens, W8 7HB 01–937 3685/7
Kenya: 45 Portland Place, W1N 4AS 01–636 2371
Korea (South): 36 Cadogan Square, SW1X 0JN 01–581 0247
Kuwait: 40 Devonshire Street, W1N 2AX 01–580 8471
Lebanon: 15 Palace Gardens Mews, W8 4RB 01–229 7265
Liberia: 21 Princes Gate, SW7 1QB 01–589 9405/7
Libya: 58 Princes Gate, SW7 2PN 01–589 5235/7
Luxembourg: 27 Wilton Crescent, SW1X 8SD 01–235 6961
Malawi: 47 Great Cumberland Place, W1H 8DB 01–723 6021/3
Malaysia: 45 Belgrave Square, SW1X 8QT 01–235 9221
Malta: 24 Haymarket, SW1Y 4DJ 01–930 9851
Mexico: 8 Halkin Street, SW1X 7DW 01–235 6393
Monaco: 4 Audley Square, W1Y 5DR 01–629 0734
Morocco: 49 Queen's Gate Gardens, SW7 5NE 01–584 8827/9
Netherlands: 33 Hyde Park Gate, SW7 5DP 01–584 5040
New Zealand: New Zealand House, Haymarket, SW1Y 4TQ 01–930 8422
Nigeria: 178/202, Great Portland Street, W1N 6BQ 01–580 8611
Norway: 25 Belgrave Square, SW1 01–235 7151
Pakistan: 35 Lowndes Square, SW1X 9JN 01–235 2044
Panama: Wheatsheaf House, 4 Carmelite Street, EC4Y 0BN 01–353 4792/3
Paraguay: Braemar Lodge, Cornwall Gardens, SW7 4AQ 01–937 1253
Peru: 52 Sloane Street, SW1X 9SP 01–235 6867
Philippines: 9a Palace Green, W8 4QE 01–937 3646/8
Poland: 19 Weymouth Street, W1N 4EA 01–580 4324
Portugal: 3rd floor, Silver City House, 62 Brompton Road, SW3 01–235 6216/8
Romania: 4 Palace Green, W8 4QD 01–937 9667
Saudi Arabia: 30 Belgrave Square, SW1 01–235 0303
Senegal: 11 Phillimore Gardens, W8 7ZG 01–937 0925
Sierra Leone: 33 Portland Place, W1N 3AG 01–636 6483
Singapore: 16 Northumberland Avenue, WC2N 5AZ 01–839 5061
South Africa: 16 Charles II Street, Haymarket, London SW1 01–930 4488
Spain: 20 Draycott Place, SW3 2SB 01–589 3284/6
Sri Lanka: 13 Hyde Park Gardens, W2 2LU 01–262 1841
Sudan: 3/5 Cleveland Row, St. James's, SW1A 1DD 01–839 8080
Sweden: 23 North Row, W1R 2DN 01–499 9500
Switzerland: 16–18 Montague Place, W1H 2BQ 01–723 0701/6
Syria: 5 Eaton Terrace, SW1W 8EX 01–730 0384
Tanzania: 43 Hertford Street, W1Y 8DB 01–499 8951
Thailand: 30 Queen's Gate, SW7 5JB 01–589 2857
Trinidad & Tobago: 42 Belgrave Square, SW1X 8NT 01–245 9351
Tunisia: 29 Princes Gate, SW7 1QG 01–584 8117
Turkey: Rutland Lodge, Rutland Gardens, SW7 1BW 01–589 0949
Uganda: Uganda House, 58/9 Trafalgar Square, WC2N 5DX 01–839 1963

Union of Soviet Socialist Republics: 5 Kensington Palace
Gardens, W8 4QP   01–229 3215/6
United Kingdom: Chief Passport Office, Clive House, Petty
France, SW1H 9HD   01–222 8010
United States of America: 5 Upper Grosvenor Street, W1A
2JB   01–499 5521
Uruguay: 48 Lennox Gardens, SW1X 0DL   01–589 3733
Venezuela: 71a Park Mansions, Knightsbridge, SW1X 7QU   01–589 9916
Vietnam: 12–14 Victoria Road, W8   01–937 1912
Yemen (Republic): 41 South Street, W1Y 5PD   01–499 5246
Yugoslavia: 7 Lexham Gardens, W8 7HG   01–370 6105
Zaire: 26 Chesham Place, SW1X 8HH   01–235 6137
Zambia: Zambia House, 7/11 Cavendish Place, W1M 0HB   01–580 0691

Consulates are also maintained in London by the following countries: Barbados, Benin, Botswana, Burundi, Cameroon, Costa Rica, Dominican Republic, Fiji, Gabon, Gambia, Guyana, Haiti, Honduras (Republic), Ivory Coast, Khmer Republic, Laos, Lesotho, Mongolia, Nepal, Nicaragua, Oman, Qatar, Salvador, Somalia, Southern Yemen, Swaziland, United Arab Emirates and Upper Volta.

The following list shows countries that have no official representation in London, but whose representatives can be contacted where indicated:

Burundi: Square Marie-Louise, 46 Brussels 1040, Belgium   733.55.93/733.57.15
Congo Republic (Brazzaville): 57 bis, Rue Scheffer, Paris 16,
France   727 77–09
Guatemala: 73 Rue de Courcelles, Paris 8, France   227.78–63
Guinea: Via Luigi Luciani 41, 00197 Rome   872007/804 505
Malagasy: 1 Boulevard Souchet, Paris 75016, France   504.18–16
Mali: 89 Rue du Cherche-Midi, Paris 6, France   548.58–43
Mauritania: 5 Rue de Montevideo, Paris 16, France   504.88–54
Niger: 154 Rue de Longchamps, Paris 16, France   504 8060
Togo: Avenue de Tervueren 264, 1150 Brussels, Belgium   770.55.63./770.17.91

British Embassies, High Commissions and Consulates Abroad

IN AFRICA	*Tel. No.*
Algeria: Résidence Cassiopee, Batîment "B", 7 Chemin des Glycines, Algiers	9502–5
Angola: Rua Diogo Cao 4, (Caixa Postal 1244), Luanda	22487
Botswana: Private Bag 23, Gaborone	2483
Burundi: BP 1344, Bujumbara	3206
Cameroon: Le Concorde, Avenue J. F. Kennedy, BP 547, Yaounde	22–05–45
Central African Republic: SCKN, PO Box 809, Bangui	2166
Chad: Conoco, BP 694, Fort Lamy	3202
Egypt: Kasr el Doubara, Garden City, Cairo	20850/9
Ethiopia: Papassinos Building, Ras Desta Damtew Avenue, Addis Ababa	151305
Gambia: 78 Wellington Street, PO Box 507, Bathurst	244
Ghana: Barclays Bank Building, High Street, PO Box 296, Accra	64651
Ivory Coast: Fifth Floor, Immeuble Shell, Avenue Lamblin, PO Box 2581, Abidjan	226615
Kenya: Bruce House, Standard Street, PO Box 48543, Nairobi	35944
Lesotho: PO Box 521, Maseru	3961
Liberia: Mamba Point, PO Box 120, Monrovia	21055
Libya: 30 Trig al Fatah, Tripoli	31191
Malagasy: First Floor, 41 Rue Choiseul, PO Box 167, Tananarive	206–50
Malawi: Victoria Avenue, PO Box 479, Blantyre	33022
Mauritania: "Somima", BP 75, Nouakchott	23–27
Mauritius: Cerne House, Chaussée, PO Box 586, Port Louis	20201
Morocco: 52 Rue d'Angleterre, PO Box 2033, Tangier	15895

Nigeria: 1st Floor, Western House, 8 Yakubu Gowon
Street, Lagos   51630
Senegal: 20 Rue du Docteur Guillet, BP 6025, Dakar   22383
Sierra Leone: Standard Bank, Sierra Leone Building,
Wallace Johnson Street, Freetown   3961
Somali Republic: Via Londra 7/8, PO Box 1036,
Mogadishu   2288
South Africa: 8th Floor, BP Centre, corner Kerk/
Harrison Streets, PO Box 10101, Johannesburg   834 6411
Sudan: New Aboulela Building, Barlaman Avenue (PO
Box 801), Khartoum   70766–69
Swaziland: Allister Miller Street, Private Bag, Mbabane 2581
Tanzania: Permanent House, Independence Avenue
(PO Box 9200), Dar-es-Salaam   29601
Tunisia: 5 Place de la Victoire, Tunis   245.100
Uganda: Parliament Avenue, PO Box 7070, Kampala   57054
Zaire: Avenue de l'Equateur, 5th Floor, Boîte Postale
8049, Kinshasa   23483
Zambia: Independence Avenue (PO Box No. RW 50),
Lusaka   51122

IN THE MIDDLE EAST
Afghanistan: Karte Parwan, Kabul   20512
Iran: Avenue Ferdowsi, Tehran   45011
Iraq: Sharia Salah Ud-Din, Karkh, Baghdad   32121
Israel: 192 Rehov Hayarkon, Tel Aviv 63405   249171
Jordan: Third Circle, Jebel Amman (PO Box 87),
Amman   41261–66
Kuwait: Kuwait Investment Company Building, Plot 6,
Area 9, Ahmad Ak Jabir Street (O. Box Safat 300),
Kuwait   39221
Lebanon: Avenue de Paris, Ras Beirut   22.15.50
Persian Gulf: PO Box 114, Al Mathaf Square,
Mahama, Bahrain   4002
      PO Box 65, Dubai   31070
      Shaikh Hamdan Street, Abu Dhabi   41305
Saudi Arabia: PO Box 393, Jedda   52849
Yemen: 28 Ho Chi Min Street, Khormaksar, Aden   24171
Turkey: Tepebasi Beyoglu, Istanbul   447545
Syria: Quarter Malki, 11 rue Mohammad Kurd Ali,
Imm. Kotob, Damascus   332.561

IN SOUTH AND SOUTH EAST ASIA AND THE FAR EAST

Bangladesh: DIT Buildings, Dilkusha, (PO Box 90), Dacca 2   243251–3
Burma: 80 Strand Road, PO Box 638, Rangoon   15700
Cambodia: 96 Moha Vithei, 9 Tola, PO 150, Phnom Penh   23974
China: 5 Kuang Hua Lu, Chien Kuo Men Wai, Peking   52–1961
Fiji: Civic Centre, Stinson Parade, PO Box 1355, Suva   311033
India: Chankyapuri, New Delhi 110021   70371
Indonesia: Djalan Thamrin 75, Djakarta   41091
Korea: No. 4 Chung-dong, Sudaemoon-Ku, Seoul   75–7341
Laos: Rue Pandit J. Nehru (PO Box 224), Vientiane   2333
Malaysia: Wisman, Jalan Semantan, PO Box 1030, Kuala Lumpur   202666
Mongolia: 36 Peace Street, PO Box 703, Ulan Bator   51033
Nepal: Lainchaur, PO Box 106, Kathmandu   11588
Pakistan: York Place, Runnymede Lane, Port Trust Estate, Clifton, Karachi   516041
Papua New Guinea: United Church Building, Douglas Street, Port Moresby   2998
Philippines: 8th Floor, 1414 Roxas Boulevard, PO Box 295, Manila   592461
Singapore: Tanglin Circus, Singapore 10   640461
Thailand: Ploenchit Road, Bangkok   53291
Vietnam: 25 Dai Lo Thong Nhut, PO Box N1, Saigon   25341

IN CENTRAL AND SOUTH AMERICA

Argentina: Dr Luis Agote 2412, Casilla de Correo 2050, Buenos Aires   3275.25
Barbados: 147 Roebuck Street (PO Box 676c), Bridgetown   63525
Bolivia: Avenida Arce 2732–54 (PO Box Casilla 694), La Paz   29401
Brazil: Edificio Flarida, Praia do Flamengo 322, Apt 601, Rio de Janeirio   225–7385
Bahamas: Bitco Building (3rd floor), East Street, Nassau 57471
Chile: Bandera 227 (Casilla 72-D), Santiago   61151
Colombia: Carrera 10, No. 19–65, Bogota   349080
Costa Rica: 3202 Paseco Colon (Apartado 10056), San Jose   21.58.16
Cuba: Edificio Bolivar, Capdevilla 101/103, e Morro y Prado, Apartado, Havana   61–5681

Ecuador: Calle Gonzalez Suarez 111 (Casilla 314),
Quito   230070–3
El Salvador: 13a Avenida Norte (Apartado 601), San
Salvador   23–2412
Guatemala: Edificio Mayo Via 5, No. 4–50, Zona 4
(PO Box No. 8), Guatemala City   61329
Guyana: 44 Main Street (PO Box 625), North
Cummingsburg, Georgetown   65881
Haiti: Shell Building (PO Box 1302), Port au Prince
Honduras: Edificio Palic, 4 Piso, Avenida Republica de
Chile 804, Tegucigalpa   22–0479
Jamaica: 58 Duke Street (PO Box 628), Kingston   932–1930
Mexico: Lerma 71, Cuauhtemoc, Mexico City 5, DF   11–48–80
Panama: Via España 120, Apartado 889, Panama City   23–0451
Paraguay: 25 de Mayo, 171 (PO Box 404), Ascuncion   491463
Peru: El Edificio Pacifico Washington, Plaza
Washington Avenida Arequipa (PO Box 854), Lima   283830
Trinidad and Tobago: 4th Floor, Furness House, 90
Independence Square (PO Box 778), Port of Spain   52861–6
Uruguay: Bank of London and South America, Cerrito
420, Montevideo   81882
Venezuela: 12th Floor, Av. Le Estancia 10, Ciudad
Comercial, Tamanaco, Chuao, Caracas   91.12.55

Tana River – crocodiles are still abundant in this unspoilt part of Kenya.

Foreign Tourist Offices in the United Kingdom

Algeria: Algerian National Tourist Office, 35 St.
James's Street, SW1   01–839 5315
Andorra: Alcoverro, 49 Wentworth Road, NW11   01–455 3978
Australia: Australian Tourist Commission, 22 Old
Bond Street, W1   01–499 2247
Austria: Austrian National Tourist Office, 16 Conduit
Street, W1   01–629 0461
Bahamas: Bahamas Islands Tourist Office, 23 Old Bond
Street, W1   01–629 5238
Barbados: Barbados Tourist Board, 6 Upper Belgrave
Street, SW1   01–235 8686
Belgium: Belgian National Tourist Office, 66
Haymarket, SW1   01–930 9618
Bermuda: Bermuda Dept of Tourism, Travel House, 58
Grosvenor Street, W1   01–499 1777
Britain: British Travel, Queen's House, 64 St. James's
Street, SW1   01–629 9191
Brazil: 35 Dover Street, W1
Bulgaria: Bulgarian National Tourist Office, 126
Regent Street, W1   01–437 2611
Canada: Canadian Government Travel Bureau, 19
Cockspur Street, SW1   01–930 0731
Cyprus: Cyprus Tourist Board, 213 Regent Street, W1   01–734 2593
Czechoslovakia: Czechoslovak Travel Bureau, 17 Old
Bond Street, W1   01–629 6058
Denmark: DFDS Travel, 8 Berkeley Square, W1   01–629 3512
Danish Tourist Board, Sceptre House, 169 Regent
Street, W1   01–734 2637
Finland: Finnish Tourist Board, Finland House, 56
Haymarket, SW1   01–839 4048
France: French Government Tourist Board, 178
Piccadilly, W1   01–493 3171
Germany: German National Tourist Office, 61 Conduit
Street, W1   01–734 2600

Gibraltar: 2 Grand Buildings, Trafalgar Square, WC2   01–930 2284
Greece: National Tourist Organisation of Greece, 195
Regent Street, W1   01–734 5997
Holland: Netherlands National Tourist Office, 143
New Bond Street, W1   01–499 9367
Hungary: Hungarian Travel Centre, 6 Conduit Street,
W1   01–493 0263
Iceland: Iceland Tourist Information Bureau, 73
Grosvenor Street, W1   01–493 7663
India: India Government Tourist Office, 21 New Bond
Street, W1   01–493 0769
Iraq: Iraqi Tourist Office, 4 Lower Regent Street, SW1   01–930 1155
Israel: Israel Government Tourist Office, 59 St. James's
Street, SW1   01–493 2431
Italy: Italian State Tourist Office, 201 Regent Street, W1 01–734 4631
Jamaica: Jamaica Tourist Board, 6 Bruton Street, W1   01–493 3647
Japan: Japan National Tourist Organisation, 167 Regent
Street, W1   01–734 9638
Kenya: Kenya Tourist Office, 318 Grand Buildings,
Trafalgar Square, WC2   01–839 4477
Lebanon: Lebanese Tourist Office, 80 Piccadilly, W1   01–493 6321
Luxembourg: Luxembourg National Tourist Office, 66
Haymarket, SW1   01–930 8906
Malta: Malta Government Tourist Office, Malta House,
24 Haymarket, SW1   01–930 9851
Mexico: Mexican National Tourist Council, 52
Grosvenor Gardens, SW1   01–730 0128
Morocco: Moroccan Tourist Office, 174 Regent Street,
W1   01–437 0073
New Zealand: New Zealand Government Tourist
Bureau, New Zealand House, 80 Haymarket, SW1   01–930 8422
Northern Ireland: Northern Ireland Tourist Board, 11
Berkeley Street, W1   01–493 0601
Norway: Norwegian National Tourist Office, 20 Pall
Mall, SW1   01–839 6255
Poland: Polish Travel Office, 313 Regent Street, W1   01–580 8028
Portugal: Casa de Portugal, 20 Lower Regent Street,
SW1   01–930 2455
Romania: Romanian National Tourist Office, 98
Jermyn Street, SW1   01–930 8812
South Africa: South African Tourist Corporation, 13
Lower Regent Street, SW1   01–839 7462
Soviet Union: Intourist Moscow, 292 Regent Street,
W1   01–580 4974

Spain: Spanish National Tourist Office, 70 Jermyn
Street, W1   01–930 8578
Sweden: Swedish National Travel Association, Swedish
Embassy, 23 North Row, W1   01–499 9500
Switzerland: Swiss National Tourist Office, Swiss
Centre, 1 New Coventry Street, W1   01–734 1921
Tanzania: Tanzania Tourist Office, 111 Grand
Buildings, Trafalgar Square, WC2   01–930 5848
Tunisia: Tunisian Tourist Office, 7a Stafford Street, W1 01–493 2952
Turkey: Turkish Tourism Information Office, 49
Conduit Street, W1   01–734 8681
United Arab Republic: 62A Piccadilly, W1   01–493 2401
United States of America: United States Travel
Service, 22 Sackville Street, W1   01–734 5805
Yugoslavia: Yugoslavia National Tourist Office, 143
Regent Street, W1   01–734 5243
Zambia: Zambia National Tourist Bureau, 163
Piccadilly, W1   01–493 5552

Metric Tyre Pressure Conversion Chart

Pounds per sq in	Kilograms per sq cm	Atmospheres
14	0.98	0.95
16	1.12	1.08
18	1.26	1.22
20	1.40	1.36
22	1.54	1.49
24	1.68	1.63
26	1.83	1.76
28	1.96	1.90
30	2.10	2.04
32	2.24	2.16
36	2.52	2.44
40	2.80	2.72
50	3.50	3.40
55	3.85	3.74
60	4.20	4.08
65	4.55	4.42

Representatives of Canadian, Australian, New Zealand and American Governments in Asia

	Afghanistan	Bahrain	Bangladesh
Canadian	c/oIslamabad Pakistan	c/oTehran Iran	House no. 69 Road no. 3 Dhamandi Resid'l Area Dacca Ph. 242652
Australian	c/o Islamabad Pakistan	Al-Fateh Commercial Bldg Al-Khalifa Road Manama Bahrain P.O. Box 252 Ph. 55011	Hotel Purbani International 9th Floor Dacca Ph. 255640/1/2
New Zealand			c/o New Delhi India
American	Wazir Abkar Khan Mina Kabul Ph. 654 3832	Manama Bahrain	Adamjee Ct. Building Montijheel Dacca Ph. 244220–9

	Burma	India	Iran
Canadian	c/o Kuala Lumpur Malaysia	7/8 Shanti Path Chanakyapuri New Delhi 110021 Ph. 619461	19 Darya-e-Noor Avenue Tehran Ph. 622623/4/5 625269 629899

Australian	88 Strand Road Rangoon Ph. 15711	Australian Compound 1/50–G Shanti Path Chanakyapuri New Delhi P.O. Box 5210 Ph. 70337	23 Avenue Arak Tehran P.O. Box 3409 Ph. 824554 822711 825698
New Zealand		39 Golf Links Rd. New Delhi 110003	Avenue Nadershah Afshin St. No. 29 Tehran
American	581 Merchant St. Rangoon Ph. 18055	Shanti Path Chanakyapuri 21 New Delhi Ph. 70351	260 Avenue Takti Jamshid Tehran. Ph. 824001, 820091

	Iraq	**Israel**	**Jordan**
Canadian	c/o Beirut Lebanon	84 Hahashmonaim St. Tel Aviv Ph. 292121–5	Third Circle P.O. Box 638 Rangoon Ph. 15700
Australian	c/o Beirut Lebanon	145 Hayarkon St. Tel Aviv Ph. 231263/4	
New Zealand			
American	Nidhal Street P.O. Box 2447 Alwiyah Baghdad Ph. 96138/9	71 Hayarkon St. Tel Aviv Ph. 54338	Jebel Amman Amman Ph. 44371/6

	Kuwait	**Lebanon**	**Malaysia**
Canadian	c/o Tehran Iran	Immeuble Sabbagh Rue Hamra Beirut Ph. 350660	American International Assurance Building Ampang Road Kuala Lumpur Ph. 98722/3/4

Australian	c/o Jeddah Saudi Arabia	S.F.A.H. Bldg. Iantari Street Beirut P.O. Box 1860 Ph. 297050–3	44 Jalan Ampang Kuala Lumpur Ph. 80166/9 80541
New Zealand			Bangunan Syarikat Jalan, Suleiman Kuala Lumpur
American	P.O. Box 77 Kuwait Ph. 424 156/8	Corniche at Rue Air Mreisseh Beirut Ph. 361800	AIA Building Jalan Ampang P.O. Box 35 Kuala Lumpur Ph. 26321

	Nepal	Pakistan	Saudi Arabia
Canadian	c/o New Delhi India	Diplomatic Enclave Plot 5 Islamabad Ph. 21101	6th Floor Office Tower Comm'l & Resid'l Bldg. King Abdul Aziz St. Jeddah
Australian	c/o New Delhi India	National Bank Bldg. Islamabad Ph. 22111–5 (also Karachi)	Villa-Ruwais, Quarter Jeddah P.O. Box 4876 Ph. 51303
New Zealand	c/o New Delhi India		
American	King's Way (Kanti Path) Kathmandu Ph. 515081	Diplomatic Enclave Ramna 4 Islamabad Ph. 26161 26180 (Also Ka'chi, Lahore, Peshawar)	Palestine Road Ruwais Jeddah Ph. 53410 54110 52188 52396 (Also Dhahran)

	Singapore	Sri Lanka	Syria
Canadian	Faber House 7th Floor 230 Orchard Road Singapore 9 Ph. 371322	6 George's Rd. Cinnamon Gdns. Colombo 7 Ph. 95841–3	c/o Beirut Lebanon
Australian	201 Clemenceau Ave. Singapore 9 P.O. Box 99 Ph. 379311	3 Cambridge Pl. Colombo P.O. Box 742. Ph. 96464/5/6	
New Zealand	13 Nassim Road Singapore 10	c/o New Delhi India.	
American	No. 30 Hill St Singapore Ph. 30251	44 Galle Road Colpetty, Colombo. Ph. 26211–17	Ave. al-Mansour Abu Rummanih Damascus Ph. 3255–7 (also Aleppo)

	Thailand	Turkey
Canadian	Thai Farmers Bank Bldg. 7th Floor 142 Silom Road Bangkok Ph. 32956/7 30746 38215	Nenehatun Caddesi 75 Gaziosmanpasa Ankara Ph. 275803
Australian	Anglo Thai Bldg. 64 Silom Road Bangkok Ph. 35970–9	83 Nenehatun Caddesi Gazi Osman Pasa Ankara Ph. 179618 181407
New Zealand	Anglo Thai Bldg. 64 Silom Road Bangkok Ph. 35970–9	

Australian, Canadian and American Embassies, High Commissions and Consulates in Africa

	Algeria	Botswana	Cameroun
Australian		c/o Pretoria South Africa	
Canadian	27Bis rue d'Anjou Hydra Algiers Ph. 60 61 90/91/92	c/o Pretoria South Africa	Immeuble Soppo Priso Rue Conrad Adenauer P.O. Box 572 Yaounde Ph. 22 22 03 22 29 22 22 19 36
American	Villa Mektoub 4 Chemin Cheikh Bachir Brahimi Algiers Ph. 60 14 25/29 60 37 70/72 (*also Oran*)	Koh-i-Nor House The Mall P.O. Box 90 Gaborone Ph 2944/5	B.P. 817 Rue Nachtigal Yaounde Ph. 33 57 33 58

	Central African Republic	Benin	Egypt
Australian			1097 Corniche el Nil Garden City Cairo Ph. 28190 28663 22862

Canadian	c/o Yaounde Cameroun	c/o Accra Ghana	6 Sharia Mohammed Fahmed el Sayed Garden City Cairo (Post: Kasr el Doubara P.O.) Ph.2 31 10
American	Place de la Republique Centrafricaine Bangui Ph. 2050 2051	Rue Caporal Anani Bernard Cotonou Ph. 29 93	5 Sharia Latin America Cairo Ph. 28219 (*also Alexandria*)

	Ghana	**Ivory Coast**	**Kenya**
Australian	Milne Close Off Dr. Amilcar Cabral Road Airport Residential Area P.O. Box 2445 Accra Ph. 77972 75671/2		AFC/DC Building Development House Government Road P.O. Box 30360 Nairobi Ph. 35666 34672 Telex: 22203 Austcom
Canadian	E 115/3 Independence Avenue P.O. Box 1639 Accra Ph. 28555 28502	Immeuble 'Le Général' 4ème et 4ème étages Av. Botreau- Roussel B.P. 21194 Abidjan Ph. 32 20 09	Industrial Promotion Services Building Kimathi Street P.O. Box 30481 Nairobi Ph. 34033/4/5 6
American	P.O. Box 194 Liberia Rowe Roads Accra Ph. 66811	5 Rue Jesse Owens P.O. Box 1712 Abidjan Ph. 32 46 30	P.O. Box 30137 Cotts House Eliot Street Nairobi Ph. 35141

	Libya	Mali	Malawi
Australian			
Canadian	c/o Cairo Egypt	c/o Dakar Senegal	c/o Lusaka Zambia
American	Garden City Shari'al-Nsr Tripoli Ph. 34021 32026	Rue Testard & Rue Mohamed V Bamako Ph. 4663 4834	

	Mauritania	Morocco	Niger
Australian			
Canadian	c/o Dakar Senegal	13 Bis Rue des Cadets de Samur Rabat-Agdal (B.P. 553 Rabat-Chellah) Ph. 713 75/6	c/o Abidjan Ivory Coast
American	B.P. 222 Nouakchott Ph. 20 60	2 Ave. de Marrakech Rabat Ph. 3036/2	B.P. 201 Niamey Ph. 2670 2664

	Nigeria	Rwanda	Senegal
Australian	Investment House (4th Floor) 21/25 Yakubu Gowon Street P.O. Box 2427 Lagos Ph. 25981/2		
Canadian	Niger House Tinubu Street P.O. Box 851 Lagos Ph. 53630/1/2/3/4	c/o Kinshasa Zaire	45 Avenue de la République P.O. Box 3373 Dakar Ph. 20270

| American | 1 King's College Rd. Lagos Ph. 57320/8 | 13 Blvd. Central Kigali Ph. 5601 | B.P. 49 BIAO Building Place de l'Indépendance Dakar Ph. 26344/5 22143 |

	Republic of South Africa	Sudan	Tanzania
Australian	302 Standard Bank Chambers Church Square Pretoria Ph. 3 7051 3 4778 (*also Capetown, Jo'burg*)	c/o Cairo Egypt	Bank House (4th Floor) Independence Avenue P.O. Box 2996 Dar-es-Salaam Ph. 20244/5/6
Canadian	P.O. Box 26006 Arcadia Pretoria Ph. 487062/3/4 (*also Capetown, Jo'burg*)	c/o Cairo Egypt	Pan Africa Insurance Building Independence Avenue P.O. Box 1022 Dar-es-Salaam Ph. 20651
American	Thibault House 225 Pretorius Street Pretoria Ph. 48 4266 (*also Jo'burg*)	P.O. Box 699 Gambouria Ave. Khartoum Ph. 74700 74611	National Bank of Commerce Building on City Drive P.O. Box 9123 Dar-es-Salaam Ph. 22775 (*also Zanzibar*)

	Tchad	Togo	Tunisia
Australian			
Canadian	c/o Yaounde Cameroun	c/o Accra Ghana	2 Place Virgile Notre-Dame de Tunis P.O. Box 606 Tunis Ph. 284950 286619 286114
American	Rue du Lt. Col. Colonno d'Ornano B.P. 413 Ndjamena Ph. 3091/2/3/4	Rue Pelletier Caventor & Rue Vauban Lome Ph. 2991	144 Ave. de la Liberte Tunis Ph. 282 566 282 549 258 559

	Uganda	Zaire	Zambia
Australian	c/o Nairobi Kenya		c/o Dar-es-Salaam Tanzania
Canadian	c/o Nairobi Kenya	Edifice Shell coin av. Wangata et boul. du 30-juin P.O. Box 8341 Kinshasa Ph. 22706 24346	Barclays Bank North End Branch Cairo Road Lusaka Ph. 75187/8
American		310 Ave. des Aviateurs Kinshasa Ph. 25881/6 (*also Lubumbashi, Bukavu*)	David Livingstone Rd & Independence Ave. P.O. Box 1617 Lusaka Ph. 50222.

Worldwide Voltage Guide

In general, all references to 110V apply to the range from 100V to 160V. References to 220V apply to the range from 200V to 260V. Where 110/220V is indicated, voltage varies within country, depending on location.

Aden 220V		Channel I. (Brit) 220V	
Afghanistan 220V		†Chile 220V	
Algeria 110/220V		China. 220V	
Angola 220V		Colombia 110V	
Anguilla 220V		Costa Rica 110/220V	
Antigua. 110/220V		Curacao 110V	
†Argentina 220V		Cuba 110V	
Aruba 110V		*Cyprus 220V	
†Australia 220V		Czechoslovakia 110/220V	
Austria 220V		Dahomey 220V	
Azores. 110/220V		Denmark 220V	
Bahamas. 110/220V		Dominica 220V	
Bahrain 220V		Dominican Rep. 110/220V	
Bangladesh. 220V		Ecuador 110/220V	
Barbados. 110/220V		Egypt. 110/220V	
Belgium 110/220V		El Salvador. 110V	
Bermuda. 110/220V		Ethiopia 110/220V	
Bhutan 220V		Fiji 220V	
Bolivia. 110/220V		Finland 220V	
Bonaire 110/220V		France 110/220V	
Botswana 220V		French Guiana. 110/220V	
†Brazil. 110/220V		Gabon 220V	
Brit. Honduras 110/220V		Gambia. 220V	
Brit. Virgin I. 110/220V		†Germany. 110/220V	
Bulgaria 110/220V		Ghana 220V	
Burma. 220V		Gibraltar. 220V	
Burundi. 220V		*Great Britain 220V	
Cambodia. 110/220V		†Greece 110/220V	
Cameroon 110/220V		Greenland. 220V	
Canada 110/220V		Grenada 220V	
Canal Zone. 110/220V		Grenadines. 220V	
Canary I. 110/220V		Guadeloupe 110/220V	
Cayman I. 110V		Guatemala 110/220V	
Cen. African Rep. 220V		Guinea. 220V	
Chad 220V		Guyana 110/220V	

Haiti	110/220V	Nicaragua	110/220V
Honduras	110/220V	Niger	220V
*Hong Kong	220V	*Nigeria	220V
Hungary	220V	Northern Ireland	220V
Iceland	220V	Norway	220V
†India	220V	Okinawa	110V
Indonesia	110/220V	Oman	220V
Iran	220V	Pakistan	220V
Iraq	220V	Panama	110V
Ireland	220V	†Paraguay	220V
Isle of Man	220V	Peru	220V
Israel	220V	Philippines	110/220V
Italy	110/220V	Poland	110/220
Ivory Coast	220V	Portugal	110/220V
Jamaica	110/220V	Puerto Rico	110V
Japan	110V	Qatar	220V
Jordan	220V	*Rhodesia	220V
Kenya	220V	Romania	110/220V
Kuwait	220V	Rwanda	220V
Laos	110/220V	Saba	110/220V
Lebanon	110/220V	St. Barthelemy	220V
Lesotho	220V	St. Eustatius	110/220V
Liberia	110/220V	St. Kitts	220V
Libya	110/220V	St. Lucia	220V
Liechtenstein	220V	St. Maarten	110/220V
Luxembourg	110/220V	St. Vincent	220V
Macao	110/220V	Saudi Arabia	110/220V
†Madeira	220V	Scotland	220V
Majorca	110V	Senegal	110V
Malagasy Rep	220V	Seychelles	220V
Malawi	220V	Sierra Leone	220V
Malaysia	220V	*Singapore	110/220V
Mali	110/220V	Somalia	110/220V
Malta	220V	South Africa	220V
Martinique	110/220V	South Korea	220V
Mauritania	220V	Spain	110/220V
Mexico	110/220V	Sri Lanka (Ceylon)	220V
Monaco	110/220V	Sudan	220V
Montserrat	220V	Surinam	110/220V
Morocco	110/220V	Swaziland	220V
Mozambique	220V	†Sweden	110/220V
Nepal	220V	Switzerland	110/220V
Netherlands	110/220V	Syria	110/220V
Neth. Antilles	110/220V	Tahiti	110/220V
Nevis	220V	Taiwan	110/220V
New Caledonia	220V	Tanzania	220V
New Guinea	220V	Tobago	110/220V
New Hebrides	220V	Togo	110/220V
New Zealand	220V	Tonga	220V

Trinidad............... 110/220V	USSR.................. 110/220V
Tunisia................ 110/220V	U.S. Virgin I............ 110V
Turkey 110/220V	Venezuela.............. 110/220V
Turks & Caicos I........ 110V	Vietnam 110/220V
Uganda................. 220V	Wales................. 220V
Upper Volta............ 220V	Yemen................. 220V
Uruguay............... 220V	Yugoslavia............. 220V
United Arab Emirates ... 220V	Zaire 220V
USA.................. 110V	Zambia 220V

*Denotes countries in which plugs with 3 square pins are used (in whole or part).
†Countries using DC in certain areas.

World Guide to Duty-Free Allowances

This list is intended as a guide to what local Customs authorities will allow into each country free of duty. Every effort has been made to ensure that the allowances shown are correct, but these are subject to alteration without notice.

KEY

V	visitors	†	all costs for *residents* deducted from personal allowance
R	residents	●	maximum two cartons if for use in New York City
ao	adults only		
oEu	who live outside Europe		
iEu	who live in Europe	x	returning residents must be 21 years old to bring in one quart of wine or spirits
fEu	from Europe		
fI	from India		
fe	from elsewhere	■	cigars of Cuban origin not admitted
n	non-Moslems only		
s	who arrive 1 Jun-31 Oct	◆	double quantity if resident outside Europe
w	who arrive 1 Nov-31 May		
g	for gifts	EECnd	from EEC *not* bought duty-free
‡	vodka, champagne and beer prohibited		
		EECd	from EEC bought duty-free
fpu	for personal use	E	entering from EEC
T	Tourists visiting Pakistan over 24 hours but under 6 months and not engaged in any gainful employment or profession	C	entering from Europe
		K	entering from countries outside EEC
		O	entering from countries outside Europe
3 mths	away for at least 3 months		
2-3 mths	away for 2-3 months	N	entering from non-EEC European countries
1-2 mths	away for 1-2 months		
*	cost deducted from gift or personal allowance	nl	no limit

		Cigarettes	Cigars	Tobacco	Wine	Spirits	Perfume
Abu Dhabi		400	or 100	or $^1/_2$ lb	Nil	Nil	fpu
Antigua		200	or 50	or $^1/_2$ lb	1 qt	1 qt	nl
Australia		200	or 50	or $^1/_2$ lb	1 ltr	or 1 ltr	nl
Austria		200	or 50	or 250 gm	2 ltr	1 ltr	value $A 1000
Bahamas		200	50	1 lb	1 qt	or 1 btl	fpu
Bahrain		100	or $^1/_2$ lb	or $^1/_2$ lb	Nil	Nil	$^1/_2$ oz
Bandar Seri Begawan		200	or $^1/_2$ lb	or $^1/_2$ lb	1 btl	1 btl	fpu
Bangladesh	V	200	or 50	or $^1/_2$ lb	$^1/_3$ gal	$^1/_3$ gal	$^1/_2$ pt
R (Banga)		200	or 50	or $^1/_2$ lb	Nil	Nil	$^1/_2$ pint
R(Foreign)		200	or 50	or $^1/_2$ lb	1/6 gal	1/6 gal	$^1/_2$ pint
Barbados		200	or 50	or $^1/_2$ lb	1 qt	or 1 qt	fpu
Belgium							
	iEu fEu	300	or 75	or 400 gm	3 ltr	1.5 ltr	75 gm
	iEu K	200	or 50	or 250 gm	2 ltr	1 ltr	50 gm
	oEu fEu	400	or 100	or 500 gm	3 ltr	1.5 ltr	75 gm
	oEu K	400	or 100	or 500 gm	2 ltr	1 ltr	50 gm
Bermuda	V	200	100	1 lb	1 qt	1 qt	fpu
	R	200	100	1 lb	1 qt	1 qt	nl*
Bulgaria		250	or 250 gm	or 250 gm	2 ltr	1 ltr	fpu
Burma		200	50	$^1/_2$ lb	1 qt	1 qt	1 pint
Canada	V	200	50	2 lb	1 qt	or 1 qt	value $10
	R	200	50	2 lb	1 qt	or 1 qt	nl*
Colombia		200	or 50	or 250 gm	3 btl	or 3 btl	2 oz
Cyprus		200	or 50	or $^1/_2$ lb	1/6 gal	1/6 gal	2 oz
Czechoslovakia		250	or 50	or $^1/_2$ lb	2 ltr	1 ltr	value 300 Kcs
Denmark	fEu	200	or 50	or 250 gm	3 ltr	$^3/_4$ ltr	75 gm
	K	200	or 50	or 250 gm	2 ltr	$^3/_4$ ltr	50 gm
Dubai		1000	or 200	1 kg	nl$1^1/_2$ ltr	nl$1^1/_2$ ltr	150 gm
† Egypt		200	or $^1/_2$ lb	or $^1/_2$ lb	1 btl	1 btl	2 btl
Ethiopia	V	100	50	$^1/_2$ lb	1 qt	or 1 qt	1 pint fpu
	R	100	50	$^1/_2$ lb	1 qt	or 1 qt	1 pint*
Fiji		200	or $^1/_2$ lb	or $^1/_2$ lb	2 qt	or 1 qt	fpu
Finland	E	200	or 250 gm	or 250 gm	1 ltr	.75 ltr	fpu
	O	400	or 500 gm	or 500 gm	2 ltr	2 ltr	fpu
France	E	300	or 75	or 400 gm	3 ltr	1.5 ltr	75 gm
	N	200	or 50	or 250 gm	2 ltr	1 ltr	50 gm
	O	400	or 100	or 500 gm	2 ltr	1 ltr	50 gm
Germany	V oEu	400	or 100	or 500 gm	2 ltr	or 1 ltr	value DM 100
	R&V iEu	200	or 50	or 250 gm	2 ltr	or 1 ltr	value DM 100
Greece		200	or $^1/_2$ lb	or $^1/_2$ lb	1 btl	1 btl	fpu
Guyana		200	or 50	or $^1/_2$ lb	‡ 1/6 gal	‡ 1/6 gal	fpu

		Cigarettes	Cigars	Tobacco	Wine	Spirits	Perfume
Hawaii	V	300	or 50	or 3 lb	1 gal	or 1 qt	1 btl
	R†	nl	100	or 1 lb	1 qt	or 1 qt	1 btl
Hong Kong		200	or 50	or ¹/₂ lb	1 qt	or 1 qt	fpu
Hungary		250	or 50	or 250 gm	2 ltr	1 ltr	fpu
India		200	or 50	or 250 gm	1 btl	or 1 btl	fpu
Iran		200	or 750 gm	or 750 gm	1 btl	or 1 btl	¹/₂ ltr
Iraq		200	50	250 gm	1 ltr	or 1 ltr	or ¹/₂ ltr
Irish	fEu	300	or 75	or 400 gm	3 ltr	1.5 ltr	75 gm
Republic	iEu K	200	or 50	or 200 gm	2 ltr	1 ltr	50 gm
	oEu K	1000	or 200	or 1100 gm	1.5 ltr	1.5 ltr	.568 ltr
Israel		250	or 250 gm	or 250 gm	³/₄ ltr	³/₄ ltr	¹/₄ ltr
Italy	V fEu	200	or 250 gm	Nil	1 btl	or ¹/₂ ltr	¹/₄ ltr
	V fe	400	or 500 gm	Nil	2 btl	or 1 btl	¹/₄ ltr
	R	60	or 60 gm	or 60 gm	Nil	Nil	Nil
Jamaica		200	or 50	or ¹/₂ lb	1 qt	1 qt	6 oz
Japan	V	400	or 100	or 500 gm	3 btl	or 3 btl	2 oz
	R	200	or 50	or 250 gm	3 btl	or 3 btl	2 oz
Jordan	V	200	or 50	or 200 gm	2 btl	or 1 btl	fpu
	R	200	or 50	or 200 gm	1 btl	or 1 btl	fpu
Kenya		200	or 50	or ¹/₂ lb	1 btl	or 1 btl	1 pint
Kuwait		nl	nl	nl	Nil	Nil	nl
Lebanon	V s	400	or 25	or 500 gm	1 btl	or 1 btl	1 oz
	R&V w	200	or 25	or 200 gm	1 btl	or 1 btl	1 oz
Luxembourg							
	iEu EECnd	300	or 75	or 400 gm	3 ltr	1.5 ltr	75 gm
	iEu EECd	200	or 50	or 250 gm	2 ltr	1 ltr	50 gm
	oEu	400	or 100	or 200 gm	2 ltr	1 ltr	50 gm
Malawi		200	or ¹/₂ lb	or ¹/₂ lb	1 btl	or 1 btl	fpu
Malaysia		200	or ¹/₂ lb	or ¹/₂ lb	1 qt	or 1 qt	value $20
Malta		200	or 225 gm	or 225 gm	1 btl	1 btl	fpu
Mauritius	V	200	or 250 gm	or 250 gm	2 ltr	75 ccs	fpu
	R	200	or 250 gm	or 250 gm	2 ltr	75 ccs	Nil
Mexico		400	or 1 kg	or 1 kg	2 btl	or 2 btl	3 btl
Netherlands		200	or 50	or 250 gm	2 ltr	1 ltr	50 gm
New Zealand		200	or 50	or ¹/₂ lb	1 qt	1 qt	fpu
Norway	iEu	200	or 250gm	or 250 gm	2 ltr	.75 ltr	fpu
	oEu	400	or 500 gm	or 500 gm	2 ltr	2 ltr	fpu
Pakistan	fl	50	or 50	or 4 oz	¹/₂ pint	¹/₂ pint	2 oz
	fe	200	or 50	or ¹/₂ lb	1 btl	1 btl	¹/₂ pint
	T	200	or 50	or ¹/₂ lb	2 btl	or 2 btl	¹/₂ pint
Panama City		300	50	3 tins	3 btl	or 3 btl	2 btl
Peru	V	200	or 1 box	¹/₂ lb	Nil	1 btl	fpu
	R	Nil	Nil	Nil	Nil	Nil	Nil
Poland		250	or 50	or 250 gm	1 ltr	1 ltr	fpu
Portugal		200	or 50	or 250 gm	1 btl	1 btl	fpu
Qatar	V fpu	nl	nl	nl	Nil	Nil	nl
	R	nl	nl	nl	Nil	Nil	nl

		Cigarettes	Cigars	Tobacco	Wine	Spirits	Perfu
Romania	V	200	or 50	or 250 gm	2 ltr	1 ltr	fpu
	R	Nil	Nil	Nil	Nil	Nil	Nil
Saudi Arabia		nl	nl	nl	Nil	Nil	nl
Seychelles		200	or 250 gm	or 250 gm	1 ltr	1 ltr	4 oz
Singapore		200	or 50	or 250 gm	1 btl	1 btl	value S$50
South Africa		400	50	250 gm	1 ltr	1 ltr	300 ml
Spain		200	or 50	or 1 kg	2 ltr	1 ltr	$^3/_4$ ltr
Sri Lanka	V	200	or 50	or 12 oz	2 btl	2 btl	fpu
	R 3 mths	200	or 50	or $^1/_2$ lb	Nil	2 qt	1 pint
	R 2-3 mths	150	or 25	or 125 gm	Nil	1 qt	$^1/_2$ pint
	R 1-2 mths	100	or 50	or 125 gm	Nil	1 pint	8 oz
Sudan		100	or 25	or $^1/_2$ lb	$^1/_2$ pint	1 pint	2 btl
Sweden	iEu	200	or 50	or 250 gm	1 ltr	$^3/_4$ ltr	fpu
	oEu	400	or 100	or 500 gm	2 ltr	2 ltr	fpu
Switzerland	iEu	200	or 50	or 250 gm	2 ltr	1 ltr	8 oz
	oEu	400	or 100	or 500 gm	2 ltr	1 ltr	8 oz
Syria		200	25	or 500 gm	1 btl	1 btl	1 oz
Tanzania		200	or 50	or $^1/_2$ lb	1 pint	or 1 pint	1 pint
Thailand		200	or 200 gm	or 200 gm	1 btl	or 1 ltr	fpu
Trinidad		200	or 50	$^1/_2$ lb	1 qt	or 40 oz	fpu
Turkey		200	or 50	$^1/_2$ lb	1 btl	1 btl	fpu
UK	EECnd	300	or 75	or 400 gm	3 ltr	1.5 ltr	75 gm
	fe EECd	200♦	or 50♦	♦ or 250 gm	2 ltr	1 ltr	50 gm
USA	Vg*	nl●	100■	nl	ao 1 gal	ao or 1 gal	nl
	V fpu	300	or 50■	or 3 lb	ao 1 qt	ao or 1 qt	nl
	R†	nl●	100■	nl	x 1 qt	x or 1 qt	nl
USSR		200	or 250 gm	or 250 gm	2 ltr	1 ltr	fpu
Venezuela		400	or 50	or $^1/_2$ lb	2 btl	or 2 btl	fpu
Yugoslavia		200	or 50	or 250 gm	1 ltr	1 ltr	.75 ltr

Worldwide Exchange Rates

Country	Currency	Rate to £	Country	Currency	Rate to £
Afara & Issas			Ecuador	Sucre	42.76
(ex–Djibouti	Franc	280	Egypt	Pound	1.21
Afghanistan	Afghani	80.00	Ethiopia	Birr	3.56
Albania	Lek	14.70	Equatorial		
Algeria	Dinar	7.15	Guinea	Peseta	119
Angola	Kwanza	n.a.	Fiji	Dollar	1.59
Antigua	Dollar	4.64	Finland	Marka	7.01
Argentina	Peso	621	France	Franc	8.52
Australia	Dollar	1.56	French Guiana	Franc	8.52
Austria	Schilling	28.90	Gambia	Dalasi	4.00
Bahamas	Dollar	1.72	Germany		
Bahrain	Dinar	0.679	(East)	Mark	4.06
Bangladesh	Taka	26.50	Germany	Deutsch-	
Barbados	Dollar	3.44	(West)	mark	4.07
Belgium	Franc	62.20	Ghana	Cedi	1.96
Belize	Dollar	3.44	Gibraltar	Pound	1.00
Benin	Franc	426	Greece	Drachma	63.83
Bermuda	Dollar	1.72	Greenland	Krone	10.31
Bolivia	Peso	34.39	Grenada	Dollar	4.64
Botswana	Rand	1.43	Guadeloupe	Franc	8.52
Brazil	Cruzeiro	23.49	Guatemala	Quetzal	1.72
Brunei	Dollar	4.23	Guinea	Sily	37.91
Bulgaria	Lev	1.63	Guyana	Dollar	4.38
Burma	Kyat	12.61	Haiti	Gourde	8.60
Burundi	Franc	155	Honduras		
Cameroun			Republic	Lempira	3.45
Republic	Franc	426	Hong Kong	Dollar	8.02
Canada	Dollar	1.80	Hungary	Forint	35.44
Chile	Peso	32.26	Iceland	Krona	331
China	Yuan	3.23	India	Rupee	15.13
Colombia	Peso	62.90	Indonesia	Rupiah	714
Costa Rica	Colon	14.80	Iran	Riel	122
Cuba	Peso	1.42	Iraq	Dinar	0.507
Cyprus	Pound	0.707	Israel	Pound	15.90
Czechoslovakia	Koruna	18.70	Italy	Lira	1,530
Denmark	Krone	10.30	Ivory Coast	Franc	426
Dominica	Dollar	4.64	Jamaica	Dollar	2.15
Dominican			Japan	Yen	478
Republic	Peso	1.72	Jordan	Dinar	0.555

Country	Currency	Rate to £	Country	Currency	Rate to £
Kenya	Shilling	14.30	Philippines	Peso	12.70
Korea (Nth)	Won	1.69	Poland	Zloty	59.00
Korea (Sth)	Won	832	Portugal	Escudo	66.57
Kuwait	Dinar	0.492	Qatar	Riyal	6.78
Laos	Kip	344	Romania	Leu	20.50
Lebanon	Pound	5.23	Rwanda	Franc	160
Lesotho	Rand	1.49	St. Lucia	Dollar	4.64
Liberia	Dollar	1.72	St. Vincent	Dollar	4.64
Libya	Dinar	0.51	Salvador	Colon	4.30
Luxembourg	Franc	62.10	Sao Tome	Escudo	66.57
Macau	Pataca	8.63	Saudi Arabia	Riyal	6.07
Malagasy	Franc	426	Seychelles	Rupee	13.33
Malawi	Kwacha	1.55	Sierra Leone	Leone	2.00
Malaysia	Ringitt	4.27	Singapore	Dollar	4.23
Maldive Is	Rupee	12.50	Somali	Shilling	10.82
Mali	Franc	852	South Africa	Rand	1.49
Malta	Pound	0.732	Spain	Peseta	119
Martinique	Franc	8.53	Sri Lanka	Rupee	23.90
Mauritania	Ouguiya	85.08	Sudan	Pound	0.599
Mauritius	Rupee	11.40	Swaziland	Lilangeni	1.49
Mexico	Peso	38.76	Sweden	Krona	7.48
Miquelon	Franc	426	Switzerland	Franc	4.34
Mongolia	Tugrik	5.64	Syria	Pound	6.75
Montserrat	Dollar	4.64	Taiwan	Dollar	65.33
Morocco	Dirham	7.55	Tanzania	Shilling	14.27
Mozambique	Escudo	56.92	Thailand	Baht	35.00
Netherlands	Florin	4.23	Trinidad &		
Netherlands			Tobago	Dollar	4.13
W. Indies	Florin	3.08	Tunisia	Dinar	0.733
New Hebrides	Dollar	1.56	Turkey	Lira	30.00
New Zealand	Dollar	1.79	Uganda	Shilling	14.08
Nicaragua	Cordoba	12.10	USA	Dollar	1.72
Niger	Franc	426	Uruguay	Peso	7.51
Nigeria	Naira	1.20	USSR	Rouble	1.27
Norway	Krone	9.08	Venezuela	Bolivar	7.38
Pakistan	Rupee	16.70	Vietnam	Dong	4.15
Panama	Balboa	1.72	Yugoslavia	Dinar	31.33
Paraguay	Guarani	215	Zaire	Zaire	1.48
Peru	Sol	132	Zambia	Kwacha	1.37

For countries with differing exchange rates the 'tourist' or 'free' rate is shown.

The above should be considered only as a rough guide.

Metric Conversion Table

Length
inch = 2.54 centimetres
foot = 0.30 metre
yard = 0.91 metre
mile = 1.61 kilometre

Weights
ounce = 28.35 grams
pound = 0.45 kilogram
ton = 0.91 metric ton

Liquid Measures
pint = 0.47 litre
quart = 0.95 litre
gallon = 3.79 litres

centimetre = 0.39 inch
metre = 3.28 feet
metre = 1.09 yards
kilometre = 0.62 miles

gram = 0.01 ounce
kilogram = 2.20 pounds
metric ton = 1.10 tons

litre = 2.11 pints
litre = 1.06 quarts
litre = 0.26 gallons

To convert from kilometres to miles, divide the number of kilometres by 8 and multiply the result by 5.

Temperature
To compute Fahrenheit, multiply Centigrade by 1.8 and add 32. To compute Centigrade, subtract 32 from Fahrenheit and divide by 1.8.

Satisfaction at high altitude after a long hike in the Sierra.

Wind Chill Chart

As wind has an important effect on the temperature it is most advisable to use a tent or bivouac shelter when sleeping in cold weather or at high altitude in windy weather.

ESTIMATED WIND SPEED IN MPH	ACTUAL THERMOMETER READING(°F.)											
	50	40	30	20	10	0	−10	−20	−30	−40	−50	−60
	EQUIVALENT TEMPERATURE (°F.)											
calm	50	40	30	20	10	0	−10	−20	−30	−40	−50	−60
5	48	37	27	16	6	−5	−15	−26	−36	−47	−57	−68
10	40	28	16	4	−9	−21	−33	−46	−58	−70	−83	−95
15	36	22	9	−5	−18	−36	−45	−58	−72	−85	−99	−112
20	32	18	4	−10	−25	−39	−53	−67	−82	−96	−110	−124
25	30	16	0	−15	−29	−44	−59	−74	−88	−104	−118	−133
30	28	13	−2	−18	−33	−48	−63	−79	−94	−109	−125	−140
35	27	11	−4	−20	−35	−49	−67	−82	−98	−113	−129	−145
40	26	10	−6	−21	−37	−53	−69	−85	−100	−116	−132	−148

(wind speeds greater than 40 mph. have little additional effect)

LITTLE DANGER (for properly clothed persons)

Increasing DANGER

GREAT DANGER

Danger from freezing of exposed flesh.

World-Wide Average Temperatures and Humidities

The information given below details temperature and humidity at important cities throughout the world. As given at ACCRA the first and second lines in each case indicate Minimum and Maximum Temperature respectively in degrees Centigrade and the third and fourth lines Humidity percentage a.m. and p.m. respectively. For conversion from Centigrade to Fahrenheit, see foot of second column.

	Jan.	Feb.	Mar.	Apr.	May	June	July	Aug.	Sept.	Oct.	Nov.	Dec.
ACCRA												
Temperature °C Min.	23	24	24	24	24	23	23	22	23	23	24	24
Max.	31	31	31	31	31	29	27	27	27	29	31	31
Humidity % a.m.	95	96	95	96	96	97	97	97	89	97	97	97
p.m.	61	61	63	65	68	74	76	77	68	71	66	64
AMSTERDAM	1	1	3	6	10	13	15	15	13	9	8	2
	4	5	8	11	16	18	21	20	18	13	5	5
	90	88	85	80	75	74	76	78	82	86	89	90
	84	79	71	66	63	63	65	66	69	75	82	86
ATHENS	6	6	8	11	16	19	22	22	19	16	11	8
	12	13	16	19	25	29	32	32	28	23	18	14
	77	77	74	70	66	61	53	53	60	73	77	79
	62	61	54	47	44	40	32	33	38	52	60	63
AUCKLAND	16	16	15	13	11	9	8	8	9	11	12	14
	23	23	22	19	17	14	13	14	16	17	18	21
	71	72	74	78	80	83	84	80	76	74	71	70
	62	61	65	69	70	73	74	70	68	66	64	64
BAHRAIN	14	15	17	21	26	28	29	29	27	24	21	16
	20	21	24	29	33	36	37	38	36	32	28	19
	85	83	80	75	71	69	69	74	75	80	80	85
	71	70	70	66	63	64	67	65	64	56	70	77
BANGKOK	20	22	24	25	25	24	24	24	24	24	22	26
	32	33	34	35	34	33	32	32	32	31	31	31
	91	91	92	90	91	90	91	92	94	93	92	91
	53	55	56	58	64	67	66	66	70	70	65	56
BEIRUT	11	11	12	14	18	21	23	23	21	16	16	13
	17	17	19	22	26	28	31	32	30	27	23	18
	72	72	72	72	69	67	66	65	64	65	67	70
	70	70	69	67	64	61	58	57	57	62	61	69

	Jan.	Feb.	Mar.	Apr.	May	June	July	Aug.	Sep.	Oct.	Nov.	Dec.
BERLIN	−1	−3	0	3	8	11	13	12	9	5	1	2
	2	3	8	13	18	21	23	22	19	13	6	3
	89	87	87	83	79	78	79	86	90	92	91	90
	81	73	63	56	50	53	55	58	60	68	79	84
BERMUDA	14	14	14	15	18	21	23	23	22	21	17	16
	20	20	20	22	24	27	29	30	29	26	23	21
	78	76	77	78	81	83	81	79	81	79	76	77
	70	69	69	70	75	74	73	69	73	72	70	70
BOMBAY	19	19	22	24	27	26	35	24	24	24	23	21
	28	28	30	32	33	32	29	29	29	32	32	31
	70	71	73	75	74	79	83	83	85	81	73	70
	61	62	65	67	68	77	83	81	78	71	64	62
BRUSSELS	−1	−1	2	4	8	10	12	12	10	7	2	1
	6	6	9	13	18	21	23	22	19	14	8	6
	94	95	93	92	93	94	95	94	96	95	96	96
	82	79	71	62	62	62	63	63	67	76	82	87
BUENOS AIRES	17	17	16	12	8	5	6	6	8	10	13	16
	29	28	26	22	18	14	14	16	18	21	24	28
	81	83	87	88	90	91	92	90	86	83	79	79
	61	63	69	71	74	78	79	74	68	65	60	62
CAIRO	8	9	11	14	17	20	21	33	20	18	14	10
	18	21	24	28	33	35	36	35	32	30	26	20
	69	64	63	55	50	55	65	69	68	67	68	70
	40	33	27	21	18	20	24	28	31	31	38	41
CALCUTTA	13	15	21	24	25	26	26	26	26	23	18	13
	27	29	34	36	38	33	32	32	32	32	29	26
	85	82	79	76	77	82	86	88	86	85	79	80
	52	45	46	56	62	75	80	82	81	72	63	55
CHRISTCHURCH	12	12	10	7	4	2	2	2	4	7	8	11
	21	21	19	17	13	11	10	11	14	17	19	21
	65	71	75	82	85	87	87	81	72	63	64	67
	59	60	69	71	69	72	76	66	69	60	64	60
COLOMBO	22	22	23	24	26	25	25	25	25	24	23	22
	30	31	31	31	31	29	29	29	29	29	29	29
	73	71	71	74	78	80	79	78	76	77	77	74
	67	66	66	70	76	78	77	76	75	76	75	69
COPENHAGEN	−2	−2	−1	3	7	11	13	12	9	6	2	0
	2	2	5	10	16	19	22	21	17	12	6	3
	89	92	87	80	73	73	77	82	87	90	89	89
	86	86	77	66	60	61	63	67	70	77	83	87
DELHI	7	9	14	20	26	28	27	26	24	18	11	8
	21	24	31	36	41	39	36	34	34	34	29	23
	72	67	49	35	35	53	75	80	72	56	51	69
	41	35	23	19	20	36	59	64	51	32	31	42
DJAKARTA	23	23	23	24	24	23	23	23	23	23	23	23
	29	29	30	31	31	31	31	31	31	31	30	29
	95	95	94	94	94	93	92	90	90	90	92	92
	75	75	73	71	69	67	64	61	62	64	68	71

	Jan.	Feb.	Mar.	Apr.	May	June	July	Aug.	Sept.	Oct.	Nov.	Dec.
FRANKFURT	-2	-1	2	5	9	12	13	13	11	6	2	-1
	3	6	9	14	19	22	24	23	19	13	7	4
	89	88	86	82	80	80	82	87	90	92	91	90
	79	70	60	52	50	51	53	54	60	69	77	82
HONG KONG	13	13	16	19	23	26	26	26	25	23	18	15
	18	17	19	24	28	29	31	31	29	27	23	20
	77	82	82	87	87	86	87	87	83	75	73	74
	66	73	74	77	78	77	77	77	72	63	60	63
ISTANBUL	2	3	4	7	12	16	18	19	16	12	9	5
	7	8	11	16	20	25	27	27	25	19	15	11
	82	82	80	81	82	78	78	79	80	82	82	82
	74	71	65	62	62	57	55	55	59	64	71	74
JOHANNESBURG	14	14	13	10	6	4	4	6	9	12	13	14
	26	25	24	22	19	17	17	20	23	25	25	26
	75	78	79	74	70	70	69	64	59	64	67	70
	50	53	50	44	36	33	32	29	30	37	45	47
KUALA LUMPUR	22	22	23	23	23	23	22	23	23	23	23	22
	32	33	33	33	33	33	32	32	32	32	32	32
	97	97	97	97	97	96	95	95	96	96	97	97
	60	60	58	63	66	63	63	62	64	65	64	61
LIMA	19	19	19	17	16	14	14	13	14	14	16	17
	28	28	28	27	23	20	19	19	20	22	23	26
	93	92	92	93	95	95	94	95	94	94	93	93
	69	66	64	66	76	80	77	78	76	72	71	70
LISBON	8	8	9	11	13	16	17	18	17	14	11	8
	13	14	16	18	21	24	26	27	24	21	17	14
	83	80	76	69	67	64	61	61	67	72	80	83
	72	66	63	58	57	53	48	46	53	59	68	72
LONDON	2	2	3	4	7	11	13	12	11	7	4	2
	7	7	11	13	17	21	23	22	19	14	9	7
	87	84	79	72	69	68	68	73	78	83	87	87
	80	72	63	58	57	57	55	58	63	70	79	81
MADRID	1	2	4	7	10	14	17	17	13	9	4	1
	8	11	14	18	22	27	31	30	25	19	12	9
	89	87	84	78	75	69	63	63	73	83	89	90
	71	64	58	52	51	43	37	36	47	57	68	73
MANILA	21	21	22	23	24	24	24	24	24	23	22	21
	30	31	33	34	34	33	31	31	31	31	31	30
	89	88	85	85	88	91	91	92	93	92	91	90
	63	59	55	55	61	68	74	73	73	71	69	67
MELBOURNE	14	14	13	11	8	7	6	6	8	9	11	12
	26	26	24	20	17	14	13	15	17	19	22	24
	58	62	64	72	79	83	82	76	68	61	60	59
	48	50	51	56	62	67	65	60	55	52	52	51
MEXICO CITY	6	6	8	11	12	13	12	12	12	10	8	6
	19	21	24	25	26	24	23	23	23	21	20	19
	79	72	68	66	69	82	84	85	86	83	82	81
	35	28	26	29	29	48	50	50	54	47	41	37

	Jan.	Feb.	Mar.	Apr.	May	June	July	Aug.	Sept.	Oct.	Nov.	Dec.
MIAMI	16	16	18	19	22	23	24	24	24	22	19	17
	23	24	26	27	29	30	31	31	31	28	26	24
	81	82	77	73	75	75	75	76	79	80	77	82
	66	63	62	64	67	69	68	68	70	69	64	65
MONTREAL	−14	−13	−7	1	8	14	16	15	11	4	−3	−11
	−6	−5	1	10	18	23	26	24	19	12	4	−3
	78	76	75	72	72	75	75	79	82	80	79	78
	73	69	62	56	54	55	52	54	57	60	70	75
MOSCOW	−13	−12	−8	−1	7	11	13	11	6	1	−5	−11
	−6	−5	0	8	18	23	24	22	16	8	−1	−5
	89	88	88	83	72	74	79	83	89	89	89	88
	85	80	70	60	50	54	56	56	62	70	81	86
NAIROBI	12	13	14	14	13	12	11	11	11	13	13	13
	25	26	25	24	22	21	21	21	24	24	23	23
	74	74	81	88	88	89	86	86	82	82	86	81
	44	40	45	56	62	60	58	56	45	43	53	53
NASSAU	18	18	19	21	22	23	24	24	24	23	21	19
	25	25	26	27	29	31	31	32	31	29	27	26
	84	82	81	79	79	81	80	82	84	83	83	84
	64	62	64	65	65	68	69	70	73	71	68	66
NEW YORK	−4	−4	−1	6	12	16	19	19	16	9	3	−2
	3	3	7	14	20	25	28	27	26	21	11	5
	72	70	70	68	70	74	77	79	79	76	75	73
	60	58	55	55	54	58	58	60	61	57	60	61
OSLO	−7	−7	−4	1	6	11	13	12	7	3	−2	−4
	−1	0	4	10	17	21	23	21	16	9	3	−1
	85	84	81	74	67	68	73	79	84	86	87	87
	82	75	65	56	51	54	57	61	65	72	82	85
PAPEETE	22	22	22	22	21	21	20	20	21	21	22	22
	32	32	32	32	31	30	30	30	30	31	31	31
	82	82	84	85	84	85	83	83	81	79	80	81
	77	77	78	78	78	79	77	78	76	76	77	78
PARIS	0	1	2	5	8	11	13	12	10	7	3	1
	6	7	11	16	19	23	24	24	21	15	9	6
	90	90	88	80	79	79	81	84	91	94	93	92
	77	69	59	50	52	55	55	54	59	68	76	80
PORT OF SPAIN	21	20	20	21	22	22	22	22	22	22	22	21
	31	31	32	32	32	32	31	31	32	32	32	31
	89	87	85	83	84	87	88	87	87	87	89	89
	68	65	63	61	63	69	71	73	73	74	76	71
PRAGUE	−4	−2	1	4	9	13	14	14	11	7	2	−2
	1	3	7	13	18	22	26	23	18	12	5	1
	85	83	83	78	76	74	77	81	85	87	87	87
	75	66	56	49	47	48	47	49	51	61	73	79
RIO DE JANEIRO	23	23	22	21	19	18	17	18	18	19	20	22
	29	29	28	27	25	24	24	24	24	25	26	28
	82	82	87	87	87	87	86	84	84	83	82	82
	70	71	74	73	70	69	68	66	72	72	72	72

	Jan.	Feb.	Mar.	Apr.	May	June	July	Aug.	Sep.	Oct.	Nov.	Dec.
ROME	4	4	6	8	13	16	18	18	16	12	8	5
	12	13	17	20	23	28	31	31	28	23	17	13
	85	86	83	83	77	74	70	73	82	86	87	86
	68	64	56	54	54	48	42	43	50	59	66	70
SAN FRANCISCO	7	8	9	9	11	11	12	12	13	12	11	8
	13	15	16	17	17	19	18	18	21	20	17	14
	85	84	83	83	85	88	91	92	88	85	83	83
	69	66	61	61	62	64	69	70	63	58	60	68
SINGAPORE	23	23	24	24	24	24	24	24	24	23	23	23
	30	31	31	31	32	31	31	31	31	31	31	31
	82	77	76	77	79	79	79	78	79	78	79	82
	78	71	70	74	73	73	72	72	72	72	75	78
STOCKHOLM	-5	-6	-3	0	5	9	13	12	8	4	-1	-3
	-1	-1	3	7	14	18	21	19	14	9	3	1
	85	82	80	77	67	66	71	79	85	88	88	87
	82	75	67	62	54	55	59	64	68	76	84	86
SYDNEY	18	18	17	14	11	9	8	9	11	13	16	17
	26	26	24	22	19	16	16	17	19	22	23	25
	68	71	73	76	77	77	76	72	67	65	65	66
	64	65	65	64	63	62	60	56	55	57	60	62
TEHERAN	-3	0	4	9	14	19	22	22	18	12	6	1
	7	10	15	21	28	34	37	36	32	24	17	11
	77	73	61	54	55	40	51	47	49	53	63	76
	75	59	39	40	47	49	41	46	49	54	66	75
TOKYO	-2	-2	2	8	12	17	21	22	19	13	6	1
	8	9	12	17	21	24	28	30	26	21	16	11
	73	71	75	81	85	89	91	92	91	88	83	77
	48	48	53	59	62	68	69	66	68	64	58	51
VANCOUVER	0	1	3	4	8	11	12	12	9	7	4	2
	5	7	10	14	18	21	23	23	18	14	9	6
	93	91	91	89	88	87	89	90	92	92	91	91
	85	78	70	67	63	65	62	62	72	80	84	88
VIENNA	-3	-2	1	5	10	13	15	14	11	7	2	-1
	1	3	8	14	19	22	24	23	19	13	7	3
	82	81	79	78	82	80	81	82	84	6	85	84
	74	68	57	51	53	54	54	55	58	67	75	78
WARSAW	-6	-5	-2	3	9	12	13	13	9	5	0	-4
	-1	0	5	12	19	22	24	23	18	12	4	0
	92	90	89	81	78	77	80	85	89	91	92	92
	87	83	70	58	55	57	58	62	66	70	83	88
ZURICH	-3	-2	1	4	8	12	13	13	10	6	2	-2
	3	6	10	14	20	23	25	24	21	14	7	3
	90	89	85	82	81	79	81	84	90	92	92	90
	76	66	58	56	58	57	58	56	62	70	78	79

Fahrenheit = C° × 9/5 + 32

UK Passports

A UK passport is valid for 10 years and is obtainable through any Employment Exchange or from regional Passport offices:

Passport Office Addresses

The Passport Office
Clive House
70–78 Petty France
London SW1H 9Hd

Branch Passport Office
5th Floor
India Buildings
Water Street
Liverpool L2 0QZ

Branch Passport Office
Olympia House
Dock Street
Newport NPT 1XA

Branch Passport Office
55 Westfield Road
Peterborough PE3 6TG

Branch Passport Office
1st Floor
Empire House
131 West Nile Street
Glasgow G1 2RY

Foreign and Commonwealth Office
Passport Agency
1st Floor
Marlborough House
30 Victoria Street
Belfast BT1 3LY
(Personal applications only)

For travel within Western Europe (excluding the German Democratic Republic and East Berlin), you can travel on a British Visitor's Passport. This costs half as much as a full passport, but is only valid for 12 months. British Visitors Passports and application forms for them are available from any main post office from Monday to Friday. The British Visitor's Passport is *not* obtainable from passport offices, and is only available to UK citizens for holiday purposes of up to 3 months.

Medical Requirements in the UK

The Department of Health and Social Security, Alexander Fleming House, Elephant and Castle, London SE1, publishes a leaflet *Notice to Travellers* which contains up-to-date inoculation requirements for travellers. This may also be obtained by telephoning the Department on 01–407 5522, ext. 6711.

Useful Vocabulary — Europe

English	French	German
1. Do you speak English?	1. Parlez-vous anglais?	1. Sprechen Sie englisch?
2. I do not understand	2. Je ne comprends pas	2. Ich verstehe nicht
3. Yes/No	3. Oui/Non	3. Ja/Nein
4. Your name?	4. Votre nom?	4. Ihr Name?
5. I, you, he, she	5. Je, vous, il, elle	5. Ich, Sie, er, sie
6. Good morning	6. Bonjour	6. Guten Morgen
7. Good evening	7. Bonsoir	7. Guten Abend
8. Good night	8. Bonne nuit	8. Gute Nacht
9. Good-bye	9. Au revoir	9. Auf Wiedersehen
10. How are you?	10. Comment allez-vous?	10. Wie geht es Ihnen?
11. How far?	11. A quelle distance?	11. Wie weit?
12. How much is it?	12. Combien est-ce?	12. Wieviel kostet es?
13. Too much	13. Trop cher	13. Zu teuer
14. Very well	14. Très bien	14. Sehr gut
15. Thank you	15. Merci	15. Danke
16. You are welcome	16. Je vous en prie	16. Nichts zu danken
17. Excuse me	17. Excusez-moi	17. Entschuldigen Sie
18. I am sorry	18. Je regrette	18. Es tut mir leid
19. Please	19. S'il vous plaît	19. Bitte
20. I want	20. Je veux	20. Ich möchte
21. Airport	21. Aéroport	21. Flughafen
22. Automobile/car	22. Auto/voiture	22. Auto/Wagen
23. Bank	23. Banque	23. Bank
24. Barber	24. Coiffeur	24. Friseur
25. Beauty salon/parlor	25. Salon de beauté	25. Frisiersalon
26. Breakfast	26. Petit déjeuner	26. Frühstück
27. Bus	27. Autobus	27. Bus
28. Change (money)	28. Change	28. Geldwechsel
29. Check (bill)	29. Addition	29. Rechnung
30. Church	30. Eglise	30. Kirche
31. Dentist	31. Dentiste	31. Zahnarzt
32. Dinner	32. Dîner	32. Abendessen
33. Doctor	33. Docteur	33. Arzt
34. Flat tyre	34. Pneu crevé	34. Reifenpanne
35. Gasoline/petrol	35. Essence	35. Benzin
36. Hospital	36. Hôpital	36. Krankenhaus
37. Information	37. Renseignements	37. Auskunft
38. Lavatory (toilet)	38. Toilettes (WC)	38. Toilette (W.C.)
39. Lunch	39. Déjeuner	39. Mittagessen
40. Men (gentlemen)	40. Messieurs	40. Männer/Herren
41. Occupied (sign)	41. Occupé	41. Besetzt
42. Pharmacy	42. Pharmacie	42. Apotheke
43. Post Office	43. Bureau de Poste	43. Postamt
44. Registered (letter)	44. Recommandé	44. Einschreiben
45. Room (hotel)	45. Chambre	45. Zimmer

Spanish	Portuguese	Dutch
1. ¿Habla usted inglés?	1. Você fala inglês?	1. Spreekt U Engels?
2. No entiendo	2. Não compreendo	2. Ik begrijp U niet
3. Si/No	3. Sim/Não	3. Ja/Nee
4. ¿Su nombre?	4. Seu nome?	4. Hoe heet U?
5. Yo, usted, él, ella	5. Eu, você, êle, ela	5. Ik, u, hij, zij
6. Buenos dias	6. Bom dia	6. Goedemorgen
7. Buenas noches	7. Boa noite	7. Goedenavond
8. Buenas noches	8. Boa noite	8. Goedenacht
9. Adiós	9. Adeus	9. Goedendag
10. ¿Cómo está usted?	10. Como vai você?	10. Hoe gaat het met U?
11. ¿Hasta dónde?	11. A que distância?	11. Hoe ver is het?
12. ¿Cuánto vale?	12. Quanto custa?	12. Hoeveel kost het?
13. Demasiado	13. Demasiado	13. Dat is teveel
14. Muy bien	14. Muito bem	14. Heel goed
15. Gracias	15. Obrigado	15. Dank U Wel
16. De nada	16. De nada	16. Tot Uw dienst
17. Dispénseme	17. Desculpe	17. Pardon
18. Lo sentio mucho	18. Perdão	18. Het spijt mij zeer
19. Por favor	19. Faz favor	19. Alstublieft
20. Yo quiero	20. Eu quero	20. Ik wil
21. Aeropuerto	21. Aeroporto	21. Vliegveld
22. Automóvil/coche	22. Automóvel/carro	22. Auto
23. Banco	23. Banco	23. Bank
24. Barbero	24. Barbeiro	24. Herenkapper
25. Salón de belleza	25. Salão de beleza	25. Dameskapper
26. Desayuno	26. Café de manhã	26. Ontbijt
27. Autobús	27. Onibus	27. Bus
28. Cambio	28. Trôco	28. Change
29. Cuenta	29. Conta	29. Rekening
30. Iglesia	30. Igreja	30. Kerk
31. Dentista	31. Dentista	31. Tandarts
32. Cena	32. Jantar	32. Avondeten (Diner)
33. Médico	33. Doutor	33. Dokter (Arts)
34. Neumático reventado	34. Pneu furado	34. Lekke band
35. Gasolina	35. Gasolina	35. Benzine
36. Hospital	36. Hospital	36. Ziekenhuis (hospitaal)
37. Información	37. Informação	37. Informatie
38. Retrete/excusado	38. Banheiro	38. Toilet (W.C.)
39. Almuerzo	39. Almôço	39. Middageten (Lunch)
40. Señores/caballeros	40. Homens	40. Heren
41. Ocupado	41. Ocupado	41. Bezet
42. Farmacia	42. Farmácia	42. Apotheek
43. Oficina de correos	43. Correio	43. Postkantoor
44. Certificado	44. Registrado	44. Aangetekend
45. Habitación	45. Quarto	45. Kamer

English	French	German
46. Shop (store)	46. Boutique	46. Geschäft
47. Sick	47. Malade	47. Krank
48. Soap	48. Savon	48. Seife
49. Stamp (postage)	49. Timbre-poste	49. Briefmarke
50. Station (railroad)	50. Gare	50. Bahnhof
51. Suitcase	51. Valise	51. Koffer
52. Telephone	52. Téléphone	52. Telefon
53. Ticket (travel)	53. Billet	53. Fahrkarte
54. Time (of day)	54. Heure	54. Uhr
55. Today	55. Aujourd'hui	55. Heute
56. Tomorrow	56. Demain	56. Morgen
57. Towel	57. Serviette	57. Handtuch
58. Train	58. Train	58. Zug
59. Waiter	59. Garçon	59. Kellner
60. Water (drinking)	60. Eau potable	60. Trinkwasser
61. Women/ladies	61. Dames	61. Frauen/Damen

Guide to International Road Signs

▲ Warning signs   ● Regulative signs   ■ Informative signs

Colors may vary from country to country, but are usually red and black on a white background. Shaded areas indicate blue.

WARNING SIGNS

Right bend

Double bend

Dangerous bend

Danger! Train

Cross roads

Intersection w/minor road

Merging traffic

Road narrows

Uneven road

Slippery road

Other dangers

Round-about

Give way

Dangerous descent

Road work

Tunnel

Opening bridge

Animals

Level crossing with barrier

Level crossing without barrier

Pedestrians

Children

Two-way traffic

Falling rocks

Traffic signals ahead

Spanish	Portuguese	Dutch
46. Tienda	46. Loja	46. Winkel
47. Enfermo	47. Doente	47. Ziek
48. Jabón	48. Sabâo/sabonete	48. Zeep
49. Sello/estampilla	49. Sêlo	49. Postzegel
50. Estación	50. Estaçâo	50. Station
51. Maleta	51. Valise/mala	51. Koffer
52. Teléfono	52. Telefone	52. Telefoon
53. Billete	53. Bilhete	53. Kaartje
54. Hora	54. Hora	54. Tijd
55. Hoy	55. Hoje	55. Vandaag
56. Mañana	56. Amanhâ	56. Morgen
57. Toalla	57. Toalha	57. Handdoek
58. Tren	58. Trem	58. Trein
59. Camarero	59. Garçom	59. Kelner
60. Aqua potable	60. Agua	60. Water
61. Señoras/damas	61. Mulheres/senhoras	61. Dames

INFORMATIVE SIGNS

 Motorway exit

  Priority road

End of priority road

  One-way traffic

  Hospital

 First-aid station

 Mechanical help

REGULATIVE SIGNS

 Road closed

No entry

 No right turn

  Direction obligatory

 No U-turns

  No entry for motorcars

 No entry for motor-cycles

 No entry for all motor vehicles

 No entry for bicycles

No entry for pedestrians

Priority to oncoming vehicles

  No overtaking

  End of no overtaking

  Maximum load

Axle weight limit

Width limit

Height limit

No parking

  Maximum speed limit

 End of speed limit

  End of all restrictions

 Halt sign

 Customs

  No stopping

 Use of horns prohibited

Useful Vocabulary — Far East

English	Japanese	Chinese
1. I do not understand	1. Wakari masen	1. Wo Pu Chih Tao
2. Yes/No	2. Hai/Iie	(Wo Pu Tung)
3. Your name?	3. Onamae wa	2. Shih/Pu Shih
4. How are you?	4. Ogenki desu ka	(Tui/Pu Tui)
5. Very well	5. Genki desu	3. Ching Wen Kuei Hsing
6. Thank you	6. Arigato	4. Ni Hao Ma
7. I am sorry	7. Sumimasen	5. Hêng Hao
8. Please	8. Dozo	6. Shieh Shieh Ni
9. Airport	9. Hikojo	7. Tui Pu Ch'i
10. Change (money)	10. Ryogae	8. Ch'ing
11. Check (bill)	11. Seikyusho	9. Fei Chi Chang
12. Church	12. Kyokai	10. Huan Chien
13. Doctor	13. Isha	11. Chang Tan
14. Hospital	14. Byoin	12. Chiao Tang
15. How far?	15. Kyori wa/	13. I Shêng
16. How much is it?	donokurai arimasuka	14. I Yüan
17. Lavatory (toilet)	16. Ikura desu ka	15. To Yüan
18. Men (Gentlemen)	17. Toire (Benjo)	16. To Shao Chien
19. Occupied (sign)	18. Dansei (Shinshi)	17. Ts'ze So
20. Pharmacy	19. Shiyochu	(Hsi Shou Chien)
21. Stamps (postage)	20. Yakkyoku	18. Nan Ts'ze So
22. Suitcase	21. Kitte	(Nan Hsi Shou Chien)
23. Ticket (travel)	22. Suutsukeisu	19. Yu Jen
24. Telephone	23. Kippu	20. Yao Fang
25. Waiter	24. Denwa	21. Yu Piao
26. Water (drinking)	25. Kyuji	22. Shou Ti Pao
27. When?	26. Mizu	23. Chê Piao (train or bus)
28. Where?	27. Itsu	Fei Chi Piao (plane)
29. Who?	28. Doko	24. Tien Hua
30. Women (ladies)	29. Dare	25. Ch'a Fang
	30. Josei (Fujin)	26. Yin Yung Shui
		27. Shih Mo Shih Hou
		28. Shih Mo Ti Fang
		29. Shih Mo Jen
		30. Nu Ts'zo So
		(Nu Hsi Shou Chien)

⊛LOWEST RELIABLE AIRFARES

Scheduled flights to over 100 worldwide destinations at special low-cost fares giving you all the money-saving advantages of belonging to a large reputable Travel Club. WEXAS uses the services of 45 well-known international airlines.

	from (return)		from (return)
Australia	**£417**	**Nairobi**	**£215**
Jo'burg	**£240**	**Tehran**	**£195**
Rome	**£55**	**Athens**	**£85**
S. America	**£203**	**Auckland**	**£575**
Seychelles	**£230**	**Cairo**	**£131**
Singapore	**£373**	**Hong Kong**	**£339**
Tokyo	**£450**	**India**	**£240**
Toronto	**£126**	**Istanbul**	**£86**
Vancouver	**£172**	**Los Angeles**	**£190**
W. Africa	**£245**	**Lusaka**	**£270**
W. Indies	**£207**	**New York**	**£126**

These fares are liable to fluctuation.

Book your flights with WEXAS for big savings. As a member you'll receive a special 28-page brochure containing full details of the WEXAS Flight Programme.

🌐 ADVENTURE HOLIDAYS

Choose from the unique WEXAS Discoverers Programme of 2, 3, and 4 week holidays for the adventurous of all ages, carefully arranged by WEXAS at special low-cost club rates. You'll travel in small (8–12) congenial groups.

Go trekking in the **Himalayas** to **Everest**, **Annapurna** or **Langtang** and stay in the famous **Tiger Tops Lodge** to see tigers and rare white rhino in the wild, go on safari in the game parks of **East Africa** including Lake Rudolph, learn to sail in the **Canary Islands** on one of **Chay Blyth**'s ocean yachts, learn to dive in the coral waters of the **Sudanese Red Sea**, try jet-boating, big-game fishing and river-rafting by inflatable in New Zealand's rugged and spectacular **Fiordland**, sail up the **Nile**, go husky-sledging in **Greenland**, journey across the legendary **Aïr Mountains** of the **Sahara**, explore darkest **Borneo**, visit the mountain jungles of **Thailand**, sail to adventure among the historic islands of **Greece**, explore the High Atlas of **Morocco**, the medieval villages of the **Yemen** or the volcanic landscapes of **Iceland** by 4-wheel drive, traverse **Spain's Sierra Nevada** on horseback, cross **Jordan** in the footsteps of **Lawrence of Arabia**.

You'll make new friends and bring back memorable pictures of wildlife and strange cultures. Groups have professional leaders chosen for their local knowledge.

WEXAS offers you now the holidays of the future in a special 24-page colour brochure sent to all members when they join.

⊛ EXPEDITION MAGAZINE

The International Exploration and Travel Magazine.
Expedition is a unique, large-format publication which takes you round the globe in the words and pictures of professional writers and photographers. Designed for the regular and off-beat traveller alike, you'll receive regular copies in the mail.

Visit Conan Doyle's 'Lost World' of Roraima and Angel Falls, climb Everest by the dangerous South West Face, read Sir Peter Scott's own account of the Loch Ness Monster, trek in Nepal with John Blashford-Snell, find out how Mark Twain travelled in Europe a century ago.

You'll also find that *Expedition* has controversial editorials, contemporary and historical explorers profiles, provocative letters from readers reporting from around the world on their experiences, expert reviews of new books, a special page giving the latest travel opportunities, *Faces and Places* — the page about who's going where and why, and a classified ads page on which readers can advertise free for vehicles, travelling companions, trips to join — anything. And of course there are ads from a wide variety of companies interested in reaching the readers of *Expedition*. And a WEXAS directory updated each issue to keep you informed of available goods and services.

Expedition can be obtained only through membership of WEXAS.

Subscribe now by joining WEXAS.

WHEN YOU JOIN WEXAS

You'll receive a free copy of this handbook (*Off the Beaten Track*) plus booking forms, your International Membership Card, all the above brochures, details of travel insurance available to members and your first copy of *Expedition* magazine. In addition, WEXAS organises free film and lecture evenings presented by distinguished explorers and travellers.

Membership Subscriptions £8.78 (Individuals) and £12 (Families) for residents of the UK and Ireland. Overseas rate £12/$26 (individuals) and £20/$42 (Families). Overseas payments should be made in dollars or by Sterling Bank Draft. UK and Irish applicants pay by Standing Order.

WEXAS – the world's largest travel and exploration club with members in 83 countries.

WEXAS MEMBERSHIP APPLICATION

For individual and family membership. If you are applying for Family Membership, please complete the first three boxes with family members' names, including your own. Only the applicant need complete the remaining boxes and the reverse side of this form. Subscription £8.75 (Individuals) and £12 (Families) in UK, £12 and £20 overseas. **1978/79** *Block Capitals Please*

First Name					*Mr/Ms*	*Permanent Mailing Address*							
Family Name													
Nationality						*Tel No*							
Occupation						*Date of Birth*							

How did you hear of WEXAS? (if a newspaper or magazine, please give its exact name)	Have you previously been a member of WEXAS? If so, give year (*e.g. 1970/71*)

FOLD HERE BUT DO NOT DETACH THIS FORM FROM THE ORDER FORM BELOW

WEXAS BANKER'S STANDING ORDER

One standing Order form per person or family : valid only for UK and Ireland. (Complete *both* sides of this form). Overseas applicants pay by cheque/draft.

To . . . . Bank   Account No. . . . .
(*Name of your own bank*)   (*Last figures at bottom of cheques*)

Address. . . . .
(*Full postal address of branch*)

. . . .

. . . .

PLEASE PAY TO 18—00—05 Messrs. Coutts and Co., Bankers, SLOANE STREET BRANCH, 1 Cadogan Place, London SW1X 9PX, for the credit of WEXAS Account No. 64333321, the sum of £8.75 (eight pounds seventy-five pence) for Individual Membership/£12 (twelve pounds) for Family Membership (*delete as applicable*) one month from the date overleaf and thereafter each year on the first of the month overleaf.

This form must be sent to WEXAS and *not* to your bank or WEXAS' bank.

⊛ WEXAS MEMBERSHIP APPLICATION

For individual and Family membership. (Only one person or family per form. Please complete both sides of the form). **1978/79**

	FOR OFFICE USE ONLY
I, the undersigned, hereby apply for Individual/ Family Membership (please delete as applicable) of WEXAS.	
Signature	MN

S/O

IM

FM

MC

SG

Stamp

FOLD HERE BUT DO *NOT* DETACH THIS FORM FROM THE ORDER FORM BELOW

⊛ WEXAS BANKER'S STANDING ORDER

One Standing Order form per person or family: valid only for UK and Ireland. Personal accounts only—not company accounts.
Complete *both* sides of this form. Overseas applicants pay by cheque/draft.

IMPORTANT

The member's bankers are requested to quote the membership number opposite against the member's name in addition to the WEXAS Bank Account Number.

Membership Number (number to be allocated by WEXAS). Members renewing their subscription will be allocated a new number.

Name. . . . .

Address . . . .

. . . .

. . . .
                                            BLOCK CAPITALS

Signature. . . . .

Date in full . . . .

. . . .

Return this form with the above membership form to: Membership Controller, WEXAS, International Office, 45 Brompton Rd., Knightsbridge, London SW3, England.

This form must be sent to WEXAS, not to your bank or WEXAS' bank. Your Standing Order form will be forwarded by WEXAS to your bank once your membership number has been allocated.

Index

Aardvark Expeditions Ltd *107,111*
Aaron Insurance Consultants *153*
Abbott Travel *107,111*
ABC Travel Guides Ltd *193*
Abercrombie & Kent (Europe) Ltd *107,111*
Actions *193*
Adventure Africa *107,111*
Adventure Associates *131*
Adventure Center *131*
Adventure Guides Inc *143,180*
Adventure International Club and Tours *122,124,125,130*
Adventure Tents *146*
Adventure Travel Magazine *143*
Adventure Travel Shop and Pan Pacific *107,111*
Adventure Travel USA *143,180*
Adventures Unlimited *131*
Africanus *107,112*
Afro Ventures *119,122,130*
Afrotrek Ltd *128*
Agfa Gaevert Ltd *151*
A.G. Venture Centre *112*
Aigas Field Centre *137*
Air Alliance *126*
Alan Hutchinson Library *156*
Albert Tours *107,112*
Allen & Dunn Expeditions Ltd *107, 112*
Alliance Européenne de l'air *126*
Alpinair Ltd *159*
Alpine Club *185*
Alpine Club of Canada *173*
Alta Holidays *107,112*
Amateur Photographer *101*
Amazon Safari Club Inc *131*
AMC Books *161*
AMC Times *193*
Amerailpass *163*
American Adventurers' Association *143*
American River Touring Association *132*
American Youth Hostels Association *198*
Amtrek Overland *107,112*
Annapurna Mountaineering and Trekking Pvt Ltd *129*

Appalachia *193*
Appalachia Bulletin *194*
Appalachian Mountain Club *132, 184,193,194*
Archaeological Institute of America *132*
Archaeology Abroad Service *137*
Arena Tours *128,131*
Argus Travel Ltd *108,112*
Asian Greyhound Ltd *108,112*
Asian Rover *155*
Assinter Voyages *126*
Association of the Experiment in International Living *137*
Atrek Travel Ltd *108,113*
Atrek Travel of London Ltd *121*
AUS Student Travel *108,113*
Austrailpass *163*
Australian Pacific Camping Safaris *121,122,123*
Australian Youth Hostels Association *143*
Ausventure *121,129,130,134*
Auto Camping Club *137*
Automobile Association *45,46,137, 157*
Avon Inflatables Ltd *145*
Backpacker *194*
Baktoo, M.S. *128*
Bales Tours Ltd *108,113*
Balloon Federation of America *194*
Ballooning Magazine *194*
Bank of England (Foreign Department) *146*
BAS Overseas Publications *145*
Beam Trading NV *162*
Bennett Travel Bureau Ltd *108,113*
Berghaus *148*
Berkeley Pump Co *161*
Bill's Coach Tours *108,113*
BIT Information and Help Service *170,189*
Black Star Inc *164*
Blacks of Greenock *146*
Brathay Exploration Group *137, 183,179*
Bray, Gill and Wrightson Ltd *153*
Bridon Fibres & Plastics Ltd *148*
British Airways Medical Centre *156*

British Antarctic Survey *137*
British Cave Research Association *172,194*
British Cave Research Association Bulletin *194*
British Girls' Exploring Society *137*
British Library *70*
British Mountaineering Council *19, 153,185,195*
British Schools' Exploring Society *138*
British Sub-Aqua Club *138,191,198*
British Sub-Aqua Club Film Library *152*
Brownchurch (Components) Ltd *159*
Bruce Coleman Colour Picture Library *156*
Budget Bus *108,113*
Bustrek *108,113*
Bustrek Australia *122*
Butterfield, AW and R *108,114*
Calgary Explorers' Club *143*
Camp Trails International Ltd *146*
Campbell Irvine Ltd *153*
Camping and Caravanning Magazine *194*
Camping Centre *147*
Camping Club of G.B. and Ireland Ltd *171,194*
Camping Gaz International *162*
Camping Magazine *194*
Canadian Camping Tours *124*
Canadian Mountain Holidays *124*
Canadian Youth Hostel Association *66*
Canatrek *124*
Canoe Arctic Inc *125*
Canoe Centre (Twickenham) Ltd *145*
Canoeing Magazine *194*
Capricorn Travel and Tours Ltd *108, 114,123,125,131*
Caravan Publications Ltd *194*
Carawagon International Ltd *159*
Caribbean Schooner Cruises Inc *132*
Caving Supplies *195*
Center for Field Research *132*
Central Bureau for Educational Visits and Exchanges *181*
Chalet Club *195*
Chalet Club Ways *195*
Charities Aid Fund *17,180*
Climber and Rambler Magazine *195*
Cli-pon Insect Screens Ltd *146*
Club Nord Sud *126*
Cogans *122*
Compendium Bookshop *145*
Concord Films Council Ltd *152*
Contiki Travel Ltd *108,114*
Continental Camping Tours (CCT) *108,114,122,123,124*
Cook Hammond and Kell Ltd *155*

Cox and Kings Ltd *108,114*
Crags Magazine *195*
C.W.F. Hamilton and Co Ltd *161*
David Hodgson *151*
Découverte du Nouveau Monde *126*
Department of Health and Social Security *72*
Deutsche Katadyn GmbH *162*
Dick Phillips *108,114,181-182,199*
Directorate of Overseas Surveys *69*
Doka Expeditions *132*
Dotation Nationale de l'Aventure *144*
Dudley Hill Engineering Co Ltd *147*
Duke of Edinburgh's Award Scheme *138,178*
Dunlop Ltd *159*
Earthwatch *132*
Eastern Mountain Sports Climbing School *132*
Ecole de l'Aventure *144*
Edward Stanford Ltd *70,155*
Egypt Exploration Society *138*
Eiselin Sport *129,131,134*
Electrolux Ltd *148*
Encounter Overland Ltd *108,114*
Endeavour Training *138*
Eurasia Overland Tours *108,115*
European Express *108,115*
Europleasure Gas Ltd *148*
Ever Ready Co Ltd *159*
Exodus Expeditions *108,115*
Expedition Magazine *100,195*
Expedition Training Institute *132*
Explorado *124,126*
Explorator *126*
Explorer Films *152*
Explorer Tours *125*
Explorers Ltd *179*
Explorers (Explore Beyond Ltd) *109, 115,127*
Explorers Book Club *164,179*
Explorers Club *143,195*
Explorers Journal *195*
Fairey Winches *159*
Fairways & Swinford *109,115*
Farfugladeild Reykjavikur *128*
Fauna Preservation Society Wildlife Library *152*
Fédération Mondiale des Villes Jumelées *124,126,128,131*
Fetco Travel *122*
Field & Trek (Equipment) Ltd *149*
Field Studies Council *138*
Firemaster Ltd *159*
FLM Pandcraft *159*
Flying Doctors' Society of Africa *138,155*
Forsmark, Carl and Anya *126*
Four by Four Ltd *158*
Foyer International d'Accueil de Paris *143*
Foyles Travel Book Club *157*

Foyles Travel Department *155*
Fram Expeditions Ltd *158*
Freighter Travel News *196*
Frontier Expeditions Ltd *109,115*
Galice Raft Rental *132*
G and H Products *150*
Gardenwork *149*
Geo Expeditions *125*
Geo Magazine *136*
Geographia *69*
Geographical Journal *199*
Geographical Magazine *101,196*
George Philip and Sons *69*
Geoslides Photographic Library *102,
103,106,156,187*
Globe Newsletter *138,196*
Globetrotters Club *138,196*
Going Places *113,132*
Goway Travel Advisors *113,125*
Grand Canyon/Canyonlands
Expeditions *132*
Great Adventure Travel Centre *122*
Great African Adventure Co Ltd *109,
115*
Guide to Adventure Travel *143*
Guilde Européenne du Raid *143,
144,179*
Guildford Travel Club *139*
Hann Overland *109,116*
Hans Ebenstein Travel Inc *132*
Harrods *70*
Harvey Hudson *158*
Highland Wildlife Enterprises *109,
116*
HM Customs *146*
Holiday Tours and Travel (Pte) Ltd
130
Hughes Overland Ltd *109,116,117*
Iceland Information Unit *139,182*
Indian Railway Tours *109,116*
Institut Géographique National *69*
International Aquatic Adventures
Inc *133*
International Explorers Journal *196*
International Explorers Society *196*
International Youth Hostel
Federation *61*
International Zoological Expeditions
Inc *133*
Intertrek Expeditions Ltd *109,116,
117*
Intrepids Club *196*
Intrepids Magazine *196*
Islands in the Sun *133*
J.C. Salt and Co *160*
Jerrycan Expédition *124,126,131*
Jet Boating Journal *196*
Jeunes sans Frontières *127*
Joe McLean *133*
John Bartholomew *69*
John Moss *157*
John O'Reilly *146*
John Piercy Ltd *151*

John Ridgway School of Adventure
139
Johnson, Jim *196*
Joyer Travel Report *126*
Karrimor International Ltd *149*
Katadyn France *162*
Kenworthy, Trevor *109,116*
Kenyan Youth Hostel Association
62
Kimbla Travel Pty Ltd *113,130*
Koala Travel *122*
Kodak Ltd *151*
L & I Equipment *148*
Lama Exp. Reisen GmbH *136*
Land-Roving Ltd *158*
L'Astrolabe *161*
Latin World Travel *113,129*
Laurence Corner *147*
Le Raid — Expéditions *127*
Librairie Ulysse *161*
Lindblad Travel Inc *133*
Long Haul Expeditions *116*
Lute Jerstad Adventures *133*
Maghreb Safaris *109,116*
Magic Bus *109,117*
Maloja Tyres *164*
Manastrek *129*
Map House *155*
Map Shop *155*
Mariah Magazine *197*
Marine Unit Technology Ltd *151*
Mary Evans Picture Library *177*
Mas Travel Centre (Pte) Ltd *130*
Matador Motor Caravans *158*
Meteorological Office (International)
160
MH Travel *122*
Michael Gibbons & Co Ltd *153*
Michelin Tyre Co Ltd *160*
Middle Fork Trips *133*
Migrator *127,131*
Mistral Safari *109,117*
Mitchell Cotts (Insurance Dept.) *153*
Moffat, Stewart, Travel *122*
Monorep Ltd *160*
Motor Caravanners' Club *139*
Mountain Leadership Training Board
184,185
Mountain Rescue Committee *185*
Mountain Travel Inc *121,129,134*
Mountain Travel, Nepal *121,131,
134,136*
Mountaineering Association *184*
National Association of Boys' Clubs
139
National Association of Youth Clubs
139
National Council of Social Service
17,180
National Geographic Magazine *101,
144,197*
National Geographic Society *144,
197*

Nature Conservancy *139*
Nature Expeditions International *134*
Naval Undersea Research and Development Center *162*
Neale and Wilkinson Ltd *153*
New Horizon Holidays Ltd *125*
New Zealand Jet Boat Association *196*
Nigel Press Associates *157*
Nomade Expéditions *127*
Nord Norge Bussen *163*
Northern Lights Alpine Recreation *125*
Northern Whitewater Expeditions Inc *134*
Norwich Union Insurance Group *154*
Nouvelles Frontières/Touraventure *127*
Oars Inc *134*
Oceanic Expeditions *134*
Oceanic Society *134*
Odyssey Ltd *134*
Olympus Optical Co (UK) Ltd *151*
Ordnance Survey *67,68,69*
Outward Bound *134*
Outward Bound Trust *139*
Overland *127*
Overland Camping Services *147*
Overland Club *144*
Overland Mart *156*
Overlander Coaches *109,117*
Overlander Expeditions Ltd *109, 117,123,125,130,131*
Packhorse Adventures *122*
Partir Magazine *197*
Passeport *127*
Paul Popper Ltd *157*
Pearl's Freighter Tips *134,163*
Penn Overland Tours Ltd *109,117*
Peruvian Safaris SA *130*
Picturepoint Ltd *157*
Pindi Contracts *150*
Pindisports *149,184*
Polywarm Products Ltd *150*
Practical Camper *197*
Press, Nigel, Associates *157*
Provoya *162*
Q Tours *122*
Quest 4 Ltd *152*
Quest Magazine *197*
Questers Tours and Travel Inc *134*
Raclet Ltd *147*
Rajata Tours *131*
Ramblers' Association *197*
Ramblers Holidays Ltd *109,117*
Ranch House Meals *148*
Rapho Agency *164*
Ravel Meals *148*
Regent Holidays (IOW) Ltd *109, 117*
Rivages Expéditions *127*

Robert Harding Associates Picture Library *157*
Robert Paxton (Travel) Pty Ltd *122*
Rocky Mountain Books *161*
Roger Lascelles *145,155,172,173, 175,181,183,186,187,188,192, 199*
Rotel-Tours *136*
Rover Company Ltd *139,158,192*
Roverhire *158*
Royal Anthropological Institute *153*
Royal Automobile Club *45,46,140, 157*
Royal Geographical Society *19-21, 70,79,151,180*
Royal Insurance Co Ltd *154*
Royal Scottish Geographical Society *140,197*
Roy Ryder Ltd *147*
Rucksack Magazine *197*
Safari Camp Services of Nairobi *112*
Safari Ecuatorianos *126*
Safari Land Tours *122*
Safari (Water Treatment) Ltd *151*
Sail Training Association *140*
Schools' Hebridean Society *140*
Schooner 'Captain Scott' *140*
Scientific Exploration Society *21-25, 150,178*
Scott Polar Research Institute *140*
Scottish Geographical Magazine *197*
Scout Association *140,186*
See and Sea Travel Service *134*
Sherpa Expeditions *110,118,129*
Sherpa Society *129*
Sherratt and Hughes *155*
Sidoc Photothèque *164*
Sierra Club *134,197*
Sierra Club Bulletin *197-198*
Skyline Travel Inc *119,135*
Slaney's *156*
Slugocki Norman & Co Ltd *154*
Snowden Smith Books *146*
Sobek Expeditions Inc *135*
SOS Voyages *162*
Sotour *126,128*
South American Explorer (Journal) *198*
South American Explorers' Club *144,198*
Special Travel *152*
Sporthaus Schuster *129,134,136*
Stevenson Motors *160*
Stewart Moffat Travel *122*
Sundowners Ltd *110,114,118,123, 125,129,130,131*
Sundowners of London Travel Centre *113,123,129*
Survival International *140*
Tamar Travel Agents Ltd *110,116, 118*
Tarpaulin & Tent Manufacturing Co *147*

Tentrek Expeditions Ltd *110,118*
Terres d'Aventure *127*
Thomas Cook Ltd *110,118,129,157*
Thor Transport Ltd *153*
Tiger Tops *129*
Top Deck Travel *110,119*
Topastrek *127,131*
Topkapi Safari *110,119*
Tour East *110,119*
Tourist Centre Pty Ltd *131*
Trail Finders Ltd *110,113,119,123, 125,128,129,135,140*
Trail Finders (Services) Ltd *152,174, 180,186,189,192*
Trail Finders Travel (Pty) Ltd *123*
Trans African Expeditions Ltd *110, 119,123*
Trans Himalayan Tour (P) Ltd *119, 129*
Transit Travel Ltd *110,119,130*
Travel and Sports Centre *150*
Travel Centers of the World *163*
Travel Information Bureau *182*
Travel-Mate of Australia *162*
Travel Rite (Pty) Ltd *131*
Travel-Time International Pty Ltd *123*
Travel Wise Club *144*
Travellers' Directory *198*
Travellers' Insurance Association Ltd *154*
Treasure Tours Ltd *117,130*
Trekamerica Inc *110,120*
Triton Magazine *138,151,198*
TVC Sales Ltd *160*
Twickenham Travel Ltd *110,120*
Ulfar Jacobsen Tourist Bureau Ltd *113,128*
Ultimate Equipment *150*
Underwater Explorers Society *124*
United States Canoe Association *198*
United States Youth Hostel Association *66*
United Travel Services *130*
University of California Berkeley Research Expeditions *135*
Vango (Scotland) Ltd *147*
Vantage Motor Co *158*

Varu Garages *158*
Venture Treks Ltd *121,130*
Viastop *162*
Visas International *164*
V.U. (International) Pty Ltd *124*
W.E. Found and Co Ltd *154*
West Himalayan Holidays Ltd *110, 120*
West London Vaccination Centre *156*
West Mercia Insurance Brokers *72, 154*
Western International Travel Pty Ltd *124*
Western International Treks *125*
Western Outdoor Adventures Ltd *125*
WEXAS *24,25-26,52-54,100,110, 120,135,141,144,149,154-155, 162-163,182-183,195,243-248, 255*
Whitewater Adventures *135*
White Water River Expeditions *135*
Wilderness Camping Magazine *198*
Wilderness Company Inc *135*
Wilderness Expeditions Inc *135*
Wilderness Southeast *135*
Wilton House Gentry *172,173-174, 177,187,188,189,190*
Windjammer Cruises *135*
Windmill Motor Caravans *159*
Winston Churchill Memorial Trust *145*
World of Learning Ltd *154*
World Wildlife Fund *141-142*
Worldwide River Expeditions *136*
Writer's and Artist's Yearbook *105*
Yachts International Ltd *160*
YHA Hostelling News *198*
YMCA *66*
Young Abroad Club *119,128*
Young Explorers' Trust *26-28,139, 156,177-178,179*
Youth Hostels Association *61-66, 171*
Youth Hostels Association Services *62,146,150,188,198*
Zebco Consumer Division *164*
Zodiac of North America Inc *161*

Notes

This Page is for You to Write

A handbook like *Off the Beaten Track* contains much information which is quickly out of date. Further editions are planned, and naturally we should be grateful for your corrections and suggestions, as well as further useful short articles for the front section of the book. (These are paid for). We'd also like to know which sections you find most interesting/useful. Please write to us using the space below, or by letter. Send to:

> The Editor
> 'Off The Beaten Track'
> WEXAS
> International Office
> 45 Brompton Road
> London SW3 1DE
> England

Name ....

Address ....

....

....

Comments ....

....

....

....

....